La Nueva California

LATINOS FROM PIONEERS TO POST-MILLENNIALS

SECOND EDITION, REVISED

David E. Hayes-Bautista

UNIVERSITY OF CALIFORNIA PRESS

University of California Press, one of the most distinguished university presses in the United States, enriches lives around the world by advancing scholarship in the humanities, social sciences, and natural sciences. Its activities are supported by the UC Press Foundation and by philanthropic contributions from individuals and institutions. For more information, visit www.ucpress.edu.

University of California Press
Oakland, California

Library of Congress Cataloging-in-Publication Data

Names: Hayes-Bautista, David E., 1945- author.
Title: La nueva California : Latinos from pioneers to post-millennials / David E. Hayes-Bautista.
Description: Second Edition, Revised. | Oakland, California : University of California Press, [2017] | Includes bibliographical references and index.
Identifiers: LCCN 2016026249| ISBN 9780520292529 (cloth : alk. paper) | ISBN 9780520292536 (pbk. : alk. paper) | ISBN 9780520966024 (ebook)
Subjects: LCSH: Hispanic Americans—California—Social conditions. | Hispanic Americans—California—Statistics. | Hispanic Americans—California—Ethnic identity. | California—Social conditions. | California—Population. | California—Ethnic relations.
Classification: LCC F870.S75 H385 2017 | DDC 305.868/0730794—dc23
LC record available at https://lccn.loc.gov/2016026249

Manufactured in the United States of America

26 25 24 23 22 21 20 19 18 17
10 9 8 7 6 5 4 3 2 1

La Nueva California

To my one true love, Teodocia Maria.

Human beings share a tradition. There is no creation without tradition. No one creates from nothing.

CARLOS FUENTES
"How I Started to Write"

CONTENTS

LISTS OF FIGURES AND TABLES

FIGURES

ix

TABLES

Are Latinos American?

Can Latinos ever be American?

Do Latinos even want to be American?

In 2000, I set out to answer those questions. I pulled together census data from 1940 to 2000 that gave me the skeleton of basic Latino demography, from the birth of the largely third-generation Chicano generation at the end of World War II to the arrival of a new wave of first-generation immigration from Mexico and Central America in 1965–1990. To this basic skeleton I added health data covering the period from 1985 to 2000.

Once I knew the basics of Latino demographics, I sought to find out how different Latino subpopulations responded to those three questions by adding in qualitative data from individual interviews and focus groups, leavened with two attitudinal surveys, all conducted between 1990 and 2000. I saw in the qualitative data that when "American" was defined as meaning a having strong work ethic, not wanting to accept welfare, forming nuclear families, establishing businesses, feeling a strong sense of patriotism, and generally enjoying good health outcomes and a long life expectancy, not only the various Latino subgroups, but also Latinos as a whole, over the period 1940 to 2000, looked more typically "American" than Atlantic Americans. I reported those findings in *La Nueva California: Latinos in the Golden State* (University of California Press, 2004.)

These sixty-year-long patterns of behavior sharply contradicted the notion that Latinos were a floundering, dysfunctional urban underclass. If anything, Latinos were the most "American" of any group in their beliefs and behaviors. Yet the supporters of California's Proposition 187 in 1994 successfully depicted Latinos in the state as unemployed, welfare-dependent, lawless criminals who were not Americans, could not ever become Americans, and did not wish to become Americans. That negative image has been perpetuated in the media ever since.

One of the joys of research is that when one seeks to answer a research question, unexpected, unsought new questions are often sparked in the process, prompting the researcher to move beyond the original set of unanswered questions. Even as I was finishing *La Nueva California* in 2004, I found myself puzzled by the nearly total lack of data-based historical studies of Latinos in California prior to 1940. The unexpectedly strong "American" behaviors that Latinos exhibited during the period 1940 to 2000 surely could not have suddenly appeared for the first time on January 1, 1940. Their very existence in the period I studied was evidence of some strong social dynamics that had become firmly rooted prior to that date. Where had they come from?

I started rereading histories of California to search for clues, but the literature was not very helpful. The general picture I gleaned was that a small number of Spanish speakers had arrived in 1769 and managed to survive life on the frontier until California was forfeited to the United States at the end of the Mexican-American War. Almost immediately after that, gold was discovered, and tens of thousands of Atlantic Americans arrived in the state, overwhelming the numerically tiny Spanish-speaking population; the latter soon intermarried with, and were assimilated into, the new population, and were basically lost to history. The very few of their descendants who lived into the twentieth century considered themselves Spanish, not Mexican, and had nothing in common with the refugees from the Mexican Revolution who arrived in the US between 1910 and 1930.

Was this historical narrative sustained by any data? As I submitted the final page proofs of *La Nueva California* to the University of California Press, I led my staff at UCLA's Center for the Study of Latino Health and Culture (CESLAC) on an adventure into California's past. Given the standard narrative's strong suggestion that Spanish speakers basically disappeared shortly after 1849, our first task was to re-create that population's demographics. We used censuses from the Spanish Colonial period (1769–1821) and the Mexican Republic (1821–1848), as well as the US decennial censuses taken between 1848 and 1910. In order to develop our data extraction methodologies—we went from handwritten sheets to Excel spreadsheets—we made a pilot study using marriage data from Santa Barbara County for the period 1850–1910. The results utterly contradicted the accepted historical narrative. At no point had

Latinos disappeared in that county; in fact, their population experienced slow but constant growth over that period. We then tried our methods on the larger population base of Los Angeles County and discovered that its increasing urbanization had facilitated tremendous Latino population growth from 1850 to 1910. We have since completed population pyramids for Latinos in Los Angeles County for every decade from 1781 to 2015.

So now it was clear that Latinos had been in the state constantly for nearly 250 years. What was that population's experience of daily life under the Spanish, Mexican, and, finally, US flags? For this question, our greatest source of information became the Spanish-language press, from its start with one-page weekly inserts in 1851, which grew to multi-page dailies within a few years. The multiple voices speaking from the newspaper pages from 150 years ago on tell an alternative version of California's history. I read Latino reactions to the Gold Rush and to the Fugitive Slave Act, their rejection of the "Greaser Law," their abhorrence of the Dred Scott decision, and their concerns about their children casually sprinkling English words into their Spanish. I read about their experiences of the American Civil War: their nearly immediate support of Abraham Lincoln and the Union cause, their enlistment in the US armed forces, their horror as Lincoln's armies initially lost battle after battle to the rebel Confederate army, and their alarm as the Confederacy expanded into New Mexico and Arizona, arriving at the Colorado River and threatening to advance into California.

Then these long-past Latino voices grew somber as they recounted how Emperor Napoleon III took advantage of Lincoln's preoccupation with the Civil War to send French troops into Mexico to overthrow a republic and install a monarch, who then might make common cause with the rebelling slave states of the US South. The invading army marched through the Mexican countryside toward Mexico City, encountering little resistance. To Latinos in California, it appeared that the dream of republican equality, freedom, and democracy in the Western hemisphere was about to be extinguished in the US and Mexico, and possibly all of Latin America.

But before the invading French could control Mexico City, they had to pass through the city of Puebla. On the morning of May 5, 1862, the battle-hardened French assaulted the walls of Puebla. Three weeks later, the news arrived in California: astonishingly, the French army had been decisively beaten by the Mexicans at Puebla on May 5—the Cinco de Mayo—and Napoleon's plan to create a friend, possibly an ally, for the advancing Confederacy received a severe setback. News of the victory electrified Latinos in California, Nevada, and Oregon. In response, they created the first regional network of community organizations, the Juntas Patrióticas Mejicanas (Mexican Patriotic Assemblies), in 129 different locations. Every year after that, Latinos paraded though the streets of towns all around the West on May 5 to let the world know where they stood on the issues of the American Civil War: they opposed slavery and supported freedom; they opposed white supremacy and supported racial equality; they supported democracy and opposed elitist rule. Latinos created the public memory of Cinco de Mayo to declare that they were totally committed to the American values of equality, freedom, and democracy. I was so surprised and impressed by this hitherto undiscovered history of the Civil War that I wrote a book to share it, in time for the 150th anniversary of the Battle of Puebla, in 2012, *El Cinco de Mayo: An American Tradition.*

Through the Spanish-language newspapers of the nineteenth century, I heard anguished Latino voices describing how Anglo-Saxonist nativists refused to believe Latino claims of being American simply because they believed the self-evident truths pronounced in the Declaration of Independence, that "all men are created equal, and endowed . . . with certain inalienable rights—life, liberty and the pursuit of happiness." Nativists instead defined an American by race, religion, and language: they had to be white, Anglo-Saxon, Protestant, and English-speaking. In the nativist view, only members of this racial-ethnic group were truly to be endowed with life, liberty, and the pursuit of happiness. Nonwhites were not created equal, could not be considered Americans, and hence did not enjoy those rights. According to the nativists, *mestizo* (mixed-race) Catholic, Spanish-speaking Latinos could not claim American identity.

Plus ça change, plus c'est la même chose. For over 150 years, Latinos have claimed to be Americans by virtue of believing in universalist American values, and their claims have been repeatedly rejected by nativists, who argue that Latinos are not, and cannot ever be, American because of their race, religion, and language.

In a lunch meeting in 2014, my editor at UC Press, Naomi Schneider, suggested that I update my 2004 book to include more recent data. I jumped at the chance to bring the data up to 2015, and now to include the historical understanding I had lacked when I wrote the first edition. Seth Dobrin, also of UC Press, encouraged me to think far beyond a simple updating of the numbers to a more comprehensive narrative.

Whether in health sciences research or historical research, Latinos today cannot be fully understood without knowing how they are linked to the Latinos of the Gold Rush, the American Civil War, and Reconstruction.

A researcher needs to understand how Latinos reacted to the nativist rejections of the American Know-Nothing Party of the 1850s, Denis Kearney's racist Workingmen's Party of the 1870s, the anti-Catholic American Protective Association of the 1890s, the xenophobic "Americanization" campaigns during World War I, the massive deportations of the 1930s, Operation Wetback of the 1950s, the English-only movement of the 1970s, the rejection of Latinos that motivated California's Proposition 187 in 1994, and the xenophobic Republican presidential primary campaigns of 2016. This updated and heavily revised book, now titled *La Nueva California: Latinos from Pioneers to Post-Millennials,* is the book I wanted to write in 2004, but did not have the historical knowledge to accomplish. I now have the knowledge, and I share it with the reader in these pages.

A NOTE ON TERMINOLOGY

Since the very first United States census in 1790, the US has attempted to categorize all inhabitants into mutually exclusive racial groups. This led to the famous, or infamous, "one drop" rule of hypodescent, by which a single black ancestor in a person's family tree makes that person officially black. These rigid, binary racial categories used by the census have collided with mixed-race Latinos in California for over 150 years, creating far more confusion than clarity about race and ethnicity. In this book, I use the terms *Latino* and *Hispanic* to mean the same group of people, but generally use *Hispanic* only when referring to data sets that contain that category. I use the terms *non-Hispanic white* and *Atlantic American* (the latter my own neologism) to refer to what some call "Euro-Americans." I most often use *Atlantic American* to refer to descendants of the society and culture that had its origins in the British, mostly Protestant, English-speaking settlements of the Atlantic coast, irrespective of a given individual's race, racial mixture, or national origin. Persons of Irish origin, Italian origin, and African origin belonging to a culture descended in large part from those early settlements can all be Atlantic Americans. Some data sets, particularly the US census, use the awkward term *non-Hispanic whites* to refer to racially white persons (whatever exactly that means) who are themselves, and whose ancestors were, not Hispanic, African, or Asian in origin. A methodological appendix gives information about the quantitative data sources used in this study, and the possible sampling error intrinsic to each source.

ACKNOWLEDGMENTS

While the writing of this book has been mostly a solitary act, the preparation of data builds upon the contributions of many colleagues, without whose efforts and expertise this book could not possibly have been written during my lifetime. My first acknowledgment is to my wife, Teodocia Maria Hayes-Bautista, RN, MPH, PhD, my research companion for decades, who during our thirty-six years of marriage has continuously surprised me with her keen insights into the lives of Latinos in the US and Mexicans in Mexico, and their relation to health care research. Werner Schink, my colleague and coauthor of *The Burden of Support: Young Latinos in an Aging Society* (Stanford University Press, 1987), took the lead on extracting data from the US censuses from 1940 to 2015. Colleague and coauthor Paul Hsu of UCLA's Division of General Internal Medicine and Department of Epidemiology took the lead in corralling the health-related data sets. Colleague and coauthor Cynthia L. Chamberlin, CESLAC's historian, undertook invaluable archival research and analysis necessary for the historical portions of this book, and took the lead in editing the manuscript and checking references. Seira Santizo Greenwood managed the implementation of focus groups and provided the administrative support (even while on maternity leave!) without which any project in a large academic center would come to a grinding halt. While they were staffers at the Center for the Study of Latino Health and Culture, Mithi del Rosario and Anabel Alcaraz provided manuscript support; both are now medical students at the David Geffen School of Medicine at UCLA. Other UCLA students who over the years helped to generate the data used in this book include Veronica Viceñas, Jennifer Monica More, Laura Ochoa, and Alexis Velazquez. The 2004 edition has been required reading in my class, Health in the Chicano/Latino

Community, and I want to acknowledge the teaching assistants over the years who have provided feedback from students: Charlene Chang, Eddie Zamora, Sarah Jane Smith, Esmeralda Snow, María del Sol Torres, and Katie Cobián. Colleagues at the David Geffen School of Medicine at UCLA whose encouragement energized me include Dr. Hy Doyle, Dr. Luann Wilkerson, and Dr. Martin Shapiro, Division Chief of General Internal Medicine.

Colleagues from other institutions who have provided data and encouragement for this update include Dr. Javier García de Alba of Jalisco Seguro Social, Guadalajara; Dr. Noé Alfaro, of the Centro Universitario de Ciencias de Salud, Universidad de Guadalajara; Dr. José Luís Talancón, of the Universidad Nacional Autónoma de México (UNAM); and José Rodolfo Hernández Carrión of the Universitat de València.

Jorge Mettey, now director of news for TV Azteca, has provided invaluable support in getting information from my books out to the general public in Spanish for nearly twenty years. He won a Peabody Award in Journalism for a twenty-part series he produced based on the 2004 edition of this book. Luis Patiño, general manager of Univision KMEX in Los Angeles, encouraged the rapid completion of this book as a public education service. Gabriela Teissier, anchor for *A Primera Hora,* has been a key supporter in spreading the book's content to the general Spanish-speaking public, as have reporters Claudia Botero and Antonio Valverde, all from Univision KMEX in Los Angeles.

I have been a member of the Governing Board at White Memorial Medical Center in Boyle Heights, East Los Angeles, for nearly four years, and would like to acknowledge the support given to this effort by many of my colleagues at that institution: Beth Zachary, President and CEO, Adventist Health Southern California; John Raffoul, President and CEO, White Memorial Medical Center; fellow board members Eileen Zorn, Raul Salinas, George Ramirez, Gabriela Barbarena, David Lizarraga, and his wife Priscilla Lizarraga; Mara Bryant, Senior Vice President, Organizational Performance, and her children, Sydney and Dylan; Mary Anne Chern, Senior Vice President, Fund Development and External Relations; Dr. Karen Hansberger, Senior Vice President, Medical Affairs/Chief Medical Officer; Dr. Azmy Ghaly, Medical Staff President Elect; Dr. Leroy Reese, Designated Institutional Official, Chair, OB/GYN; Dr. Cinna Wolmuth, Residency Director, OB; Dr. Hector Flores, Co-Director, Family Medicine Residency Program; Georgia Froberg, Director, Medical Education; and Cesar Armendáriz, Associate Vice President, Community and Public Relations.

I would like to thank a number of friends who offered encouragement and feedback along the way: Jeff and Ana Valdez, Federico and Gloria Peña, Cástulo de la Rocha and Zoila Escobar of AltaMed health care services, and Joel and Judy Garcia.

Family is the geography beneath the history of this book, and I would like to thank those who gave ideas and encouragement: Raúl and Ana Bracamontes in Guadalajara, and Dr. Hugo Wingartz and his wife Patricia Jiménez in Mexico City. My greatest thanks must go to the love of my life, Teodocia Maria Hayes-Bautista; to our children, Catalina Mercedes, Diego David, Ana Raquel, and Marta Ynez; and our grandchildren, Gael Hayes-Bautista Rodriguez and Levi Francisco Edsinger.

ONE

America Defines Latinos

THE CLASH OF NARRATIVES BEGINS

> Proclamation abolishing racial categories and slavery among
> Mexicans ... They will not be called Indian, mulatto, or any
> racial category, but rather all, in common, Americans.
>
> —JOSÉ MARÍA MORELOS,
> November 17, 1810

ON THE THIRD DAY OF THE 1849 California Constitutional Convention, one of the delegates from Los Angeles, José Antonio Carrillo, rose to address the assembly, speaking through an interpreter, as he was not yet proficient in English. Carrillo had heard a fellow delegate say that the constitution being developed for the new state of California was not going to be for Latinos— the "native Californians," or Californios—but only for the "American" population. He begged leave to say that he considered himself "as much an American citizen" as the delegate who had made that remark. William M. Gwin of San Francisco patronizingly replied that the constitution was being made for the Atlantic Americans because they constituted the majority of the population, but that its purpose was also to "protect" the Latino minority. At this, Kimball H. Dimmick, an Atlantic American delegate representing San José, informed the convention that his own Latino constituents also considered themselves just as American as the rest of the population in the soon-to-be state. "They all demanded their title of 'Americans'. They would not consent to be placed in the minority. They considered themselves to be in the class 'Americans' and had the right to belong to the majority.... The Constitution had to be made for their benefit, just as it was for that of the native Americans [i.e., Atlantic Americans]."[1]

When Miguel Hidalgo, Simón Bolívar, José de San Martín, and others roused the populations of Central and South America to fight for independence from Spain in the early nineteenth century, "America" was largely a geographical expression, for the modern nation-states of Mexico, Venezuela,

Argentina, and the rest did not yet exist. These revolutionary leaders could not generate patriotism by invoking an imagined community with flags, national anthems, and other standard symbols of national unity.[2] Yet many, if not most, of the leaders and the people did share a mental model of a territorial idea that could rally soldiers, craftsmen, merchants, slaves, and farmers: *América*.

In a speech in 1814, Simón Bolívar used that mental model to inspire the troops of one of his commanders, Rafael Urdaneta: "Para nosotros, la Patria es América" (For us, the homeland is America).[3] A writer from Buenos Aires, José Antonio Miralla, who lived in Lima and Havana during Central and South America's wars for independence, declared, "Es uno el corazón americano" (The American heart is one). Vicente Rocafuerte, an independence activist from Guayaquil, Ecuador, whose dreams of liberty took him to Lima, Havana, and Mexico City, later remembered that in his youth, he had considered *"toda la América"* (all America) under colonial Spanish rule to have been *"la patria de mi nacimiento"* (the homeland of my birth).[4] Seeking to ignite the fires of independence, Mexican priest Miguel Hidalgo in 1810 made his famous proclamation addressed to *"la nación americana"* (the American nation), with the invocation, "Rise up, O noble spirits of Americans! . . . for the day of glory and public happiness has arrived."[5]

In their respective struggles for independence from a European colonial power, both Mexico and the United States declared to the world their intention to create an independent republic based on notions of equality. Each subsequently fought a war against its colonial power, then formalized its own governing principles and structure. After Mexican independence, Alta California was part of the new Republic of Mexico, whose first constitution was written for *"la América Mexicana"* (Mexican America);[6] and a generation of leaders grew up shaped by these ideals of Mexican independence. Yet some forty years after Hidalgo called on the "noble spirits of Americans" to fight for self-governance, the subsequent generation of Californios found itself confronting a competing vision of America from the United States of America, after the Treaty of Guadalupe-Hidalgo (1848) ceded nearly half of Mexico's territory, including Alta California, to the US at the end of the Mexican-American War.

José Antonio Carrillo was joined at the 1849 California Constitutional Convention by other Latinos who had been active participants in government when Alta California was still part of Mexico, such as Pablo de la Guerra, Mariano Vallejo, Antonio María Pico, José María Covarrubias, and

Manuel Domínguez. Their vision of California's future as part of the United States was based on their understanding of Mexico's constitution and government, and their vision of "America" presumed the values of self-government with freedom and equality for all.[7]

On the other hand, many of the Atlantic American delegates to the California Constitutional Convention probably were surprised by Latinos calling themselves "Americans" simply because they believed in ideals of equality, freedom, and democracy. The early leaders of the United States independence movement felt they had developed a plan for self-governance and political equality that would serve as a model for the rest of the world.[8] But between the Declaration of Independence in 1776 and California's Constitutional Convention in 1849, the definition of "American" had largely changed in the US, from the universalist idea of individual liberty and freely chosen self-governance to a nativist definition that limited "American" to members of a self-perceived national ethnic group: white, preferably Anglo-Saxon, Protestant, and English-speaking. Kaufman has detailed the stages in this shift. The French and Indian War (1754–1763) highlighted differences between the white, British-origin, English-speaking Protestant population and perceived "others"—Catholic, Francophone, and of French origin; or Native American, either Catholic or pagan; or black, African-origin slaves—even before the American Revolution was fought, for self-governance ostensibly based on universalist ideas such as life, liberty, and the pursuit of happiness. Yet contemporary and subsequent Whig historians asserted that these "universal" values had been born deep in the German forests and taken to England by the Anglo-Saxons. With the "desire for freedom in their veins," the Anglo-Saxons' English descendants had brought these values to North America's shores. Many early American statesmen, including Benjamin Franklin, Samuel Adams, and George Washington, subscribed to this ahistorical notion of the Anglo-Saxon origins of republican values. For instance, Thomas Jefferson wrote to John Adams in 1776 that the "political principles and form of government" guiding the new republic were derived from "the Saxon chiefs." A nativist narrative in which the American government was the product of a white, Anglo-Saxon, Protestant people, "descended from the same ancestors, speaking the same language, professing the same religion," competed with the universalist narrative that American governmental values and institutions were open to peoples of any language, origin, or religion.[9] This nativist definition of America was strengthened by the "Black Legend" of Spain. Dating from the sixteenth-century Protestant Reformation, the

Black Legend depicted the Catholic Spanish to British Protestants as "unusually brutal and avaricious barbarians of a mixed race, a combination of African and European ... who then went on to mix with the Native Americans and other non-European peoples in the New World." By contrast, English Protestants liked to see themselves as a "civilized and uncontaminated race" descended from the Anglo-Saxons, an inaccurate but nonetheless firmly held concept of identity they bequeathed to their white, Protestant descendants in North America.[10]

As ideas about race, ethnicity, and government began to coalesce in the US between 1776 and 1849, whites increasingly considered nonwhites incapable of self-government; they believed it was their duty to impose their model of government and society upon nonwhites for the ultimate "benefit" of those lesser races. Horsman sees in the US expansion into Texas an example of how the definition of "American," already shifted from a universalist one based on lofty ideals to a nativist one based on Anglo-Saxonism, was used to further Manifest Destiny over nonwhite ethnic groups who happened to live in the way of US territorial expansion—lofty rhetoric about freedom and democracy to the contrary.[11] Kaufman posits that by 1849, citizens of the United States had learned a dual definition of who was American. On the one hand, in the universalist narrative, an American was any inhabitant of the western hemisphere who believed in freedom, equality, individual liberty, democratic self-government, and similar values. On the other hand, in the nativist narrative, an American was a white, English-speaking Protestant descended from Anglo-Saxon ancestors either literally or fictively, via cultural assimilation.[12]

Carrillo and the other Latinos participating in California's Constitutional Convention in 1849, however, believed that the universalist ideals they shared, of equality, freedom, and self-government, made them as American as the Atlantic Americans, whose rhetoric, at least, indicated that they shared similar ideals. These Latinos' adherence to the universalist values of Mexican independence made them advocates for the abolition of slavery and for racial equality in voting.[13] Considering their own cultural heritage just as valid as the Atlantic American tradition, they also supported the publication of all public documents and announcements in Spanish as well as English, and the continuation of Iberian and Mexican legal traditions protecting married women's property rights.[14] From their universalist point of view, inclusion of these policies in California's new constitution would spread the blessings of freedom, equality, and democracy to even more people: African Americans also would be endowed with life, liberty, and the ability to pursue happiness; adult male African Americans, Native Americans, and their descendants would be able to vote; traditional property rights would be secured; and Spanish-speaking citizens would be informed of new laws, so as to respect and comply with them.

But the prevailing Atlantic American, nativist view on these policy issues was nearly the opposite of the Californios' universalist vision. It considered slavery a valid legal institution (whether one personally condoned it or not), limited the vote to adult white males, and believed all US citizens should speak English. Thanks to this nativist narrative, by the mid-nineteenth century African Americans, Native Americans, and their descendants in the US had been formally excluded from the enjoying the same political and social rights as white persons, and the enslavement of nonwhite human beings was constitutionally permitted. Although not yet enforced by legislation, the idea of publishing official communications in any language but English mocked the goal of the cultural assimilation of nonwhites to an "Anglo-Saxon" model.

For six weeks, the issues of slavery, racial restrictions on suffrage, the right of married women to own property independently of their husbands, and the use of the Spanish language were debated at the convention, with the nativist narrative clearly driving many Atlantic American delegates' positions on these issues. But by the end of the convention, the universalist vision of "American California," championed by the Latino delegates and a significant portion of the Atlantic American ones, largely prevailed on these policy issues. The 1849 Constitution of the State of California abolished slavery, (theoretically) opened suffrage to nonwhites, guaranteed legal protection for married women's property rights, and stipulated that all legal documents be published *"en inglés y en español"* (in English and in Spanish).[15]

A CONTINUING CLASH OF NARRATIVES

Ever since the conclusion of the California Constitutional Convention in 1849, Latinos in California, and in the rest of the US, have experienced periodic clashes between these opposing views of their place in American society. Latinos have very much adhered to the universalist outlook, and this view consistently has driven their ideas of the American Dream. Data presented in this book will demonstrate that, in terms of adherence to the universalist values that hold US society together, Latinos have been, and are, entirely

American. Moreover, they have shown themselves to be at times even more American than any other group in the US, in terms of traditional individualist values and behaviors, such as workforce participation, family formation, and independence from public assistance. Despite these facts, Latinos have over and over again run up against the competing nativist narrative, which insists on defining "American" in terms of membership in a single ethnic group—white, Anglo-Saxon, Protestant, and English-speaking—and therefore argues that Latinos have not been, are not, and never can be truly American.

The Nativist Narrative in California

California was admitted to the United States with a state constitution based largely on the universalists' concept of American identity. The abolition of slavery in California, however—a universalist ideal with a precedent in the Mexican government's abolition of slavery in 1813—nearly proved to be a deal breaker. California's admission as a free state upset the carefully crafted balance between free and slave states established by the Missouri Compromise; and the slave states, perceiving their political power as endangered, threatened to leave the Union. Civil war loomed in 1850, and for a good part of that year the federal government virtually ceased to function, as members of the US Congress deadlocked over how to respond to California's proposed admission as a free state. After nine months of acrimonious debate, Stephen Douglas and his congressional allies managed to negotiate a series of compromise bills, known in their totality as the Compromise of 1850. This compromise essentially saved the United States for another decade, but the price required for California's admission as a free state was high. Slavery would not be banned in any other territory taken from Mexico, but instead would be decided in the future by a territory's voters, in a process dubbed "popular sovereignty"; and the Fugitive Slave Act greatly strengthened the hand of slave owners, who now could legally pursue their escaped "property" into any state, free or slave.[16]

After California gained admission in 1850, nativist arguments about citizenship and identity commanded further public attention in California, strengthened in part by the Black Legend, in a narrative of Anglo-Saxon superiority over the mixed-race Catholic Latino. A common image in English-language papers during the Gold Rush portrayed Catholic, Spanish-speaking, mixed-race Latinos as having been culturally and economically inert, or "asleep," in California "before this Anglo-Saxon race broke upon them, and woke them from their lazy slumbers."[17] Latinos were aware that US nativists saw English-speaking, white, Protestant "Anglo-Saxons" as racially superior. A Latino newspaper in San Francisco chided its English-language counterparts for constantly printing stories about *"la superioridad de la raza sajona"* (the superiority of the Saxon race), with its self-proclaimed ableness, moral perfection, and generosity, compared to the allegedly backward, vice-ridden Latinos, incompetent to govern themselves.[18] Most filibustering expeditions into Mexico in the same period were overtly predicated on such Anglo-Saxonism. A pro-filibuster editorial in the English-language Stockton *Weekly Democrat* was excerpted, in Spanish translation, by Francisco P. Ramírez, editor of Los Angeles's *El Clamor Público,* to show his readers the filibusters' nativist braggadocio: "The Anglo-Saxon race will take away from it the richest portion of our continent, and will make Mexico into what Nature intended it should be, whilst its wretched inhabitants will be obliged to flee to the tropics; or we will make them our slaves, as their color well justifies it."[19] In another anti-filibuster editorial, Ramírez said scornfully that "the Anglo-Saxons, in their origins, were robbers and pirates," adding that this "piratic instinct" was still alive in their own day and age.[20] Meanwhile, legislators guided by the Anglo-Saxonist narrative taking root in the state lost little time in attempting to move California away from its original universalist principles.

Slavery. Although California had been admitted as a free state, the Fugitive Slave Act, negotiated as part of the Compromise of 1850, emboldened some Southern slave owners to bring their slaves to California. At least one slave owner, Thomas Jefferson Green, was elected a member of the state legislature shortly after he brought fifteen slaves from Texas to the Yuba River in California. By 1852, sympathies for slave ownership facilitated passage of the 1852 California Fugitive Slave Act, which aimed to restrict the antislavery scope of the California Constitution and to commit state resources to hunting down fugitive slaves. This act was renewed in 1853 and 1854.[21]

Race. It was proposed at the constitutional convention to limit the vote to adult white males, but Latinos strongly objected to being excluded from voting in a state in which even those among them who had "received from Nature a very dark skin" had voted and held public office. Pablo de la Guerra y Noriega of Santa Barbara assured his fellow delegates that, under Mexican law, no racial group had been excluded from voting. The point sparked a bitter debate, during which the Anglo-Saxonists, to their dismay, found they could not define with legal precision what the word "white" meant, even though thirty other state constitutions contained such wording. They nevertheless tried to insist that courts of law understood who was "white" and who not. De la Guerra, not convinced that the new US courts should be allowed to define whiteness for voting purposes, proposed an amendment that kept the door open just a crack for at least some nonwhites in the future. This specified that nothing in the new constitution would prohibit that the legislature "might concede the right of suffrage to Indians or to the descendants of Indians," to be approved by a two-thirds vote.[22]

Language. Although California had been admitted to the United States as an officially bilingual state, the nativists resisted this constitutional provision. As early as 1850, a writer in San Francisco, clearly influenced by Anglo-Saxonism, argued that "for the sake of our nationality and brotherhood," society should have "unanimity of language" and should "encourage the general and universal extension, throughout California, of our mother tongue, the good, old, strong, nervous, poetical, heroic Anglo-Saxon."[23] In 1854, Governor John Bigler, in his annual message to the state legislature, suggested revising the state constitution so that, among other things, "it may not be absolutely necessary that all laws be published in Spanish"; at that time, however, no such revision was made.[24] In 1858, Ramírez reprinted a letter to the editor of San Francisco's *El Éco del Pacífico* complaining that recent official translations were of such poor quality as to be worthless to Spanish speakers in understanding new laws.[25] Despite such protests, the bilingual provision of the 1849 constitution continued to be a legal mandate—albeit sometimes honored more in the breach than in the observance—throughout the first generation of California's statehood.

The Know-Nothing Party, 1850s

In 1854, the Know-Nothing Party swept out of New York, providing a political party for dedicated nativists in the United States, as its platform was strongly anti-immigrant and anti-Catholic. The Know-Nothings established themselves in California in 1855, threatening to upset the existing Whig and Democratic Parties. For the first time, California's Latinos faced a concerted political battle driven by the nativist narrative and directed at them.

Francisco P. Ramírez, the eighteen-year-old California-born Latino editor of Los Angeles's *El Clamor Público,* emerged as one of the state's first public defenders of the universalist narrative against this nativist narrative, on behalf of his fellow Latinos.[26] Publishing his translation of the Know-Nothing Party's national platform in 1855, Ramírez informed his readers that the Know-Nothings planned to restrict immigration, to ban Catholics from holding political office, and to ensure that "only Americans will govern America!" In addition, their platform supported a state's right to determine the legality of slavery within its borders, without interference from the federal government.[27] Ramírez ran articles against the Know-Nothings almost every week that year, using sarcastic humor to educate his readers about the dangers this nativist party posed. He mocked the fact that the Know-Nothings called themselves "Native Americans" when, in fact, their ancestors had immigrated to America from Europe. He pointed out that they sought to take the vote away from anyone who had the "misfortune" to profess the Catholic religion.[28] When a Know-Nothing leader named Rayer declared, in typically nativist fashion, "Brethren, let us have American liberty and American religion," Ramírez observed with mock surprise that no one had ever before suspected that "Jesus Christ was a native [i.e., Anglo-Saxon] American." He then mused that the Christian faith therefore could not be the "American religion" Mr. Rayer and the Know-Nothings wished for, as it "is incompatible with their character."[29]

On the day before the 1855 elections, however, Ramírez turned entirely serious, contrasting the universalist narrative he personally held, as a Latino who was a citizen of the United States, with the nativist, Anglo-Saxonist narrative of the Know-Nothings. While the constitution of the United States and its laws extended rights and privileges to all citizens naturalized under its principles and institutions, the Know-Nothing Party wanted to restrict these rights, under the nativist doctrine that those rights were reserved only for white, English-speaking, Protestant adult males born in the US.[30] The Know-Nothing Party swept the California elections that year, electing their slate of state officers and winning a majority in both the state Assembly and the Senate.[31] The following year, they turned their eyes to the national elections. Antonio María Pico, who had been a delegate to the 1849 California Constitutional Convention when he was mayor of San José, served as Santa Clara County's delegate to the Republican National Convention in 1856. In a letter to voters back home, he warned that the Know-Nothing, "wrapping up together self-centered notions of nativism and opposition to Catholicism, sets himself against the interests of the individuals who have adopted the United States of America as their homeland."[32]

Yet just as rapidly it rose, the Know-Nothing Party fell in California. Resentment against immigrants and Catholics temporarily united many mutually antagonistic factions in California, particularly the anti-Nebraska Democrats, the pro-Nebraska Chivalry Democrats, and the rapidly disappearing Whigs. Yet once the Know-Nothings were in power, latent sectional disputes ripped the different factions of the party apart so thoroughly that they could not use their fragile majority to elect a Know-Nothing senator to represent the state in Washington. In a matter of weeks, the Know-Nothings "divided into groups of selfish politicians," lost their mandate in California, and by the end of 1856 were virtually extinct.[33]

Temporarily relieved of the need to fight the nativist narrative, Ramírez concentrated his efforts instead on building up the universalist narrative to which Latinos subscribed. In the summer of 1859, he began publishing some articles in his Spanish-language newspaper in English, to encourage the "young and rising generation" to become bilingual, urging them to read "the Spanish in their mother tongue, then ... read the English side by side." A major goal of this bilingualism was to enable California's Latinos to learn the universalist constitutional precepts of the United States, the laws by which the country was governed, by which "life, liberty and property are held sacred and secure."[34]

Reginaldo F. del Valle was one of the young Latinos born after California became a state. He was raised in the very fashion Ramírez later suggested, as a bilingual, bicultural loyal American citizen. Born in 1854, in a house facing the plaza in Los Angeles, Del Valle, like Ramírez, was actually trilingual, in Spanish, English, and French. Educated at St. Vincent's Academy in Los Angeles (later Loyola Marymount University), then at Santa Clara College (later Santa Clara University), he read law with the firm of Winans and Belknap in San Francisco and was admitted to the state bar in 1877. He then returned to Los Angeles and entered politics. He also subscribed to the universalist narrative that Ramírez championed, and would battle three waves of nativist politics during his eighty-four years of life.

Civil War and Reconstruction

By the close of the American Civil War, Abraham Lincoln held out a universalist vision for America in which slavery would be abolished, racial equality would confer citizenship and voting rights irrespective of race (for men, at least), and government would be "of the people, by the people, for the people." The Confederates, on the other hand, firmly espoused the nativist narrative throughout, fighting to maintain race-based slavery and white supremacy. The majority of Latinos in California supported Lincoln's universalist ideals; those who were citizens voted for Lincoln, and even some who weren't nevertheless joined the Union's military. Major José Ramón Pico helped recruit four units of the Spanish-speaking Native California Cavalry, who manned forts in the Arizona Territory and tracked down English-speaking Confederate bandits and sympathizers in different parts of California.

In 1862, Emperor Napoleon III sought to take advantage of the American Civil War to halt US expansion and in its place expand French influence into Mexico by overthrowing democratically elected President Juárez and installing a monarch. Napoleon also made friendly overtures to the rebelling slave states. But his grand design met its first setback in the unexpected victory of the Mexican army over the French at the first battle of Puebla, on May 5, 1862. Latinos in California celebrated this triumph for freedom and democracy with a new American holiday, the Cinco de Mayo, thereby also constructing a new public memory enshrining Latino devotion to universalist values in the US and throughout the Americas. During the Civil War and after, Latinos in many California cities marched, sang, made speeches, and conducted public ceremonies every May 5, reminding the world where they stood on the issues of both wars. They opposed slavery and supported freedom; they opposed white supremacy and supported racial equality; they opposed elite rule and supported an ethnically inclusive democracy. With the surrender of the Confederate army and the passing of constitutional amendments that abolished slavery throughout the country, declared racial equality in citizenship, and protected racial equality in voting, it appeared that Lincoln's universalist vision had triumphed in America.[35]

But this universalist victory was short-lived, even in California. "White men must rule America!" screamed an advertisement in the English-language *Union Democrat,* published in Sonora, California, in 1869, claiming that the country "demands the restoration of the White Republic."[36] The *Union Democrat* shared with many of its readers, and with many Atlantic Americans in California, a strong belief in "the distinctions of race fashioned by the hand of the Creator," and the consequent duty of white men to avoid amalgamation with the "inferior races" by not "forcing different species of men . . . to enjoy impartial freedom." To demonstrate that "mongrelism" would lead to the downfall of society, the paper pointed to the fate of Mexico, a "Mongrel Republic" where the extension of basic civil rights to "mixed breed, Indians and Negroes in common citizenship" allegedly had led to the country committing "social suicide."[37] Unsurprisingly, the *Union Democrat* also thundered against the Fifteenth Amendment as an attempt to "give the inferior races new rights," arguing that its passage would lead to a "mongrelization" of the US.[38] The *Amador Dispatch* also opposed racial equality in voting rights, urging that "white men who are trying to preserve this government for the benefit of white men and their posterity forever" oppose this legacy of the late President Lincoln.[39] In this renewed nativist atmosphere, Pablo de la Guerra—the delegate who at the 1849 constitutional convention had informed nativist delegates that no race had been excluded from voting under Mexican law, and who had served as acting lieutenant governor of California in 1861–1862 and was now a district court judge in Southern California—was sued in 1870 for attempting to "exercise the rights of a White citizen" in spite of his Native American ancestry. Although de la Guerra succeeded in winning his own case, the California Supreme Court nevertheless used the lawsuit to assert its prerogative of determining which persons of Native American origin would or would not be allowed to vote.[40]

Spanish-language newspapers in California protested against this resurgence of nativist sentiment. Reponding to a report on an incident of cattle rustling that appeared in an unnamed English-language newspaper in Los Angeles, which had "supposed" that the rustlers were Mexicans, a Spanish-language paper in the same city, *La Crónica,* replied sarcastically, referencing known local outlaws, "It's obvious that only Mexicans steal—and here are the Gassens, the Katzes, and others as proof."[41] Spanish-language newspapers kept their readers up to date on instances of racial discrimination, for example publicizing the fact that even though Latinos made up nearly one-third of the voters in Santa Barbara County and over a quarter of those in Los Angeles County in 1873, both the Republican and Democratic Parties failed to nominate a single Latino candidate that year.[42]

The threats of police abuse and mob lynching hung over Latino communities. In Fairfield, Pancho Valencia, sentenced to death, had been granted a new trial by the State Supreme Court, but the Solano County sheriff ignored the appeal process and hanged him anyway. The editor of Los Angeles's *La Crónica* publicly opined that the sheriff should be tried for murder.[43] After a "shamefully drunk" mob burned five prisoners alive in the Bakersfield jail, the editor of *La Crónica* sarcastically suggested that state legislators be asked to carry a bill authorizing the lynching of all thieves, with the proviso "that such an edifying act should be committed by drunk American citizens, and that the victims be of the Latino race."[44]

One assurance Latinos had, however, that they were still part of a universalist American society in California was the constitutional right to have laws, regulations, reports, and other official materials from state, county, and city authorities printed in the Spanish language. But by the 1870s, even this was under threat. There was no oversight of the quality of these official translations into Spanish; on one occasion, the editor of *La Crónica* complained that the Spanish translation of a new city ordinance in Los Angeles was so poor it seemed to be written "in a new language, in an unknown tongue which—by right of invention—belongs to the Council's translator," and questioned its validity if no one could understand it.[45] In 1874, the mayor of Los Angeles, citing a need to cut costs, refused to authorize payment to *La Crónica* for printing a list in Spanish of persons who owed back taxes, even though the city council had unanimously approved the expenditure.[46] Later that same year, the governor declared that he had decided to save the state money by ceasing publication of Spanish translations. *La Crónica* objected that some older Latino citizens, including persons who had helped write the 1849 state constitution, did not speak or read English—through no fault of their own, as the state had not provided schools with any bilingual staff. Ignoring or abolishing the Spanish-language provision of the state constitution, therefore, was fundamentally unjust.[47] A Latino state legislator in Colorado and a Spanish-language newspaper in New Mexico publicly applauded *La Crónica's* efforts to uphold the bilingual provisions of California's constitution.[48]

Denis Kearny and the Workingmen's Party

This renewed nativist narrative, made more strident in reaction to the legal racial equality federally mandated under Reconstruction, fed the establishment of the Workingmen's Party, a new political action group formed in 1878 by Denis Kearney. A demagogue, he rose to power during one of California's periodic economic depressions, initially by denouncing capitalism and railroad monopolies. He subsequently fueled nativists' resentments by attacking the presence of Chinese immigrants in California, making famous the phrase "The Chinese must go!" He touted the unrealistic dream that if California were rid of the Chinese, all white men in the state would have work. Kearney rabble-roused on this nativist theme, demanding that California write a new constitution to alleviate the problems the average working man faced. As had the earlier Know-Nothing Party, Kearney's nativist Workingmen's Party swept the state, sidelining the Republican and Democratic candidates, and was able to call a new constitutional convention, to which not one Latino was chosen as a delegate. The resulting 1879 California Constitutional Convention has been called the "runaway convention" because the delegates took up topics far beyond the original issues that had prompted its convening.[49]

Their nativist agenda included Latinos among its targets. The 1849 constitution had provided for the publication of all official communications in English and in Spanish; but from the nativist perspective, Spanish was a foreign language, spoken by a foreign population, and thus ought not to be officially recognized in the state. Old Atlantic American resentments against the recognition of Spanish erupted during the convention, expanding into more general nativist complaints about Latino "foreigners" in California. Wiley James Tinnin—originally from Jackson, in the former Confederate state of Mississippi and now a representative from Weaverville in Modoc County— announced to the convention, "This is an English-speaking Government," and declared himself upset that documents should be published, at government expense, "in Spanish for the benefit of foreigners." Surprised to hear Latinos being called "foreigners," Judge Horace Cowan Rolfe of San Bernardino County asked Tinnin, "Do you call the native population of this state foreigners?" Rolfe was an acquaintance of the Rubidoux family, descendants of a Frenchman who had married a Latina woman from New Mexico and become a naturalized citizen of Mexico in the 1830s. Rubidoux's children and grandchildren still lived in Southern California, were fluent in Spanish, and openly celebrated Mexican Independence Day. Tinnin, however, avoided the real point of the question and, in typically nativist fashion, declared, "They had ample time to learn the language."[50] The nativist narrative prevailed and was enshrined in the 1879 constitution. Article IV, Section 24, read, "All laws of the State of California, and all official writings and the executive, legislative and judicial proceedings shall be conducted, preserved and published in no other than the English language."[51]

After returning to his native Los Angeles in 1877, Reginaldo del Valle opened a law office, and in 1879 he ran successfully for the state Assembly. In January 1880, he was sworn in as its only Latino member. He was perfectly fluent in English, but apparently spoke with a slight accent, as a later *Los Angeles Times* article noted that he pronounced English "with just a suave hint of Castilian [Spanish]."[52] The turmoil stirred up by the Workingmen's Party, with its radical demands for economic and racial reform in California, and by the raucous 1879 constitutional convention, had left the 1880 state legislature the enormous task of redesigning all the state's governing and administrative structures to comply with the new constitution, within just ninety days. One of these tasks, of course, was to remove the bilingual provisions that had been in place for over thirty years. A portion of this task fell to Del Valle, who promptly used his parliamentary skills to contest this removal of Spanish from its status as an official state language.

When a legislator is opposed to a bill, there are many ways to express it. For example, if a bill requires funding for its enforcement, the dissatisfied legislator can reduce the accompanying budget request so drastically as to make its enforcement impossible to carry out. Assembly Bill 184 was introduced to "provide for the keeping of accounts in the English language." Del Valle, the only Latino in the chamber, was the only assemblyman to express opposition to the bill. He was just beginning his political career, and in general, first-time legislators are reluctant to annoy other members by opposing popular bills, but Del Valle made one of his first motions on the floor of the Assembly an oppositional one, in effect announcing his anti-nativist stance. AB 184, however, had no budget that he could attack; in fact, Tinnin had argued during the constitutional convention that eliminating the printing of Spanish-language translations would save the state money. Yet many bills have an enacting clause, to provide direction as to how a law is to be carried out. Del Valle chose to oppose AB 184 by moving to strike out the enacting clause, which would have essentially rendered the bill ineffective. His motion was voted down, and the bill was passed—California moved to the linguistically nativist position of mandating English only—but Del Valle had made the first of many public statements that he would oppose Anglo-Saxonist nativism whenever he could.[53]

The American Protective Association, 1890s

After the furor of the Workingmen's Party died down, immigration from Europe continued to flow into the United States during the 1880s and 1890s. Now, however, the immigrants came increasingly from non-Anglo-Saxon regions, largely from southern and eastern Europe: Italy, Greece, the Austro-Hungarian Empire, the Balkans, Poland, and Russia. In California, immigration from Mexico also began to surge, supplying labor to build the state's rapidly expanding railroads and agricultural sector. Many of these new immigrants, both Mexican and European, were Catholic, and the US Catholic church at this time was vigorously establishing parishes and building parochial schools to meet the needs of its expanding membership.[54]

Henry F. Bowers was a Baltimore native who had lived through the Know-Nothing movement and American Civil War. In the post-Reconstruction era, he took nativism to a new level. Not only did he believe that men of pure Anglo-Saxon stock were solely responsible for founding the United States government, but he was further convinced that the Catholic Church was masterminding a plot to overthrow the Anglo-Saxon–authored US government and impose a Catholic regime, which would take orders from Rome. In 1887, Bowers formed a secret, anti-Catholic, anti-immigrant group called the American Protective Association (APA).[55] By 1894, APA membership had grown to over half a million persons, and APA candidates were running for office.[56] Antonio J. Flores, editor of Los Angeles's *Las Dos Repúblicas,* one of the Spanish-language newspapers published in California during the 1890s, penned a strongly worded editorial on *"esa execrable sociedad"* (that execrable society), the APA. If, by misfortune, it should happen to win the upcoming elections, he warned, Latinos would become pariahs in their own land, treated worse than the Chinese had been treated a generation earlier.[57]

Hoping to motivate Latino voters to turn out to vote against the APA, Flores also sought an interview with Reginaldo del Valle. Since his brush with the nativist Workingmen's Party in 1880, Del Valle had been reelected to the state Assembly, and then elected to the state Senate, where he served as president pro tem of the upper house. By 1894, he had become something of an elder statesman and was also a member of many Latino organizations, by whom he was often invited as a speaker at Cinco de Mayo and Mexican Independence Day celebrations. Understanding the threat of another nativist movement, Del Valle warned Flores's Spanish-speaking readers that the APA was a secret society whose members had taken an oath to keep Catholics from political office. An APA member would only vote for Protestants, swore to do everything in his power to ensure that Catholics were not employed in any government position, and promised personally never to hire a Catholic for any job, if a Protestant could be found instead. Del Valle then listed historical Catholic contributions to the United States, including the European discovery of the Americas by *"un católico ayudado por los Reyes Católicos"* (a Catholic helped by the Catholic Monarchs), and Catholic France's aid to the fledgling United States during the American Revolution. He pointed out that a number of Union generals in the American Civil War had been Catholics, along with a great many of their soldiers, whose defense of the United States was a more than sufficient answer to APA claims of a Catholic plot against the US. Del Valle ended the interview by urging *"los de la raza latina y los que creen fielmente en las libertades de esta gran República"* (those of the Latin race and those who faithfully believe in the freedoms of this great Republic) to defend the constitution by voting for non-APA candidates.[58]

The APA fell apart by the late 1890s. At its height of success, it was rent by an internecine struggle for leadership. Bowers was deposed, and an "opportunistic Michigan publicist" led it through a "brief, flamboyant career of hysteria and political manipulation," after which it collapsed in 1896, deserted by its followers.[59] Unfortunately, its decline did not signal the end of nativist political thinking in either California or the nation as a whole.

Ku Klux Klan Revival and Jim Crow Laws in California in the 1920s

The Mexican Revolution erupted in 1910, and nearly a million Mexicans fled their homeland during the next twenty years. About half of them came to California, creating a Latino population explosion that coincided with a period of renewed nativism. During World War I, however, the induction of men into the US Army created employment opportunities for the refugees, and for a short time the new immigrants flourished. Then the Ku Klux Klan, revived in the early twentieth century, made its appearance in California, where its opposition to nonwhites included not just African Americans but also multiracial Latinos. Klan chapters formed in Los Angeles, San Francisco, Oakland, Sacramento, Santa Barbara, San Diego, the Imperial Valley, and the San Joaquin Valley, especially in Tulare, Fresno, Kings, and Kern Counties.[60] Jim Crow–style segregation, strengthened by the Supreme Court's decision in *Plessy v. Ferguson,* also arrived in California around this time. The nativists' desire to live separately from "inferior races" led to segregation in schools, housing, and public facilities.[61] As Latinos constituted the largest nonwhite ethnic group in the state, they became a particular target of segregation and hate crimes. Upon the return of soldiers to civilian life after World War I, and given the nativist tendencies of the time, many Mexican immigrants lost their jobs. Juan de Heras, editor of Los Angeles's Spanish-language newspaper *El Heraldo de México,* described Mexican immigrant families reduced to living in open fields, suffering during the winter without fuel or warm clothing. Their search for gainful employment frequently met with, "¡No hay trabajo!" (There's no work!).[62]

Seeing the need to address the immigrant community's needs, De Heras founded the Liga Protectora Mexicana (Mexican Protective League) in 1918, on the general model of the *mutualista* movement, to provide food, shelter, and emergency relief for those Latinos who had nowhere else to turn. The Liga was membership based, with dues of fifty cents a month. In addition to trying to provide basic necessities of life, the Liga offered to represent workers in cases of employer-employee conflict and to press for compensation for workplace accidents resulting in injury. As the Liga's financial resources were not extensive, it committed itself to special philanthropic fund-raising efforts when legal or medical situations exhausted available funds.[63] The Liga also concerned itself with resisting violations of Latinos' civil rights. One of its earliest efforts was the attempt to obtain a commutation of the death sentence passed on Ladislao Guerra in 1918. The Liga hired bilingual attorney Antonio Orfila, a contemporary of Del Valle and, like him, a second-generation Latino born in California during the Gold Rush–Civil War era. Orfila called on the governor and contacted the Mexican ambassador in Washington, DC, to try to get the White House to weigh in on the case.[64] As legal costs mounted, the Liga mounted a fund-raising effort, and contributions came in from a number of communities in California—including Los Angeles, Bakersfield, Paso Robles, San Diego, and Santa Paula—as well as from Texas, Arizona, Kansas, and even Baja California.[65] After several weeks' effort, the Liga was able to convince California's governor to commute Guerra's death sentence to life imprisonment.[66]

The Liga also began to offer cultural and educational activities. A reading room was established at its Los Angeles headquarters, and English-language classes were part of its programs.[67] One evening of fund-raising, for instance, included an appearance by a local musical group, the Banda Mexicana Islas Hermanos, which played classical pieces by Von Suppé, Donizetti, Sarasate, and Saint-Saëns, as well as a stirring rendition of the "Himno Nacional Mexicano" (Mexican national anthem). The evening included speeches and ended with a dance.[68]

The needs of unemployed Mexican immigrants were so great, however, that the Liga Protectora Mexicana exhausted its funds within a few years, and by 1921 accepted the assistance of Conrado Gaxiola, the Mexican consul in Los Angeles, and of a sister organization from Arizona, the Liga Protectora Latina. This enabled it to create a more robust response to community needs, the Comité Mexicano de Auxilios (Mexican Aid Committee), which eventually opened a soup kitchen to feed needy immigrants.[69] The Liga Protectora Latina had been founded in Phoenix, Arizona, in 1914, and chapters quickly spread.[70] More importantly, the Liga Protectora Latina had more experience at raising and managing funds, and had a membership familiar with *mutualista*-type organizations. In 1921, de Heras merged the Liga Protectora Mexicana into the Liga Protectora Latina, as Chapter 30 of the latter organization.[71]

Reginaldo del Valle seems to have been involved in the activities of the Liga Protectora Latina, most likely as a fiscal contributor and possibly also as a legal advisor. In 1925, the president of the Liga, Julio Zegner Uriburu, bestowed upon him the Medalla al Merito (Medal of Merit), to recognize his efforts *"en bien de la Raza"* (for the welfare of the [Latino] race). Since 1880, Del Valle had been doing his best to defend Latinos from nativist attacks, and his activities thus embodied the Liga's motto, *Protección—Igualdad—Justicia* (Protection—Equality—Justice).[72] But Del Valle's efforts against nativist attacks were not yet over.

Taking a more universalist approach to protecting their civil rights, Latinos in Texas formed the League of United Latin American Citizens (LULAC), setting forth to claim their constitutional rights by virtue of being loyal, law-abiding US citizens who sincerely believed in the principles of the United States Constitution. Their 1927 bylaws recorded their vow to educate their children about the "duties and rights, language and customs" of this country. Once its membership staked out its universalist position as citizens, LULAC stood on these rights to fight nativist efforts to "create racial prejudices against our people." As American citizens, LULAC members promised to combat the "infamous stigmas being imposed upon them," all the while vowing to be "proud and respectful" of their Mexican "racial origin."[73] Inspired by this example, Daniel Dominguez became the secretary of the San Gabriel Spanish American League, with the goal of organizing a group similar to LULAC in California. By 1934, the California group had drafted bylaws that paralleled LULAC's. The San Gabriel group, comprised of US citizens, claimed the universalist "inalienable rights of all citizens, as set forth in the Constitution of the United States." They undertook to educate their community about "equality, justice, tolerance and American patriotism," supported by a vigorous voter-education campaign, so that via the ballot box they would attain "recognition of said rights by all men." By asserting their rights as US citizens, members of the San Gabriel Spanish American League vowed to combat the discrimination inherent in the "granting of special privileges," by which they most likely meant restrictive covenants and the segregated schools, swimming pools, and restaurants that had become common in California by the 1930s. Dominguez sent a draft of these bylaws to Reginaldo del Valle in 1936, asking him to make a financial donation to the San Gabriel group.[74] Del Valle's response to this request has not survived, but the fact of the request illustrates that throughout his professional life, Del Valle was a leader in battling the nativist narrative in California.

Deporting the "Mexican Problem"

In 1928, California governor C.C. Young directed the state departments of Industrial Relations, Agriculture, and Welfare to find a solution to what he termed "the Mexican Problem" plaguing the state.[75] Employees of these departments, assisted by "Americanization teachers," conducted surveys and collected data on the perceived problem.[76] Meanwhile, the US census declared that Mexicans were a nonwhite race completely different from whites, and were to be enumerated along with other nonwhite races in the 1930 census: Negroes, Indians, Chinese, Japanese, Filipinos, and the newest racial group, "Mexican."[77] Governor Young's Mexican Fact-Finding Committee followed the lead of the US census and "racially segregated" state and country records so as to discover clues about the "intelligence of the group" they called "Mexican."[78] Two years later, the committee's tautological report on "the problem of Mexican immigration into California" concluded that the problem, in essence, lay in the immigration of Mexicans into California. Governor Young reported to the state in 1930 that the Mexican Problem required a "solution" at the national level.[79]

By the time the report was released, the Great Depression was forcing millions out of work, which created serious strains on state and local welfare departments. Consequently, the nativist "solution" to the Mexican Problem called for deporting the "problem" population back to Mexico, which would open up jobs for "real Americans" and thereby reduce welfare costs. As a result, during the 1930s over 1 million legal US residents and American citizens of Mexican descent were forcibly removed from their homes and transported to Mexico. The trauma of this abrupt uprooting and expulsion from the only country they had ever known scarred a generation of Latinos so deeply that, sixty years later, many US citizens came forward in 2003 to testify at the California State Senate Hearings on Unconstitutional Deportation and Coerced Immigration. Sometimes in tears, they shared their stories of how they, US citizens, were deported, and their lives broken, in order to solve Governor Young's "Mexican Problem."[80] For a decade and more, a generation of Latinos—whom I call the deportation era generation—grew up learning to hide their Mexican roots, so as not to stand out and be liable to sudden deportation.

Nativism Permeates Research on Latinos

A flood of new immigrants from southern Europe from 1880 to 1910 had to be assimilated into American life, a goal Theodore Roosevelt described in 1915 in terms redolent of nativism: "There is no room in this country for hyphenated Americanism. . . . There is no such thing as a hyphenated American who is a good American. The only man who is a good American is the man who is an American and nothing else."[81] Roosevelt had written a multivolume series, *The Winning of the West,* which laid out an Anglo-Saxonist historical narrative of a small group of English-speaking settlers arriving on the Atlantic shore and expanding their territory to the Pacific Ocean. This narrative depicted them boldly picking up their rifles, traveling in successive waves to the farthest, wildest edge of the American wilderness, and taking the land from malevolent Indians, treacherous and corrupt Spaniards, and ignorant, indolent French. In common with many of his Atlantic American contemporaries, Roosevelt worried that the plunging birth rate of the "White American race stock" might result in "race suicide," unless the non-Nordic immigrants arriving were to completely assimilate into and join the core national ethnic group, laying aside all prior allegiances, languages, and cultures.[82] Roosevelt's historical account implied that if immigrants rejected nonwhite, Catholic, Latinate cultures—such as the ones from which many of them came—they might be admitted to membership in the privileged white, Anglo-Saxon,Protestant, English-speaking core national group.

Based on similar cultural assumptions, social researchers in the 1920s developed a theoretical model of the "assimilating immigrant" and created scales—for example, "Do they speak English Very Well, Well, Not Well, or Not At All?"—to calculate the degree to which immigrants, and their children and grandchildren, "unlearn their inferior cultural traits" in order to be fully accepted in American society.[83] Park and Burgess, two of the major theorists of the "assimilating immigrant" model, marveled at the speed and ease with which the children of Poles, Lithuanians, and Norwegians assimilated into American society, so thoroughly that soon they could not be distinguished from Americans "born of native parents." They assumed that this unidirectional, linear assimilation would be the future of all immigrants in

America, resulting in a melting pot that would tolerate "every sort of normal human difference," except, of course, differences of culture, color, and race.[84] When applied to Latinos, the assimilating immigrant model presumes that they, despite having had a settled presence in what is now the United States since 1526, are somehow intransigently foreign and un-American because they do not exhibit "sufficiently" the cultural traits of the core national ethnic group as defined by nativists. As long ago as the California Constitutional Convention in 1849, José Antonio Carrillo contested this narrow definition of "American," championing instead a universalist definition based on adherence to core values derived from the Latino-Catholic experience of Western society and generally shared by English-speaking Protestants. Ignorant of such historical contestations of the definition of "American," most researchers in the twenty-first century unthinkingly continue to measure Latino acculturation and assimilation by nativist standards of language and culture, in the mistaken belief that Latinos are largely "foreign immigrants." In fact, for over 160 years, the majority of Latinos in California have been born in the state, and hence are not immigrants (see chapter 7 for demographic details).

By the 1970s and 1980s, however, the new nativism appeared to expand its definition of "American" from merely being a white, Anglo-Saxon, English-speaking Protestant to holding individualist mores such as the work ethic, independence from welfare, family values, and good health behaviors—all of which, not coincidentally, were represented as characteristic of white, Anglo-Saxon, English-speaking, Protestant culture. By these standards, a "true American" was one who worked hard, did not use welfare, formed families, and exhibited good health behavior and outcomes. For the period covered by this book, 1940 to 2015, data from the US census and other sources make clear that Latinos have shown by their high labor force participation, low welfare use, strong families, strong entrepreneurial activity, and superior health behaviors and outcomes that they consistently exhibit these individualist values and behaviors; indeed, so much so that Latinos now are reinforcing these basic building blocks of society throughout the US as a whole. Despite this, researchers unwittingly perpetuate nativism in nearly all research conducted on Latinos, through their unexamined use of assimilation and acculturation scales based on nativist assumptions about language and cuture. Debates about the "American-ness" of Latinos, begun over 160 years ago, continue to drive elections, policy, and research on Latinos in the twenty-first century.

Nativism's Survivors

In the late 1990s, the United Way of Greater Los Angeles wanted to issue a research-based Latino Report Card to highlight progress that Latinos in the region were making and to identify roadblocks to greater progress, to which the United Way could then turn its philanthropic focus. As an initial step in that project, during the summer of 1998, the Center for the Study of Latino Health and Culture (CESLAC) at UCLA convened a number of middle-aged Latinos in an effort to understand how nativist rhetoric had affected them during their lives. Born in the 1940s and 1950s, these participants had grown up in a world far different from the one they lived in by the late 1990s. They were old enough to remember a much more overtly segregated, exclusionary society. Still expressing hurt and pain forty years later, they described growing up in situations in which Latino claims to American identity were not validated by the rest of society. As one participant expressed it, "Back then [1950s] . . . who cares? You're just a Mexican, you're a 'beaner,' you know, you're a 'greaser.'"[85]

During the postwar period, these older participants remembered, the Spanish language was largely suppressed, especially in the public sphere. There was no Spanish television, very little radio, only one newspaper, and certainly no billboards or bus placards in Spanish. "It's real easy to live here now and speak Spanish. It wasn't when my mother was growing up, in the fifties and the sixties. I don't think it was."[86] While Spanish was merely absent from most aspects of public life, it was actively rooted out in the schools these participants had attended. Many older respondents remembered being punished if they spoke Spanish at school, which was a disincentive to developing fluency in that language. "In high school . . . you wanted not to speak Spanish, and [teachers would] punish us. . . . I didn't want to hang around anybody that spoke Spanish."[87] The longer they stayed in school, the more the idea that Spanish was somehow bad worked into the images these respondents had of their families, their culture, and themselves; and those images were themselves largely negative. Anglo-Saxonist rhetoric had wormed its way into their personal lives, into their own feelings about self and family. If Spanish was bad, those who spoke it must be bad, and the culture they came from, by association, must also be bad. "[My] own language, in a way, for me, was invalidated. We were punished if we spoke Spanish. So, as a kid, your values, all of a sudden is [sic], 'What I have known—my parents, my grandmother, all these people that I've loved—were speaking wrong.'"[88]

In the days before the emergence of Chicano studies on college campuses, a passive ignorance of Latino culture and history reinforced this active invalidation. The California school curriculum of the 1940s, 1950s, and 1960s tended to present a triumphant Anglo-Saxonist expansionist version of state history, with almost no mention of Latinos in California or of relations with Mexico in US history. As a result, many older Latinos grew up knowing very little, if anything, about Latino or Latin American culture with which to balance nativist claims. "My great-grandma was born in Mexico, but I don't know anything about it."[89] As a result, these older Latinos grew up with a void in their identity. For some, particularly those who did not go to college and therefore missed out on the heyday of the Chicano movement, that void continued up to the day of their participation in the focus group. "Supposedly I'm Mexican, but I don't know the background. I don't know anything about the Aztecs or anything, so I don't have anything to say 'This is me.' I don't know who I am, as far as culture."[90] At its most virulent, this constant downgrading of things Latino led some to actively deny their Latino families and friends. "Yeah, I mean, I knew I was Mexican; but then I had my mother tell me, here, because of her experiences, that 'People ask you, you tell them you are white. You're tall; you can pass for white. You're light-skinned. Don't say you are Mexican.'"[91]

For nearly a century prior to 1965, the nativist narrative defined Latinos as the opposite of the WASP population: mixed-race, Catholic, Spanish speakers—and hence not American. This nativist narrative powered a political impetus to limit the languages Latinos could speak, the schools they could attend, the houses they could buy, the public facilities they could use. All these restrictions were imposed externally, by a society that defined anyone who was not white—and hence, by nativist definition, not able to be a "real American"—as thereby inferior to those who were. One focus group participant remembered how these externally imposed definitions had become internalized in her own family, to the extent that they had determined which boys she could date. "All my life my mother has told me, 'If somebody asks what you are, you tell them you're white. . . . Don't tell anyone you're a Mexican. Don't like Mexican boys, because you're never gonna get ahead. Like a white boy.' Okay? I've had that drilled in me."[92] This struggle between Latinos holding to a universalist vision of America and those persons espousing a nativist vision would continue into the twenty-first century.

TWO

Latinos Reject America's Definition

1965–1975

The thing that strikes me [as] funny is that . . . a lot of people who
are my contemporaries . . . talk about "in the days of the Chicano
movement," like it's past tense, like it happened and it's over. . . .
To me, it's present and alive [in 1999]. . . . It's more like a glimpse
of the future, if we understand it.

IN REACTION TO ANGLO-SAXONIST NATIVISM in California during
the Gold Rush, the American Civil War, the Workingmen's Party, and the
American Protective Association, Latinos commonly asserted their rights as
Americans because they were believers in the universalist definition of
"American" shared by nearly all Latin American governments during the
nineteenth century. Yet the rise of "scientific racism" in the early twentieth
century codified Anglo-Saxonist race-based definitions of "American" into
law, starting with the landmark *Plessy v. Ferguson* case, which mandated
second-class citizenship for nonwhites. Racial restrictions tightened on
California's Latinos in the 1920s, as public and private facilities increasingly
were restricted to whites only, and then the 1930 census officially declared
Latinos to be members of a nonwhite race called "Mexican." In response,
Latinos continued to fight Anglo-Saxonism by insisting that they enjoyed
the same rights as any other loyal American citizens, irrespective of race. But
the Latino response to such nativism changed dramatically in the 1960s and
1970s, as Chicano-era Latinos essentially rejected the Anglo-Saxonists and
Anglo-Saxonism.

During the tempestuous 1960s, various groups sought a more significant
place in American policymaking than they had previously occupied: the
African American civil rights movement, the anti–Vietnam War movement,
the women's movement, the first wave of the gay and lesbian movement, the
Native American movement, the disability rights movement . . . the list of
aggrieved groups seeking public redress seemed to go on and on. Among the

new currents of political activism of the time, Chicano Power registered on the public consciousness, too, albeit feebly. While this Latino movement appeared to be only one of many competing for attention in those heady days when change was the only constant, it was powerful enough to change Latino self-consciousness permanently. "It was a time where there was a lot of political awareness, not just in the Chicano community, because it was during the Vietnam War. People were very active at the time. It was the flower generation, peace generation, a lot of activism."[1]

I was a participant-observer in the events of that era (1965–1975), and in fact changed my doctoral dissertation topic—from a study of Latino patient behavior to a study of the socialization processes experienced by the first generation of Latino medical, dental, nursing, and professional students—so that I could better understand the social world we were creating with the formation of the National Chicano Health Organization (NCHO). Thirty years after those events, trying to understand the role that the Chicano generation continues to play in Latino daily life, I returned to many of those original informants for my dissertation and reinterviewed them. I was curious how their participation in the Chicano movement had marked them, their professional decisions, their family lives, their roles now as parents, providers, key economic nuclei in various communities, and high-impact political participants. Between 1997 and 2001, I interviewed forty-six of these *veteranos* (veterans of the Chicano movement), adding a few interviews with members of the older deportation-era generation who had interacted with these "young Turks" during the sixties and seventies. The quotations in this chapter are from those interviews. "All of this activism had an interesting effect on the community and what I consider the mental health of the community. It gave us a purpose; it gave us a reason to be; it gave us a sense of community. And sometimes we felt like it was us against the world."[2]

NOT QUITE AMERICAN

By the late 1960s, the Latino population in California numbered nearly one and a half million, a tremendous upsurge from the one-third of a million just thirty years earlier. Despite the increasing prosperity of the postwar era, Latino families did not fully share in the economic boom. For example, at the beginning of the 1950s, 60.6% of Latinos lived in poverty, compared to

25.5% of non-Hispanic whites.[3] "I was raised in what was then call [sic] Jingle-town, which was the barrio of Whittier. That's where the Mexicans lived. . . . It was a little barrio with dirt streets and no light, all that sort of stuff. It was very primitive."[4]

Having grown up in a more racially segregated California, postwar-generation young Latinos were aware that they were different, and somehow separate, from the non-Hispanic white majority around them. "I am very dark; I am very brown. I had more identity problems growing up as a teenager here in the U.S. I used to think that nobody was ever going to marry me because I was so dark. I was in a very white school."[5] Particularly for those few who later went to college, schooling often took place outside of barrio schools, which only heightened their sense of difference, even exclusion. "We went to that school until high school. So, for me, life was always being the oddball, the cute little Mexican kid among all these Anglos. My brother and I were the only Latinos, so it put us in a very difficult situation sometimes."[6]

Population pressure created by the baby boomers had pushed the construction of new elementary and high schools in California, culminating in the formulation of the California Master Plan for Higher Education and a building boom at the community college, state university, and University of California levels. These new educational facilities, however, were out of reach for most Latinos. By 1960, fewer than one out of every four Latino adults had graduated from high school (24.2%), and very few had graduated from college (3.2%).[7] Yet despite the lack of societal incentives, a small number of Latino high school students in the 1950s and 1960s caught the state's educational fever and were determined to go to college. "Well, I'm the first in my family to get a college education. . . . When I announced to my parents, my senior year in high school, that I wanted to go to college, they were shocked. No one in their family had ever gone to college, and they were very proud and very supportive."[8]

When they arrived on the college campuses, though, these Latino students continued to feel out of place. Even the campuses located in Latino barrios, such as California State University, Los Angeles, had very few Latino students. "I got out of college early on in 1966 . . . at Cal State L.A. . . . You have to recall, at that point in time, Los Angeles had the biggest Latino population outside of Mexico City. You had 45 Spanish-surname students in a population of 24–25,000 students."[9] In 1964, there were seventy Latino students at UCLA; this figure had increased to three hundred by 1967. There were seventy-eight Latino students at UC Berkeley in 1966, and a total of two hundred Latinos enrolled at San José State University that same year.[10] The number of Latinos in the graduate and professional schools was even smaller.

> The first month I was at USC medical school, I did get the alumni list—and USC med school has been there since 1885—and I could pick out about twenty Spanish-sounding surnames over the eighty-year period. [There was] some overlap—Portuguese, Italians, or could be González straight from Zaragoza, Spain, who ain't got nothing to do with the 'hood. So, for an eighty-year period, it was around twenty Latino possible [medical students].[11]

By the mid-1960s, a small number of soon-to-be highly influential Latinos had made their way onto the state's college and university campuses, acutely aware that, from the nativist perspective, they were not quite American, with a gnawing outrage at the injustices Latinos had endured for being "different."

> In the '64, '65, '66 period . . . I knew that there was a difference in the way the system functioned for Latino people and for non-Latino people. . . . One of the dynamics . . . molding me . . . was really anger and revenge. I felt that the Latino people were not getting their fair share, and I tried to turn those energies into positive energies, to work on issues that would enhance Latino power and give us a fair share of what our community was entitled to.[12]

Although the Chicano movement had roots that ran generations deep, it was very much influenced by the spirit of the times. President Lyndon B. Johnson launched the War on Poverty as part of the civil rights agenda of the mid-1960s. For five successive years, urban America witnessed riots and disturbances. Social change was in the air. "I would say my first overtly political experience was the Vietnam Summer, based on the Mississippi Summer when they registered black folks in Mississippi. The summer of 1967, I got involved in Vietnam Summer. I got trained; I focused on fundraising, media, and did a lot of draft counseling."[13] The Chicano movement would have happened without that context, but such an invigorating social environment certainly made the entrée to social activism more acceptable than it had been for deportation-era Latinos.

> In the middle of my college career, coming home for the summer, I had to deal with the Chicano moratorium . . . and that helped kind of crystallize . . . this sense of the Chicano movement and what Chicanos were looking for, why they were protesting and why they felt certain injustices existed. And of course, the highlight of that whole experience was the unfortunate death of Ruben Salazar, the [Los Angeles] *Times* reporter.[14]

Latinos of the 1920s and 1930s had battled discrimination in their own way, suing to end segregated schools and military segregation, and organizing labor unions and community service organizations. The major generational difference was that Chicano-era Latinos insisted on asserting a cultural presence that had been conspicuously lacking during deportation-era efforts. This sudden insistence on being unmistakably Latino was, at first, upsetting and confusing for the deportation-era generation, as described by one interviewee in his eighth decade of life: "The younger generations of that particular time [1960–1970] preferred to be called Chicanos, and my [1930s] generation preferred not to be called Chicanos. It's just a matter of choice between the two distinct elements, because we were completely distinct."[15] The term *Chicano,* used to assert that cultural identity, was a shock for some members of the earlier generation. They had soft-pedaled their Mexicanness; moreover, for them *Chicano* was derogatory. It meant *pachuco;* it meant zoot-suiter; it meant juvenile delinquent.

Cultural self-determination—the right to express oneself in the terms one thinks fit—was a touchstone for Chicano-era Latinos.[16] That cultural assertion was key to rejecting the definitions imposed by Anglo-Saxonist American society. Yet this cultural assertion was, at times, accompanied by a number of cultural contradictions. For instance, despite the emphasis on bilingual education, the stark reality was that very few Latinos of that era had developed fluency in Spanish; the vast majority—80.6% in 1960—had been born in the United States, where there were significant pressures to learn English and suppress Spanish.[17] An elderly, deportation-era Latino physician offered his views on Chicanos' Spanish-speaking abilities: "The Californian Mexican-American very seldom know [*sic*] Spanish enough to communicate with [immigrant] people, so that is one of the deficits I see.... They say that 'I'm going to help my people.' So how can you help your people if you can't communicate with them? If they [immigrants] feel comfortable coming to talk to you in Spanish, and you don't understand?"[18]

Participants in the Chicano movement invariably described their involvement as an emotional, cathartic experience. The spirit of the times seemed to bind together those active in the movement. Many described feeling free to be "brown and proud"; it was a touching experience that few have forgotten. "These marches seemed to give [me] a means of expression, a means of pride. Because it is at this time, 1968 forward, that I became comfortable in my own skin, that I became proud to be identified as a Chicana."[19] This was a catharsis of pent-up resentment and anger at many injustices suffered, both personally and collectively. The emotional release was described by respondents as being extremely intense. "And it felt like . . . this was the first time . . . that people were advocating for welfare rights, for health, for education, for real participation in a political arena. And I became, you know, very passionate, you know, very, *very,* VERY, *VERY* passionate about these issues."[20]

But the downside of such passionate involvement in a movement that combined the cultural with the political was the emergence, at times, of a streak of intolerance for those who were considered not sufficiently "Chicano," whether culturally or politically. In that era, a medical student who had just had his Chicano-ness questioned by another Chicano medical student confided to me that such remarks seemed to be a game of *Soy más chicano que tú* (I'm more Chicano than you). The personal became political. What one wore, what one ate, the friends one associated with, the music one listened to: all were symbols of being a good, or bad, Chicano. Usually, an intense cultural nationalism was difficult to sustain beyond a few months or a couple of years. Even the most ardent nationalists during that time later relaxed their demanding standards to more reasonable levels. "I mean, I got fairly nationalist, you know—1968, 1969, 1970. . . . You know, cultural nationalism, [as] in 'Latinos as the center of the universe.' . . . You go through a nationalist phase. Thankfully, I'm over it. I mean, it only lasted, in my view, a few years."[21]

Of course, the political was political, too. Marxism and Marxist-inspired literature were on many reading lists, and even science students found themselves reading and pondering many variations of Marxism.

> At that time I was reading a lot of . . . Marxist philosophy, and was interested in social justice and ideas of distributive justice. I wasn't really ever, you know, a hard-core Marxist. I was always a little nervous about some of the things that happened in some of the socialist countries and the communist countries. But as a philosophy, I was interested.[22]

Often, Chicano-era groups used the imagery of Latino revolutionary figures—Emiliano Zapata, Pancho Villa, Che Guevara—as a way of asserting presence in the face of huge institutions, such as university campuses. At times, this inspirational imagery was misinterpreted by non-Latinos unaware of the emotions the images touched.

I should tell you a side story. Our [student group] emblem at that time—remember, we are going through the sixties and the Vietnam War and all of that stuff—was the face of Che Guevara, with his beret and his star in the middle. Some of our faculty, who were ex-military, became alarmed . . . [and] informed me that the FBI was investigating the organization because it could be subversive. Of course, nothing was farther from the truth. I think we just wanted an equal opportunity.[23]

Even thirty years later, the reinterviewed Chicano-era Latinos felt a sense of pride in that rebellious period in their lives. The rebellion was not that of a lonely "rebel without a cause"; rather, it made individuals feel they were part of a larger, dynamic social movement that provided concrete meaning in their lives, both then and thirty years later. "I am very comfortable with the term *Chicano,* but I recognize that it's a loaded word in some people's minds. They don't like it, but for me it was a political word that had political significance during my days as an undergraduate student."[24]

STRUCTURING THE REJECTION

The decade 1965–1975 was the heyday of the early Chicano movement: César Chávez and the United Farmworkers; Corky Gonzalez's Crusade for Justice; the new Raza Unida Party, which promised to bring the boys home from Vietnam; the high school "blowouts" in East Los Angeles; the student strikes at various college and university campuses around the state to agitate for courses in Chicano studies; the Chicano moratorium in San Francisco and Los Angeles; the Brown Beret occupation of Catalina Island.

Rejecting the expectations social analysts had of Italian, Irish, or Jewish immigrants of earlier generations, Latinos of the Chicano generation did not slip quietly into the American mainstream, culturally speaking. Researchers on European immigrant groups, such as Gordon (1964), had expected that the grandchildren of these immigrants would be, in nearly all things, "American," with a mild "third-generation return" resulting in a thin residuum of St. Patrick's Day parades and other pro forma ethnic festivals once a year.[25] Chicano-generation US-born Latinos overtly and publicly rejected this expectation as the only possible outcome. Instead, they burst onto the state's cultural and political scene with the energy of waters that had long been pent up behind a dam athwart a natural riverbed. "It was one of those, I guess, youth rebellion things, where people would tell you not to do [something] is more of the reason why you would do it. And on top of that, we didn't . . . know what we couldn't do. And so we said, 'Let's try it.'"[26]

Like flood waters spilling over the cement channels of the Los Angeles River, the energies of the Chicano generation overran attitudes and institutions that had been built regarding the Latino presence in the state. The Chicano activists scoured the surface of more than a hundred years of nativist definitions.

> There were several arenas. One was the whole area of police and police brutality, concerns about how the police were beating Chicanos. There was a whole lot of work done on welfare rights. . . . And there was a whole other arena that was concerned about the role of the [Catholic] church and its inclusion of Latinos in its work. And out of that were concerns about the quality of education.[27]

Angered by the high percentage of Latino high school dropouts, Chicano activists applied pressure on schools for better educational outcomes. They insisted that this new educational environment include bilingual and bicultural education. Thirsty to learn the Mexican and Latin American history their schools had not taught them, they pushed schools, colleges, and universities to offer courses, and then to establish centers and departments of Chicano studies. "My commitment . . . goes back to the student movement, as I mentioned, in Santa Barbara. And we had what was called a *Plan de Santa Bárbara* . . . which is really about higher education."[28] Fed up with years of nativist-inspired insults and segregation, they established civil rights organizations such as the Mexican American Legal Defense and Education Fund (MALDEF), the Southwest Council of La Raza, and California Rural Legal Assistance, which doggedly defended Latino civil and cultural rights whenever they were attacked. "We did form our Brown Beret chapter. I was the minister of health. It was a health problem if the goddamn cops take a Mexican out at 3:00 in the morning, take him behind the K-Mart, and beat the shit out of him and dump him into a canister [dumpster]. . . . A bunch of Mexicans were pissed off about having the cops beat the shit out of them."[29]

Outraged by years of neglect by basic public institutions—schools, highways, parks, streets and lighting, health care services—they established hundreds of alternative community health centers, bilingual libraries, job-training centers, mental health programs, community development centers, and the like. "I think the *Zeitgeist,* the spirit of the times, was that all of us were aware of our roles and responsibilities in issues of social justice in general.

Everybody . . . did their own personal things, but that was one sort of uniting feature that was part of the culture of the times."[30]

Given the overtly political nature of many Chicano-era organizations, culture and politics were intertwined. The muralist movement, for example, saw itself as both aesthetic and political. Murals were meant to move Latinos emotionally, to motivate them to become involved. Mural art spread like wildfire; soon murals covered walls up and down the state. The radio waves were another medium for organizing, and a small Chicano public radio movement began. In rural areas of California, such as Santa Rosa and Fresno, small FM stations started up, whose target audiences were rural agricultural workers. In urban areas, public radio stations introduced Chicano programming for an hour or two per week: a lowrider program with a political message in Berkeley, a Saturday night soulful-oldies show in Pasadena, a day of salsa music on a Jesuit college station.

Some Chicano-era Latinos threw themselves, body and soul, into *la causa* (the cause). The needs were so great that they could consume every waking hour. Rather than being daunted at the enormity of the task ahead of them, however, some Chicano-era Latinos recalled that, in those days, they took to it with relish. Their very involvement was invigorating, refreshing, and all-consuming. "It felt good. It was a lot of fun, to be honest with you. . . . I mean, basically, we were tied together by a common ethic about what we wanted to do. And we still had a lot of other things that we did, studies and work. And [we] had fun, you know. We had good parties, all that. So it was really pretty exciting."[31] Thanks to such enthusiasm, a tremendous amount of social infrastructure was created. But this high level of involvement could not be sustained forever.

NOT QUITE MEXICAN

When they were younger, this generation had been told in many subtle nativist ways that they were not truly American. Now they embraced the Mexican aspect of themselves that they had once felt compelled to hide. They enrolled in courses in the newly instituted programs of Chicano studies and Latin American studies. For some, this embrace included traveling to Mexico, the "motherland," expecting to be welcomed as long-lost relatives. Once there, however, they were quickly disabused of the notion that Mexicans considered them fellow Mexicans. Often, when Chicanos traveled to Mexico for the first time, relatives, friends, and even hotel maids would be quick to let them know that they did not speak Spanish properly; that they dressed like Americans; that their values, attitudes, and opinions were not "really Mexican." They were *pochos* (US-born persons), from the other side of the border.

> I remember, in about '71, a group of students from UCSF, Chicanos who had never been to Mexico, climbed in a Volkswagen bus, drove to Tijuana to go visit the "motherland." They told me about it afterwards. . . . Literally, the minute they got across the border, they stopped and got off and kissed the ground. "Motherland, we're here." And they got robbed, and they got cheated and stolen; their van was picked clean. . . . They got treated miserably. . . . The motherland rejected them.[32]

Thus, many Chicanos were caught in a quandary: too Mexican to be American, too American to be Mexican. They felt they were somewhere between two worlds.

By and large, Chicano activism came from the state's college and university campuses, but there were very few Latinos in higher education during the 1960s and early 1970s. "We were this passionate little rag-tag group of activists, and yet the majority of these people have gone on to become very productive professional leaders in their own areas . . . doctors, writers, professors, lawyers, movie producers. I mean, they're artists; they've become everything."[33]

In their assertion of cultural presence, this generation also attempted to awaken their 1930s deportation-era Latino parents, who, some Chicanos felt, had sold out their cultural heritage in an effort to blend in. "I'd be at these demonstrations. I had long braids, and I'd wear what my mother called funny clothes; and she said, 'Lucia, you look like an *india* [Indian].' I said, 'But, Mother, we *are* Indians.' And my mother would just go, 'Absolutely, this one is hopeless.'"[34] Some respondents described how their initial resentment at their parents' lack of support mellowed over the years, as they came to understand that their parents had had their own issues to deal with during the deportation era, which the Chicano era, in its zeal, had overlooked.

> So, for me, it was a romantic notion. Here's César Chávez trying to improve the lot of the farmworker. And for my mother, it was a painful memory . . . because I had forgotten, in my own zeal, that my mother had to work the migrant [farmworker] streams too, as she was a child. She never graduated . . . because she'd be taken out of school [to work].[35]

As the militant, more confrontational Chicano activity gradually mellowed, even the older deportation-era generation grudgingly allowed that some important things had been accomplished. Even the word that once meant "juvenile delinquent" had become a part of the Latino lexicon. "You didn't want to be called a Chicano in my day [the deportation era]. There would be a fight if you called me a Chicano. But today [1999], it is acceptable."[36]

In the spring of 1971, about twenty Latino medical and dental students met in the Millberry Student Union at the University of California Medical Center, San Francisco. While the student conference rooms in the building enjoyed a panoramic view of the Golden Gate Bridge and the rolling Marin County headlands, none of the young Latinos looked out the window. Their attention was riveted to the business at hand: a peace conference, of sorts. They had come from medical and dental schools in the Southwest: California, Texas, Colorado, New Mexico, and Arizona. Only two years earlier, there had been a total of three Latino medical students in all nine of California's medical schools, and similarly small numbers in the other states. But in 1969, under pressure from the American Association of Medical Colleges, health professional schools in the country began to admit significant numbers of Latino applicants. Once they entered the medical and dental schools, they organized themselves into affinity groups, with names like Chicanos for Health and Education (CHE) at UCMCSF, Chicanos for Creative Medicine (CCM) at UCLA and USC, Mexican American Students for Health (MASH) in Arizona, and the Texas Association of Mexican American Medical Students. The organizations differed slightly, but they had arrived at the same conclusion: there was a need to press health professional schools for ongoing Latino recruitment, admissions, retention, and financial aid. The meeting in San Francisco was an attempt to create a new organization out of these separate groups, to be called the National Chicano Health Organization (NCHO). Those from Colorado invoked the organizing ability of the boxer Corky Gonzalez; those from Texas extolled the political power base of the Raza Unida Party established by José Angel Gutiérrez to take the mayorship in Crystal City; those from New Mexico reveled in the armed rebellion of Reies Tijerina to reestablish the old Spanish land grants; and those from California pointed with pride to the achievements of César Chávez and the farmworkers. Those able to do so sprinkled their English with Spanish phrases.

Late in the tense, nonstop day, without a meal break, one of the San Francisco host students suggested the group grab a burger and some fries down at the corner stand, then get back to battling over ideological turf. Eyes flashing with fury, a pony-tailed medical student from Southern California, wearing an embroidered Mexican peasant shirt and huarache sandals, stood up and said, "That's what I would expect from a bunch of *vendidos* [sellouts]—going out for a hamburger. Eating a hamburger is committing cultural genocide. We eat tacos, or we eat nothing." A debate ensued, and meeting participants voted to find a Mexican restaurant, a show of solidarity with the Latino community and a reinforcement of their cultural heritage. A *real* Chicano, it was decided, would never eat a hamburger. This incident encapsulates the quandary felt by not a few Latinos of this generation: Am I really Chicano? After all, I don't speak Spanish. My parents were not farmworkers. In fact, they were middle class. I didn't go to high school in a barrio. I don't own a lowrider, and no one in my family is a *vato loco* (gang member) or a *pinto* (former prison inmate). I studied science while my classmates were boycotting grapes. What does a "real" Chicano act like?

The National Chicano Health Organization was finally founded, in the summer of 1971, as an umbrella organization aiming to satisfy the needs and demands of medical, dental, and other health professional students from San Francisco to Houston. A governing board of representatives from each of the states met often to set policy, develop programs, and provide guidance to each group of incoming medical students. As with many organizations, the more important policies were never written down but were passed orally from one class of students to the next. Each year, this lore became increasingly succinct, providing an informal model of what a "real" Chicano physician should be like:

—Use the Chinese "barefoot doctor" as a community service model.

—Swear never to set up a private practice, because that is capitalist medicine.

—Swear to avoid the specialties, because the Latino community needs primary care physicians, and few Latinos can afford specialty care.

—Be an employee physician, ideally with a farmworkers' clinic. If that is not possible, at least be a salaried employee of a community clinic.

—Never, ever be caught dead talking to a member of the California Hispanic American Medical Association. They are the enemy. After all, they aren't even Chicano—they're *Hispanic*.

DEMOGRAPHICS OF CULTURAL CHANGE:
THE NEW IMMIGRANTS

Two policy changes at the national level had an impact on the Latino community as profound as the energies of the Chicano generation had had: the ending of the *bracero* (agricultural guest worker) program and the elimination of national-origin quotas for immigration. Like the Chicano movement, these policy initiatives contributed to emerging Latino self-confidence, but in a different way. The Chicano movement—angry young people with rhetoric, theory, and plans—took the path of confrontation. Federal decisions on immigration policy initiated changes in a quieter, less self-conscious, but very basic way: the way of the immigrant Latino.

The bracero program began in 1942, the result of an agreement between the United States and Mexico to provide emergency labor for designated employers, usually in agriculture, who were suffering from World War II's drain on the labor force. Braceros were not immigrants; they were temporary guest workers, with none of the rights of immigrants. They were under contract for a limited period, and their movements were heavily restricted; they could not leave farm labor camps without permission; they could not rent or buy property; they could not bring their families with them; and they could not marry a resident of California. Nevertheless, they were the first tendrils of later, more voluminous, immigration. As seasonal guest workers, braceros were often not captured in public enumerations such as the census.

Agricultural interests profited from this cheap, docile labor force, which was essentially bound labor, contracted to a specific employer. For twenty-two years, prospective employers sent recruiters to Mexico; for twenty-two years, repeated journeys between specific villages in Mexico and specific employers in California gradually solidified these routes, and a tremendous annual seasonal immigration took shape. An entire generation of Mexican workers grew up dreaming of work opportunities *en el norte* (north of the border).

The end of the bracero program in 1964 did not mean that the need for Mexican labor had expired. Rather, coupled with the 1965 changes in immigration law, which finally allowed immigration from Mexico and the western hemisphere, it meant that former braceros could return to their old jobs, but increasingly as immigrants rather than as guest workers. For nearly the first time since the late 1920s, immigrant Latinos returned in force to familiar neighborhoods in East Los Angeles, east San José, the Mission District of

San Francisco, and scores of other neighborhoods around the state where settlers from Mexico had established themselves ever since 1769. Once jobs were secure, they brought their wives and children. Slowly they began to settle down and raise their families. Unlike US-born Chicanos, who were acutely aware of their cultural choices, immigrants rarely thought about what a "real" Latino would do; they simply were parents, workers, neighbors, godparents, cousins, and parishioners. Immigrant Latinos did not feel that they committed cultural genocide by eating a hamburger. They did not feel the need to wear huaraches or peasant clothes to feel Mexican. By and large, they did not see themselves consciously as "Latino," much less as a group with a political agenda. Daily life was consumed by making a living, and their aspirations rarely reached beyond the four walls of their houses.

Among the trickle of immigrant Latinos beginning to arrive in California in the post–World War II era were physicians trained in medical schools in Mexico, Argentina, Peru, the Dominican Republic, and other Latin American countries. During that period, immigrant Latino International Medical Graduate (IMG) physicians entering the state comprised close to 90% of all Latino physicians, as all the state's medical schools combined managed to graduate only one or two Latino physicians each year until the mid-1970s. Fluent in Spanish and comfortable with a Latino clientele, they established thriving practices in east San José, Fresno, East Los Angeles, the Mission District of San Francisco, and other barrios densely populated by a quietly increasing number of Latinos. "If you went to the east side [of Los Angeles] in the late fifties and sixties, you found out that health care was provided by foreign-trained [Latino] physicians, not American-trained [Latino] physicians."[37]

A number of these immigrant Latino IMGs wound up practicing at Monterey Park Hospital, east of Los Angeles. They commiserated with one another over the issues all Latino immigrants, even highly educated immigrant physicians, faced in California: the travails of forming a family and buying a house, limited Spanish-language television or radio programming, the paucity of Spanish-language newspapers, the challenges of raising children in a state that was largely non-Hispanic white, the difficulty of finding the types of food they really enjoyed, the difficulty of having their children speak Spanish, the subtle indignities of living in a state that still practiced widespread but informal segregation.

Their most common ground, however, was in the professional world. Their medical education in Mexico and other parts of Latin America, they felt, was as good as the training offered in California; yet they were told, in many different ways, that they were merely second-class doctors. They continued to have difficulty gaining privileges at other hospitals. Not sure they would be welcome, very few had joined their local medical associations or the state-level California Medical Association. In the early 1970s they formed their own professional group, the California Hispanic American Medical Association (CHAMA), whose official business language was Spanish. "CHAMA was founded in 1975 . . . by a group of Latin American doctors who had received their medical education in either Mexico, Argentina, Peru, in Latin America, who trained outside of the United States and then immigrated . . . and were called at that time Foreign Medical Graduate."[38]

Beginning in the early 1970s, the informal group affiliated with the Monterey Park Hospital had the idea of organizing a small social get-together for immigrant physicians and their spouses as a way of combating the loneliness they felt. Various pharmaceutical companies offered to help sponsor the event. Before long, the informal social gathering had grown in size to a full-fledged dinner and dance, a dressy black-tie event held at various top hotels in Southern California. Bands played danceable music they remembered from their student years in Latin America: rumba, cha-cha, tango, merengue. A trio would wander through, playing old favorites written by Agustín Lara or Los Panchos. Friendships would be rekindled, conversations about the latest novels from Mexico or Argentina flowed spontaneously, young children scampered around, and for an evening the difficulty of establishing a medical practice in California could be put aside. In an event rare for that time, a Chicano-generation US-born Latino medical student was invited to a CHAMA dinner to receive a CHAMA scholarship. He afterward reported being impressed by a group whose existence he had not suspected. "I was able to go to a big banquet [in the late 1970s] at the Los Angeles Athletic Club, downtown. And it was a real eye-opener for me to see doctors out there [who were Latino], but they weren't U.S.-born like I was. They were Latin American, like my parents, but they were educated, not laborers."[39]

With the next generation in mind, CHAMA established a scholarship fund for future medical students. Members who had children hoped that their offspring would want to follow in their footsteps and study medicine. They had heard vaguely about the Chicano movement but did not personally participate in it. Indeed, to them Chicanos appeared to be hot-headed political radicals, probably not too different from members of the various leftist militant movements that had been part of the context of their education in Mexico or elsewhere in Latin America.

In the late sixties and early seventies, US-born Latinos and newly arriving Latino immigrants tended to live in different worlds. Those involved in the Chicano movement fought daily for the right of "cultural self-determination," but the world they lived in was predominately English-speaking. Chicanos generally did not watch the first imported Spanish-language television shows or the six o'clock news in Spanish that reported events in Mexico and, increasingly, Central America; nor did they listen to Spanish-language radio. Meanwhile, in the period from 1970 to 1975, 69.5% of Latino population growth was due to immigration rather than births.[40] Immigrants not only significantly increased overall Latino population numbers; they also had far higher fertility rates than did US-born Latinos. Once immigrants started to give birth, their children would quickly outnumber the children of US-born Latinos. Somewhere down the road, the children of the Chicano generation and those of the new immigrants were bound to meet.

MARIACHIS OR BEETHOVEN?

In 1970, Alec Velasquez was an unusual participant in the Chicano movement at UC Berkeley. He was an immigrant, born to an upper-middle-class family in Mexico City. He had been educated there in private schools, and through his university-educated parents was familiar with the capital's rich cultural offerings: the Mexico City Philharmonic, the Teatro de Bellas Artes (Fine Arts Theater), museums, art galleries, and bookstores. As a child, Alec had joined a junior *charro* (Mexican cowboy) association and learned the traditional art of horsemanship, occasionally performing dressed in the *charro*'s glittering outfit. Then, after a family dispute when he was age thirteen, he was sent to live with a grandmother in San Francisco. To finish high school there, he became fluent in English in a matter of months. Thanks to his intellectual drive, he became one of the few Latino undergraduates at UC Berkeley in the late 1960s, where I met him in a biology class.

Familiar with student politics in Mexico City, he joined the Chicano movement at Berkeley and was an active leader. Yet he was an unusual member of *el movimiento* (the movement). For one thing, he dressed in sport coats, while other militants preferred the paramilitary Che Guevara look. He smoked a pipe, rather than hand-rolled, lumpy cigarettes, and was comfortable with a wine list, yet he did not hesitate to volunteer for extra duties *por la causa* (for the cause).

One spring morning, he heard that the Mexican conductor Carlos Chávez was to be a guest conductor for a local performance of Beethoven's Third Symphony. He invited me to accompany him. We spent an enjoyable afternoon, and Alec reminisced about the last time he had heard the conductor; years earlier, he had joined his parents for a preconcert cocktail beneath a Diego Rivera mural in the lobby bar of the Hotel Prendes, had heard the concert, then had had a typical late-night dinner in a sophisticated Zona Rosa restaurant. A week after our outing, Alec hosted a breakfast meeting of the local Chicano student group leadership at his apartment. As he and I waited for the others to arrive, he shared with me a treasure he had just found in a used record bin on Telegraph Avenue in Berkeley: a recording of the same symphony, conducted by the celebrated German conductor Wilhelm Furtwengler. He put it on, and we discussed the differences in conducting style between the Mexican and German conductors. An incredulous US-born Chicano wandered into the room, mouth agape, and watched us, lost in our appreciation of classical music. Unable to contain himself any longer, the young Chicano blurted out, "Hey, you can't do that. Chicanos can't listen to classical music!" "What do you mean, 'Chicanos can't listen to classical music'?" Alec replied. "I mean, classical music isn't Chicano. Chicanos can only listen to mariachi music. That's what I was told, that a real Chicano does not listen to white man's music." Alec then launched into an impromptu lecture on Mexican classical music composers, starting with the baroque music of Gutiérrez de Padilla, written in 1652, and winding up with Silvestre Revueltas. Chastened, the young Chicano slunk away, still muttering that real Chicanos should not listen to Beethoven.

Still too small to register on corporate America's radar screen, at best considered "America's second-largest minority," and at times referred to as a "sleeping giant," Latinos of the period 1965–1975 existed in the public consciousness as simply another political group pushing for its civil rights. Yet all the growth dynamics for the remainder of the twentieth century were in place, beginning their work. Latinos and non-Latinos alike were blithely unaware of what was about to happen. Demographic and cultural changes were about to propel California into the multicultural twenty-first century.

THREE

Washington Defines a New Nativism

1965–1975

Those discussing the underclass are usually referring to people who are concentrated in urban neighborhoods and who are predominately black or Hispanic.

DURING THE "LONG HOT SUMMERS" from 1966 to 1969, major American cities—from the South Bronx to Newark, from the South Side of Chicago to Philadelphia—seemed ready to explode, just as the Watts area of Los Angeles had in 1965. Leather-jacketed advocates of Black Power strode through the charred inner cities, denouncing America's treatment of African Americans and demanding that something be done. In guilty response to the anger, programs flooded out of Washington to quench the burning urban cores. A minority group had found its voice, and the federal government responded. Other groups—women, gays and lesbians, those with disabilities, Asian Americans, and American Indians—likewise sought to make their private grievances public. To most policy makers, it appeared as if Latinos, too, numbered among the aggrieved minorities seeking notice. But among Latino communities, something much more fundamental was at work than the identity politics of an aggrieved minority.

Today, *minority* has come to suggest a host of negative images—poverty, unemployment, welfare dependency, broken homes, crime, poor health—which, taken together, paint a picture of community dysfunction, an impaired ability to engage in the patterns of behavior commonly expected by the majority of society. Policy makers in Washington, DC, saw these "minority" dysfunctional outcomes as the result of the absence of individualist values—the work ethic, independence from welfare, and family formation—that normally undergirded the positive outcomes of the "majority" population. Between 1965 and 1975, these individualist values were enshrined as the ideals of a new nativism that largely defined an "American" as someone who adhered to them Any group that did not have the income or success of the majority population came to be seen as rejecting these new nativist American values. It was believed that this rejection inevitably resulted in unsuccessful outcomes such as poverty, dependence on welfare, and illegitimate births, which marked that group as in some sense not truly "American."

AMERICAN VALUES, MINORITIES, AND PUBLIC POLICY

Anthropologist Oscar Lewis, studying poor families in Mexico and Puerto Rico from the 1940s to the 1960s, created the theoretical model of a "culture of poverty."[1] The culture of poverty, he claimed, is "an [individual] adaptation to a set of objective conditions of larger society"; in other words, the existence of poverty creates a culture of poverty in the minds of poor individuals.

> Once it [the culture of poverty] comes into existence, it tends to perpetuate itself from generation to generation because of its effects on the children. By the time slum children are six or seven, they have usually absorbed the basic values and attitudes of their subculture, and are not psychologically geared to take full advantage of changing conditions or increased opportunities which may occur in their lifetime.[2]

Key features of this culture of poverty include lack of impulse control, present-time orientation, inability to defer gratification, and inability to plan for the future. Psychological consequences include a sense of failure, resignation, fatalism, marginality, helplessness, dependence, and inferiority. This cultural maladaptation was universal and worldwide, he argued, not confined to underdeveloped countries. Even in a modern society, and even in the United States, Lewis claimed to find groups who had all the characteristics of the culture of poverty. "[In] the United States . . . [the] culture of poverty . . . would consist of very low-income Negroes, Mexicans, Puerto Ricans, American Indians and Southern poor whites."[3]

Another seminal text in the evolution of the culture of poverty construct was Michael Harrington's 1962 classic, *The Other America: Poverty in the United States,* which asserted that there were more than 50 million poor people in the world's richest economy, living a life the better-off could not understand. "Poverty in the United States is a culture, an institution, a way of life. . . . There is, in short, a language of the poor, a psychology of the poor, a worldview of the poor. To be impoverished is to be an internal alien, to grow up in a culture that is radically different from the one that dominates society."⁴ The manifestations of this subterranean culture, so different from "mainstream" American culture, were unstable families, female-headed households, teen pregnancies, inadequate medical care, more and longer illnesses, lost wages, lost jobs, and poor housing, all of it perpetuated through generations. It was a dire portrait.

In the late 1960s, Daniel Patrick Moynihan, then working in the US Department of Labor, prepared an analysis of poverty in urban communities that focused on the "tangle of pathology" present in "the Negro family in urban ghettos." In the crumbling African American family, he found high divorce rates, a high percentage of unwed mothers, and a high percentage of female-headed households. Trapped in segregated housing, such communities spawned socially costly behaviors: the failure of youth to perform in school, juvenile delinquency, crime, unemployment, drug addiction, isolation, and alienation.⁵ Nothing short of a massive national program could ever hope to address this tangle of pathology, then seen as limited to a population that had been segregated from mainstream America since the days of Reconstruction. Against a media backdrop of shattering glass, wailing sirens, and mobs chanting "Burn, baby, burn," President Lyndon B. Johnson enlisted the nation to help fight the "War on Poverty." The phenomenon of minority politics was born in this era, and rivers of federal largesse were routed to those involved in bettering the "minority condition."

Two decades after the long hot summers had passed, William Julius Wilson's powerful 1987 book *The Truly Disadvantaged: The Inner City, the Underclass and Public Policy* further linked African Americans and life-shattering poverty and continued to define the inner-city ghetto as a community "increasingly isolated from mainstream patterns and norms of behavior."⁶ Guardedly, he used Moynihan's twenty-year-old phrase "tangle of pathology in the inner city" to highlight how economic restructuring had, once again, crippled the black family. Lack of job skills, long-term unemployment, out-of-wedlock births, female-headed families, crime and other aberrant behavior, persistent poverty, and welfare dependency yielded what he termed "the underclass." The inner city, its pathological poverty, and black Americans were firmly linked in the American imagination.

Helen Rowan's 1970 "A Minority Nobody Knows" incorporated Latinos into the culture of poverty framework, likening their situation to that of

African Americans. For more than a century, she said, many Latino communities also had endured conditions of segregation, discrimination, poverty, low educational achievement, and low income:

> Census statistics and other studies show the Mexican Americans in the Southwest to be worse off in every respect than the non-whites (Negroes, Indians, Orientals).... They are poorer, their housing is more crowded and more dilapidated, their unemployment rate is higher, their average educational level is lower.... In California, Mexican Americans outnumber Negroes by almost two to one, but probably not one Californian in ten thousand knows that simple fact.[7]

Activists of the Chicano era saw that if the scope of "minority" were enlarged to include Latinos, federal resources could be put to use in Latino barrios. Their intense lobbying spurred President Johnson to send representatives of his administration to El Paso, Texas, in 1967, where they held the first-ever Cabinet hearings on Mexican American affairs. A number of federal agency directors and Cabinet members listened to speaker after speaker discuss major problem areas for Latinos: health, education, welfare, labor, agriculture, housing, and economic development.[8] For the first time, Washington officials were made aware that Latinos could be legitimately considered a minority. The purpose of these and other hearings, goaded by many peaceful demonstrations, was to enroll Latinos in the African American–oriented minority policy agenda: increased War on Poverty funding, more federal job hiring, greater participation in Manpower Development Training programs,[9] and more hiring by federally financed contractors. One immediate result of the hearings was the establishment of the Southwest Council for Mexican Americans, whose purpose was to pressure various federal programs to include Latinos in their minority-oriented initiatives.[10] "Across the board the barrios of Aztlan are victimized by increasing poverty, unemployment, inadequate education, scarcity of affordable housing, crime, gang violence, drug and alcohol abuse. These social problems threaten to relegate Chicanos to a permanent underclass status."[11]

The New Nativism Measures Minority Status

In 1973, President Richard Nixon mandated that all federal records henceforward include an identifier for "Hispanic." The new definition sidestepped earlier concerns about determining the "race" of a largely mestizo Latino population by

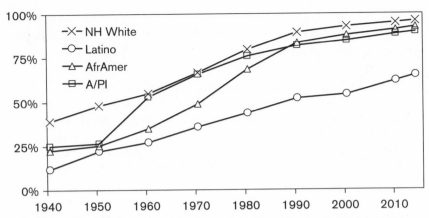

FIGURE I. Percent of adults 25+ years that graduated from high school, California, 1940–2014. Source: IPUMS-USA, University of Minnesota, http://www.ipums.org.

defining that contentious issue out of existence, as "a person of Mexican, Puerto Rican, Cuban, Central or South American or other Spanish culture or origin, regardless of race."[12] Latinos finally had been designated a federally recognized group, but it was not a racial group. Slowly and sketchily at first, federal, state, and local offices revised their records systems to include the category "Hispanic" on birth, marriage, and death certificates. Once data were available that identified Latinos, analysts could see if Latinos exhibited the socially dysfunctional risk factors characteristic of the "typical minority" community.

There is no question that Latinos, historically, have been poorly served by the nation's educational structures. In general, the percentage of adults who graduate from high school is a good indicator of a community's educational status. Low Latino educational attainment can be expressed in a number of other ways as well: average years of schooling, percent of students attending college, percent graduating from college, and so on. However it is expressed, there is no denying that Latino adults have the lowest educational levels of any group of Americans. Figure 1 shows that during the seventy-four-year period from 1940 to 2014, a consistently lower percentage of Latino adults graduated from high school than any other group. While African American adults once had a low percentage of high school graduates, by 2000–2010, they had nearly caught up with non-Hispanic whites. Similarly, Asians once had a low graduation percentage, but had nearly reached non-Hispanic white levels by 2000–2010.

Low income, coupled with high poverty, is another major risk factor mentioned in "minority policy" analyses. Figure 2 shows the percentage of

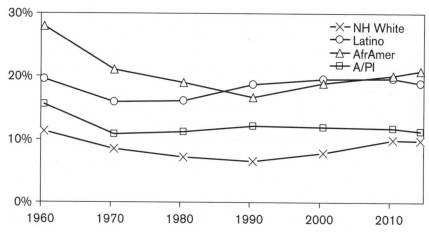

FIGURE 2. Percent of adults below poverty level, California, 1960–2014. Source: IPUMS-USA, University of Minnesota, http://www.ipums.org.

California's population from 1960 to 2014 living in poverty. During that period, Latinos consistently had far higher poverty levels than non-Hispanic whites or Asian/Pacific Islanders, close to African American poverty levels. Whether measured in percent living in poverty, household income, or per capita income, Latinos have had the smallest portion of the state's economic pie.

As Latino-specific information gradually became available after President Nixon mandated the identification of "Hispanic" data, it appeared that the Latino population matched the African American population in low educational and income levels. Policy analysts assumed that since the Latino population so closely matched African Americans in the risk factors of low income, poor education, and high poverty, Latinos also would match African Americans in terms of other "minority characteristics." By the early 1990s, the General Accounting Office stated unequivocally that Latinos constituted a large portion of the urban underclass.[13]

Minority Health Disparity

Just as the national discourse on poverty from 1965 to 1975 tended toward a new nativist definition of poverty, so did discourse in health care, although there it took longer to develop. The seminal 1979 report *Health Status of Minorities and Low-Income Groups* was an initial attempt to pull together what had been learned about the effects that low income and being a racial or ethnic minority in the United States had on health status.[14] Because there was almost no information available about Latino health profiles, researchers had to tiptoe around a lack of data. New aggregations of data were created for a new series of categories presented in the report, which were supposed to include Latinos: "Minority," "Black and other," "Non-white," "Black and minority," "Racial minority," "Persons of color." No matter how the other-than-white category was denominated, the conclusion was the same: minority groups suffered from higher mortality rates than whites for nearly all conditions, including heart disease, cancer, stroke, accidents, influenza and pneumonia, diabetes, cirrhosis, and infant mortality. Of the top ten causes of death listed in that report, in nine categories "minorities" had a higher death rate than whites. Only for suicides was the "minority" rate lower than the white one. "Nonwhites . . . continued to experience an excess mortality, relative to whites, of 39 percent in 1975."[15] From the new nativist perspective, it seemed obvious that minorities did not share basic American health values and behaviors.

In 1984, Margaret Heckler, secretary of the Department of Health and Human Services, appointed the Task Force on Black and Minority Health, which provided information on the health of African Americans and "other minority" populations in urban America. The task force also introduced the concept of "excess deaths," defined as those deaths in a minority group above the number observed in a white population of similar size and age. Most data available for analysis in the early 1980s only identified whites and African Americans; hence, most of the policy recommendations were based on a comparison of whites and blacks. Other minorities were automatically included nonetheless, on the assumption that low income and low education would have similar effects on their health. In African American populations, nearly half of all deaths in 1979–1981 were classified as "excess deaths," those which presumably would not have occurred if this population had fit the white mortality profile. Secretary Heckler extended the African American death profile to other minority groups and expressed her concern that "there was a continuing disparity in the burden of death and illness experienced by Blacks *and other minority Americans* as compared with our nation's population as a whole."[16] Her policy response was to establish the Office of Minority Health, charged with removing the disparities in health status between blacks and other minorities and the "general" (i.e., white) population.

The prevailing health model used by the Office of Minority Health in preparing its publications has been the "race/ethnic health disparity model," in which a number of health problems appear to be related to race and ethnicity alone. In 1998, the Office of Minority Health, in its report *Eliminating Racial and Ethnic Disparities in Health,* noted "compelling evidence that race and ethnicity correlate with persistent, and often increasing, health disparities among U.S. populations."[17] Continuing in this vein, a press release in 2000 baldly announced, "African American, American Indian/Alaska Native, Asian and Pacific Islander, and Hispanic citizens suffer poorer health and higher rates of premature death than the majority population."[18] Since the late 1960s, therefore, social policy analysts have concluded that Latinos are a minority group and exhibit all the dysfunctional behavior attributed to minority groups, which according to new nativist views ultimately stems from Latinos' rejection of American values. But this conclusion is wrong.

Minority Fatigue: The New Nativist Backlash

When Harrington described the plight of the poor in the early 1960s, America responded with compassion, as well as with practical solutions. While the public was watching cities burn in the mid-1960s, few dissented openly about the need for policy aimed at minority issues—to save America's cities, if nothing else. Republican president Richard Nixon not only embraced the minority policy agenda but also implemented many of Johnson's "Great Society" programs. Affirmative action, for example, was a major program of the Nixon administration, starting with the Philadelphia Plan, which mandated minority participation in unions and construction.

The election of President Ronald Reagan in 1980, however, signaled a change in social policy direction. The problems of minority groups—poverty, unemployment, broken families, welfare dependency—were no longer seen as the result of an uncaring society. Instead, these problems came to be seen as the result of minority groups rejecting "American" behaviors constructed around a strong work ethic, rejection of welfare "handouts," and family formation. Charles Murray's 1984 book, *Losing Ground. American Social Policy, 1950–1980,* posed a simple question: Why, after the expenditure of billions of dollars on social welfare programs, were conditions getting worse for minorities? More people were living in poverty, more were on the welfare rolls, families were crumbling, crime was rising, and cities were less safe. He answered that question in a way compatible with the new Republican president's political philosophy: programs such as public assistance were making the situation worse, not better, by subsidizing, possibly even rewarding, dysfunctional behavior. "It was wrong to take from the most industrious, most respectable poor ... so that we could cater to the least industrious, least responsible poor. ... [S]tatus was withdrawn from behaviors that engender escape from poverty. ... [F]or the first time in American history, it became socially acceptable within poor communities to be unemployed."[19] A new policy began to solidify, emphasizing that poor minorities' own behavior contributed to their plight. Drug addiction was not a maladaptive response to alienation caused by poverty; it was a personal choice, which, by driving out decent folk, destabilized neighborhoods. Unwed pregnancy was not a maladaptive response to poverty but a personal choice that created poverty. In the rising economy of the 1980s—now often referred to as the "me decade" or the "greed decade"—unemployment was cast as a personal choice. "The greatest cause of today's poverty may simply be that the attempts in recent decades to equalize opportunity have *failed to persuade many Blacks and Hispanics that it is worth working.*"[20] Mead argued that easy access to a wide variety of welfare and medical benefits discouraged people from working and, over time, actually robbed them of initiative. Programs designed to eliminate poverty, his argument went, were actually creating it. "Underclass poverty stems less from the absence of opportunity than from the *inability or reluctance to take advantage of opportunity.*"[21] The situation did indeed appear worse after fifteen to twenty years of policy effort. Minority need seemed to be a bottomless pit. Rising crime rates and incidents of public disorder—panhandling, urban gangs, graffiti, drug dealing, and so on—were interpreted as the acts of an ungrateful population biting the hand that had fed it. "Minority fatigue" began to set in.

Murray had given words to the new nativist definition of American. According to this new nativism, universalist American values of equality, freedom, and democracy came to be defined in terms of individualist values and behaviors, and it was declared that poverty-stricken urban neighborhoods were poor because too many people in those areas chose to reject such basic American values as hard work and individual responsibility. And by extension, if a group rejected these new nativist American values, just how American could that group really be? The poor, the unemployed, broken families, and the poorly educated were increasingly believed by new nativists to be essentially rejecting American values; hence, they could not be American.

During the presidential elections of 1980, 1984, and 1988, the term "minority" served as a code word for dysfunction, itself the result of "rejecting

American values." As War on Poverty veterans fought a rearguard action to keep the flame of 1960s compassion alive, their increasingly dire descriptions of the poor and minorities were taken by the Reagan administration as greater reason to abandon those efforts. For example, there was Lisbeth Schorr's description of minority families in poverty: "These families are so devoid of structure, or organization, they can disorganize *you!* When you leave after a visit, *you* have a headache."[22] Schorr's words were meant to elicit empathy, but they also engendered antipathy and opposition to the poor in new nativist circles. Policy makers began to polarize into two camps: Great Society holdovers, who painted an increasingly negative picture of minority dysfunction in order to argue for more programs, and Reagan reactionaries, who used those same portraits to inveigh against lax morals and the erosion of societal standards. "The solution [to poverty] is within the reach of most people. Marriage and family prevent poverty. Schooling prevents poverty. Working at almost any job prevents poverty," wrote Murray Weidenbaum.[23]

In 2012, Charles Murray's book *Coming Apart: The State of White America, 1960–2010* not only repeated Weidenbaum's analysis of American values but also sounded the new nativist alarm that even white Americans were being infected by the rejection of fundamental national values communicated to them by dysfunctional minorities. Murray argued that "virtuous" Americans, who still held those values, had prospered in 1960–2010, while those who rejected those values had failed to thrive.[24] The slide of white Americans into the endless cycle of unemployment, poverty, welfare dependency, and disintegrated families, so typical of nonwhite minorities, was threatening to tear America apart. The only salvation would be for white America to return to good old new nativist American values.

REFRAMING LATINOS

As an undergraduate in the social sciences at the University of California, Berkeley, in the 1960s, and later as a graduate student in medical sociology at the UC Medical Center in San Francisco during the early 1970s, I had been taught the prevailing wisdom about minorities and dysfunction. I started my academic career firmly convinced that theoretical models of minority dysfunction were appropriate for understanding Latino patterns of behavior. I had been led to believe that the low income and poor education so often observed in Latino populations led inevitably to maladaptive behavior, including low labor force participation, welfare dependency, disintegrating families, health-harming behavior, excess deaths, increased infant mortality, greater drug use, and the like. It was only years later, as data for Latinos gradually became available, that I was able to see that this model of minority behavior—which continues even today to undergird most federal social policy—is completely inappropriate for most Latino populations.

From 1970 to 1974, I was the founding executive director of La Clínica de la Raza, a small, grassroots community clinic established, in the heat of the Chicano movement, in the Fruitvale District of Oakland, California. The clinic still operates today (2016) as a major provider of health services in the East Bay area. Although reliable data on the health of Latinos, and even census data on them, were virtually nonexistent at the time, I wanted to know what health needs La Clínica should be addressing. I began by listing what I already knew about the situation, which in my earlier preparation in engineering is called "listing the knowns." I knew, firsthand, that female patients at La Clínica were giving birth to a great number of babies and seemed to have a much higher fertility rate than non-Hispanic whites. It was also clear that many of La Clínica's patients were recent immigrants. Administrators of other community clinics around the state were reporting a similar pattern of high fertility and significant immigration. I knew that the baby boom had ended around 1964 and that non-Hispanic white fertility rates were falling rapidly. I also knew that immigration from Europe had largely ceased by 1926.

I roughed out a demographic model, using sketchy 1970 census data and spotty subsequent birth data, supplemented by my observations of immigration patterns, and saw a disturbing pattern. The non-Hispanic white baby boomers, a huge population numbering some 85 million Americans, would start to retire by 2010. The younger working-age population who would have to support their retirement through public means (Social Security and state, county, and municipal pension plans) or private ones (pensions, investments) likely would be increasingly comprised of Latinos. California seemed to be headed for a future population highly stratified by age and ethnicity. The older, graying population would be largely non-Hispanic white, and the younger population, whose earnings would support the future elderly via either public or private means, would be largely Latino. When I first announced this pattern publicly, in a paper I gave at a meeting of the American Public Health Association in Los Angeles in the fall of 1978, it was greeted with disbelief.[25] I was given many reasons why this projected growth was not likely to occur. The data were wrong; immigration had ceased long ago; even if there were immigration in 1978, it would soon stop; Latino fertility could not *possibly* be as high as I assumed; if it were, it could not continue for more than a year or two. And so on.

As soon as the 1980 census data—the first comprehensive data set to systematically use a Hispanic identifier—became available in 1982, I began to refine those earlier roughed-out demographic projection models. Together with Werner Schink, then of the California Employment Development Department, and Jorge Chapa, then a doctoral student at UC Berkeley, I created a set of more precise projections, which pointed to an inescapable conclusion: there would be significant growth in the state, largely in the Latino population. In *The Burden of Support: Young Latinos in an Aging Society,* we provided Latino demographic projections for California to the year 2030 and presented two possible scenarios for the future of a state with a population that by then would be about half Latino.[26] One was a scary, *Blade Runner*–like worst-case scenario in which the state would be economically bankrupt, riven by ethnic rivalry, and on the verge of civil insurrection. The other was a somewhat Pollyannaish best-case scenario in which everything ended up serene and productive, but we did not specify how such a happy state of affairs was to be achieved.[27]

I was unprepared for the negative commentary the book elicited. The criticism was not directed at the methodology; the projections were sound, defensible, and virtually irrefutable. Rather, the criticism was directed at the *fact* of Latino growth. If the state were to become half Latino, critics maintained, it would be the end of California. Such a poorly educated, poverty-stricken minority population had little that was positive to offer. This view presumed, of course, that Latinos were largely gang members, welfare mothers, high school dropouts, and drug users; some, therefore, feared a significant erosion of quality of life for non-Latinos. In essence, the critics argued that if a small minority population was bad enough, a state with a "majority-minority" population would be a disaster.

I had to admit that I had not thought about the social effects of Latino population growth. My effort had been limited to creating a set of fairly simple demographic projections. By the time the book was released, I had left UC Berkeley and the East Bay, where Latinos were a very small minority population, to take up an appointment at UCLA's School of Medicine and residence in Los Angeles, where in 1986, 2.9 million Latinos comprised more than one-third of the county's population.[28] As I watched the English-language eleven o'clock news in the "Southland" at night, I noticed that, generally, when a Latino was in the news, it was in the familiar context of dysfunctional minority—as a school dropout, drug dealer, welfare mom, or the like. Curious about the effects of so many Latinos on society, I embarked on a survey with two colleagues, Aida Hurtado from UC Santa Cruz and Robert Valdez, then at the School of Public Health at UCLA, to see what, if anything, Latinos had to contribute to society. As we developed a survey—questionnaire items, sampling methods, a data analysis plan—I began to worry about the policy implications of what we might find. What if the public stereotypes of Latinos were borne out by the data? What if most Latinos, in fact, were antisocial miscreants? Would our research fuel every nativist anti-Latino group in the state? My professional side was in conflict with my personal convictions. Yet, as a researcher, I wanted to see this project through to the end. Even if my research proved the hate groups correct, I had no alternative but to practice the best science possible.

At that time, my wife, Maria, as part of her work at UCLA's School of Nursing, was engaged in a project concerning drug-exposed infants born in Los Angeles County. One morning, before I began collecting field data for my own survey, I made my way to her office, planning to take her out to lunch. As I waited for her to return from the Academic Computing Center with a run of data, I glanced at her desk, curious how her project was turning out. There I saw a report, just issued by the Los Angeles County Department of Health Services, on mortality patterns in the county for the year 1985. That report was one of the first to use data that separated Latinos from non-Hispanic whites and African Americans.[29] My attention was caught by a seemingly anomalous finding: Latino infant mortality was *lower* than that of non-Hispanic whites, and *far lower* than that of African Americans. This favorable statistic contravened all the minority health models I had been taught. I remember thinking, "Well, even if we Latinos turn out to be social misfits, at least we can bear healthy children." Curious, I turned to the section on causes of death and mortality rates. My attention was suddenly and completely riveted by the pattern that emerged from the data. Compared to non-Hispanic whites and African Americans, Latinos had far lower death rates for heart disease, cancer, stroke, and, indeed, nearly every other cause of death. This highly unexpected result ran counter to the prevailing wisdom about the poor health of minorities, which allegedly was the result of their rejection of individualist American values.

Puzzled by finding data in an official report that flew in the face of conventional thinking, I dug around Maria's desk until I found her raw data on drug-exposed infants. A baby born to a drug-using mother is a reportable incident—that is, the attending physician must submit that information to health authorities—and Maria had collected the birth certificate data of drug-exposed babies born in the county the previous year. During the late 1980s, much of the public viewed Latino immigrants as drug dealers and heavy drug users. What pattern would we see in the drug-exposed infants? I arrayed her data by ethnicity; then, using the population estimates provided by the Los Angeles County Health Department report, I created a comparative cross-tabulation. I saw a similar, puzzling pattern: Latina mothers gave birth to drug-exposed infants at only one-third the rate of non-Hispanic white mothers, and at about one-tenth the rate of African American mothers. I could not argue with the data. With such a low rate of drug-exposed infants, Latina mothers had to have an equally low rate of drug use.

Lower infant mortality. Fewer heart disease deaths, fewer cancer deaths, and fewer stroke deaths. Lower rates of drug-using mothers. The health profile did not seem to be that of a dysfunctional minority group. Yet Latinos did exhibit the minority pattern of high rates of poverty and poor education. Something did not compute. Suddenly, I remembered a data source that could provide additional insight. Although Latinos had not been identified as "Hispanic" or "Latino" in the 1940 through 1970 censuses, their surnames were recorded, although they had not been much used for analysis. But in 1986, the US Census Bureau had released a post-coded set of Public Use Microdata Samples (PUMS) from 1940 to 1980, in which Spanish-surnamed individuals were separated out from non-Hispanic whites.[30] I had a copy of that data set at my office, and in fact had used it a little to develop the methodology for the survey on which I was about to embark. I rushed to my office—to this day, I still owe Maria that lunch date—opened up the data set, and saw a pattern that completely changed my thinking about Latinos and their contributions to California society.

LATINO SOCIAL BEHAVIOR PARADOX

Chronic unemployment, labor force desertion, loss of a work ethic, welfare dependency, failing families: these key features of the minority urban

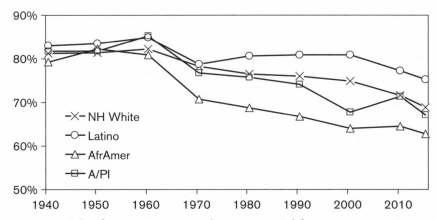

FIGURE 3. Labor force participation, males 16+ years, California, 1940–2015. Sources: 1940–1990, IPUMS-USA, University of Minnesota, http://www.ipums.org; 2000–2015, custom analysis by Werner Schink of data from Sarah Flood, Miriam King, Steven Ruggles, and J. Robert Warren, Integrated Public Use Microdata Series, Current Population Survey: Version 4.0 [machine-readable database] (Minneapolis: University of Minnesota, 2015), https://cps.ipums.org/cps-action/samples [accessed 2 August 2016; spreadsheet stored at CESLAC].

underclass were generally reflected in media images of Latinos. These dysfunctions were cited by new nativists to bolster their claim that minority groups rejected (individualist) American values, and therefore were not truly American. Would forty years of Latino-coded data prove them true?

According to the theory of the "urban underclass," one defining characteristic of such populations is male nonparticipation in the labor force, also called "labor force desertion." These males, lacking skills, ambition, and proper attitude, become "discouraged workers," unemployed for so long that they cease seeking employment and begin to depend instead either on welfare programs or on illicit economic behavior, such as drug dealing or violent crime. At this point, the underclass male has become structurally unemployable.

Labor force participation is measured by the US census for males over sixteen years of age, both those who are currently employed and those seeking work. In the period from 1940 to 1980, Latino males had either the highest labor force participation rate of any group—higher than that of Asian/Pacific Islanders, African Americans, or even non-Hispanic whites—or a rate virtually identical to the highest. I have aggregated data from 1990, 2000, 2010, and 2015 census files; figure 3 shows that, for nearly three generations, from 1940 to 2015, Latino males have been the most active workers in California's labor force.

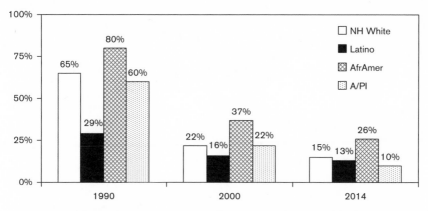

FIGURE 4. Public assistance as percentage of poverty population, California, 1990–2014.
Source: IPUMS-USA, University of Minnesota, http://www.ipums.org.

Another characteristic of the urban underclass is heavy welfare dependency. The census provides data on sources of income, including cash income from public assistance. Public assistance is means-tested; that is, one must live in poverty in order to receive welfare. Between 1990 and 2000, the US welfare system was drastically reformed, leading all groups to reduce their use of welfare programs. Figure 4 shows those receiving public assistance as a percentage of those living in poverty. It indicates that, contrary to nativist stereotypes, from 1990 to 2014, Latinos had a lower rate of welfare use than either non-Hispanic whites or African Americans.

The deterioration of the nuclear family in inner cities is another classic characteristic of the urban underclass. In another reversal of expectations, Latinos in California have the highest percentage of households composed of couples with children; this pattern held true from 1940 to 2014. In this seventy-four-year period, Latino households were more likely than non-Hispanic white, African American, or Asian/Pacific Islander households to be composed of couples with children. Beginning in the 1960s, the percentage of couples with children fell for all groups, including Latinos. By the turn of the century, the couple-with-children household was a minority in all groups, but was still more common in Latino and Asian/Pacific Islander households than in either non-Hispanic white or African American households (fig. 5).

According to current social policy theory, a vigorous work ethic should prevent poverty among a population. "Poverty is common among non-workers, but is rare among workers."[31] Yet here, too, Latinos in California

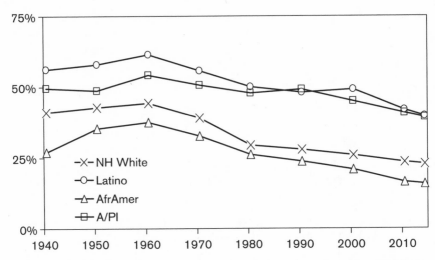

FIGURE 5. Percent of households composed of married couples with children, California, 1940–2014. Source: IPUMS-USA, University of Minnesota, http://www.ipums.org.

contradict the dysfunctional minority policy model used by both Republicans and Democrats for the last forty years. Since 1940, Latino males in California have demonstrated the highest labor force participation, the lowest use of public assistance, and the greatest propensity to form and maintain families. In fact, they demonstrate the very social behavior that Murray and other new nativist analysts claimed was missing from poor communities. Yet what has been their reward for their hard work? Latinos have one of the highest poverty levels of any segment of American society. Latino poverty, however, is not the result of any rejection of societal values regarding work and family, despite what the new nativists are quick to claim. Rather, it is the community's reward for their vigorous involvement in an economy that, in the throes of globalization, offers them low wages and few, if any, benefits such as health insurance. While Latino poverty is very much a reality, its cause is not the result of Latinos rejecting the work ethic; instead, it is the result of increased inequality in the twenty-first-century American economy.

As a result of these unexpected data about California's Latino community, my attitude to the findings of our forthcoming survey began to change. While still concerned about low income and poor education, factors worrisome to all policy makers, I began to consider that perhaps Latinos, as a population, had things to contribute to the state: strengthening of the work ethic, independence from welfare, a new injection of family values. In terms of social behavior, Latinos are far from being the antisocial miscreants still depicted on the nightly news and in movies and television shows.

The Latino Epidemiological Paradox

An analysis of census data for 1940 through 2015 reveals an obdurate social behavior paradox. While extant policy models concluded that a low-income, poorly educated population must be socially dysfunctional, the expected dysfunctions were not observed in Latino populations. Health data, however, were not so immediately clear. Data on the health of Latinos, identified as such, has only been collected in California since the 1980s, and were just being reported in the 1990s. Were the Los Angeles County data I had seen on my wife's desk, which contradicted the minority dysfunction model, perhaps some sort of local aberration? Perplexed by these Los Angeles County data on health, I hunted through state-level health data. Yet in other data files with Hispanic identifiers, I saw the same pattern. In a state with, at that point, 7.6 million Latinos, I had a very robust population platform for these patterns.[32] I have continued to track these trends for more than two decades now, and they have remained stable; meanwhile, by 2014 the Latino population had grown to 15.0 million.[33]

Every year, nearly a quarter of a million persons die in California. The top ten causes of death for the year 2013, and the number of deaths due to each cause, are shown in figure 6. The number-one cause of death in that year was heart disease; more people (59,832) died from some form of heart disease than from any other cause. Cancer (malignant neoplasms) caused the deaths of 57,504 Californians. Strokes (cerebrovascular disease) accounted for 13,603 deaths. These three causes—heart disease, cancer, and stroke—accounted for a majority of all deaths in the state. The remaining top ten causes of death, in descending order, were chronic lower respiratory diseases, Alzheimer's, unintentional injuries (accidents), diabetes, influenza and pneumonia, liver disease, and hypertensive diseases.

Yet not all groups have had the same mortality rate, which is the number of deaths in a given year out of every one hundred thousand persons. Non-Hispanic whites, Latinos, and African Americans have significantly different age-adjusted death rates for each cause of death. These mortality rates have been adjusted for age, so that the youth of the Latino population and the aging of the non-Hispanic white population have been controlled, making a more valid comparison. Figure 7 provides a close-up view of the top three age-adjusted

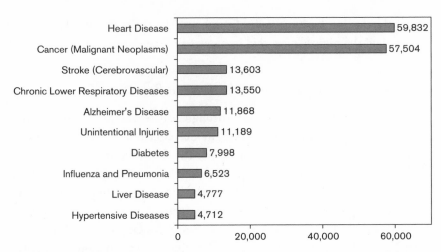

FIGURE 6. Total deaths for top ten causes of death, California, 2013. Source: http://informaticsportal.cdph.ca.gov/chsi/vsqs/ [updated 20 November 2015; accessed 8 January 2016].

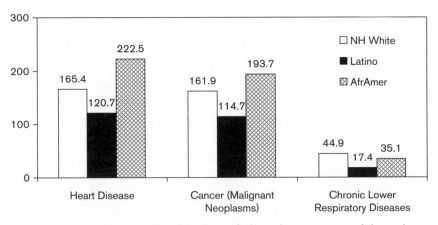

FIGURE 7. Comparative age-adjusted death rates for heart disease, cancer, and chronic lower respiratory diseases, California, 2013. Source: http://informaticsportal.cdph.ca.gov/chsi/vsqs/ [updated 20 November 2015; accessed 8 January 2016].

mortality rates. A pattern quickly emerges: compared to non-Hispanic whites and African Americans, Latinos have far lower age-adjusted death rates for heart disease, cancer, and chronic lower respiratory diseases. This pattern defies the classic minority health disparity model, which predicts that, based on having the lowest income and education, Latinos should have the highest death rate of all three groups. How does a population with lower incomes and poorer

TABLE 1 Age-Adjusted Death Rates for the Top Ten Causes
of Death, California 2013

	Non-Hispanic White	Latino	African American
Heart Disease	165.4	120.7	222.5
Cancer (Malignant Neoplasms)	161.9	114.7	193.7
Chronic Lower Resp Disease	44.9	17.4	35.1
Unintentional Injuries	36.5	23.3	32.6
Alzheimer's Disease	34.8	22.0	33.8
Stroke (Cerebrovascular)	34.0	32.3	50.4
Influenza and Pneumonia	16.4	15.6	21.3
Diabetes	16.3	29.8	38.6
Liver Disease	12.2	16.6	2.4
Hypertensive Diseases	11.5	11.0	22.9

SOURCE: http://informaticsportal.cdph.ca.gov/chsi/vsqs/ (updated 20 November 2015, accessed 29 January 2016).

NOTE: Beginning with the year 2000, the California Department of Health Services shifted from the 9th edition of the *International Classification of Diseases* (ICD-9) to the 10th edition (ICD-10). Therefore, direct comparisons with categories used in earlier years are not possible. Furthermore, these age-adjusted rates were calculated using the 2000 Standard Million, so comparisons with previous rates adjusted with the 1970 or 1940 Standard Million are also not possible. Nevertheless, the differences between Latinos, non-Hispanic whites, and African Americans have remained relatively constant, irrespective of disease classification or standard population used.

education levels than non-Hispanic whites and African Americans manage to have fewer deaths due to heart disease, cancer, and chronic lower respiratory diseases than the wealthier and better-educated groups?

Table 1 provides comparative age-adjusted death rates for the top ten causes of death in California in 2013. They are sorted by the rate for non-Hispanic whites, in descending order. Again, the pattern is that although Latinos have lower incomes and levels of education than non-Hispanic whites, somehow they have achieved lower age-adjusted death rates for eight of the top ten causes of death in the state: heart disease, cancer, chronic lower respiratory diseases (CLRD), stroke, unintentional injuries (accidents), Alzheimer's, influenza or pneumonia, and essential hypertension/hypertensive renal disease. The Latino rate is higher than the non-Hispanic white rate for only two of the top ten: diabetes and liver disease, both relatively rare in comparison to heart disease, cancer, and CLRD.

A global view of the state's mortality can be seen in figure 8, which shows the comparative mortality rates for all causes of death for Latinos,

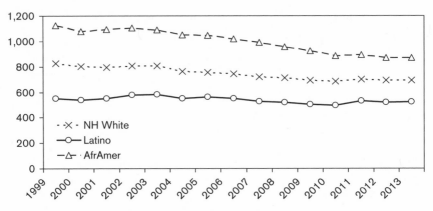

FIGURE 8. Age-adjusted death rates for all causes, California, 1999–2013. Sources: 1999–2001, custom analysis by Paul Hsu, data from California Department of Health Services (CA DHS), Death Statistical Master File 2002 [CD-ROM] (Sacramento: CA DHS, 2002); 2002–2005, VSC-2005-0501.pdf, table 5-1, http://www.cdph.ca.gov/data/statistics /documents/vsc-2005–0501.pdf [accessed 3 August 2016]; 2006–2009, VSC-2009–0501. pdf, table 5-1, http://www.cdph.ca.gov/data/statistics/documents/vsc-2009–0501.pdf [accessed 3 August 2016]; 2010, VSC-2010–0501.pdf, table 5-1, http://www.cdph.ca.gov /data/statistics/documents/vsc-2010–0501.pdf [accessed 3 August 2016]; 2011–2013, custom analysis by Paul Hsu, data from the California Vital Statistics Query (CA-VSQ) system, "all causes vsqs 2011–13.pdf," http://informaticsportal.cdph.ca.gov/CHSI/VSQS/ [accessed 1 August 2016].

non-Hispanic whites, and African Americans for the years 1999–2013, giving a long-term, multi-year picture of the mortality of each of the three groups. Over that fourteen-year period, the Latino death rate for all causes was significantly lower than the non-Hispanic white or African American rate. In 2013, the Latino age-adjusted mortality rate for all causes of death was 523.8 deaths per every 100,000 Latinos in the state. The non-Hispanic white age-adjusted rate for all causes was 692.8 deaths per 100,000 individuals, and the African American age-adjusted death rate was 869.4 deaths per 100,000. While the minority health disparity model would predict Latino age-adjusted rates much higher than those of non-Hispanic whites, and possibly even higher than those of African Americans, the fact is that the Latino age-adjusted death rate is around 25% *lower* than the non-Hispanic white rate and close to 40% lower than the African American one.

Along with low income and poor education, lack of access to health care has long been considered a risk factor for birth outcomes. In 1985, the Health Resources and Services Administration summarized the role of prenatal care in birth outcomes. "It is clear that mothers who seek care early, who have an appropriate number of visits ... have better outcomes than others."[34] That same year, the Task Force on Black and Minority Health concluded, "Risk factors associated with poor perinatal outcome among minorities that appear to be related to low socioeconomic status include: low income; limited maternal education; and inadequate health insurance that often reduce access to appropriate medical care."[35] Data from the California Department of Health Services show that from 1990 to 1998, Latina mothers in California have been among the most likely to receive late prenatal care, either in the last trimester of pregnancy or not at all.[36] According to the model of minority health disparities, these facts should result in very high Latino infant mortality.

Yet the data from California definitely show otherwise. Over forty years of infant mortality data (1970–2011) show that Latino infant mortality in California is virtually identical to that of non-Hispanic whites. In any given year, the two are very close, with Latino infant mortality lower in some years and non-Hispanic white lower in others. Non-Hispanic white mothers have the highest education and the highest income, yet Latinas, with the lowest income and the least education, have virtually identical infant mortality rates. African American infant mortality is nearly twice as high as either Latino or non-Hispanic white rates (fig. 9).

In March 2000, the American College of Physicians released a report on minority health, focusing especially on Latino health. Titled *No Health Insurance? It's Enough to Make You Sick—Latino Community at Great Risk,* the report showed that Latinos were far more likely to be without health insurance than non-Latinos. The report extrapolated from this underinsurance that Latinos must necessarily be in poorer health, suffer from more crippling illness, and die younger in life. "Because Latinos are more likely to be uninsured, they are at far greater risk than other population groups of ... poorer health outcomes, increased suffering, and even premature death."[37] No one can argue against the finding that Latinos are the group most likely to be without access to health care. Even after the implementation of the Affordable Care Act, 20.9% of Latinos in the US still do not have health insurance, more than twice the rate of 9.1% among non-Hispanic whites.[38] The 43% of Latinos in California who do not have a regular source of health care is about twice the rate of non-Hispanic whites (19%) and African Americans (18%).[39] Yet this lack of both insurance and a regular source of care does not necessarily translate into shorter lives for Latinos. In California, a non-Hispanic white baby born between 2010 and 2012 has an average life expectancy of 80.1 years. An African American baby born during the same

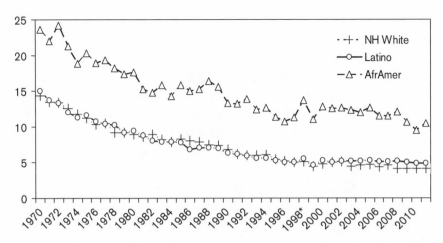

FIGURE 9. Infant mortality, California, 1970–2011. Sources: 1970–1984, CA DHS, *Vital Statistics of California, 1987,* 1989, p. 130, table 4–3; 1985–1992, CA DHS, *Vital Statistics of California, 1994,* 1996, p. 144, table 4–3; 1993–1997, 1999, CA DHS, "Age-Adjusted Perinatal and Infant Mortality Rates for Single Births," 2000, table 4–6; 1998, CA DHS, "California's Infant Mortality Rate, 2000," 2002; 1998 calculated with birth and death records, not linked birth cohort; 2000–2010, MO-MCAH-StatewideInfantMortalityData.pdf, p. 3, https:// www.cdph.ca.gov/data/statistics/Documents/MO-MCAH-StatewideInfantMortalityData .pdf [accessed 3 August 2016]; 2011, VSC-2011–0407.pdf, table 4–7, http://www.cdph.ca.gov /data/statistics/Documents/VSC-2011–0407.pdf [accessed 3 August 2016].

time period has a shorter life expectancy, 75.6 years, which fits the American College of Physicians' conclusion that urban populations will "live sicker and die younger." Yet Latinos, who now make up the majority of the inner-city population of Los Angeles County, offer a sharply different picture. With a life expectancy of 83.7 years, a Latino baby born during those years can expect to live more than three and a half years longer than the non-Hispanic white baby and about eight years longer than the African American baby (fig. 10).

After I became thoroughly familiar with these health and behavioral data, rather than seeing California's Latinos as a helpless, incapable, fragile, endangered species, I realized they were a robust, dynamic, vigorous population, and soon to be a majority, one whose basic values and behavior could contribute greatly to strengthening the civic society of California.

The health data are obdurate, long-term, and stable. Latino health profiles cannot be described by the minority health disparity model, which assumes a rejection of core individualist American values. Yet Washington continues to define Latinos as a minority and to treat them as dysfunctional.

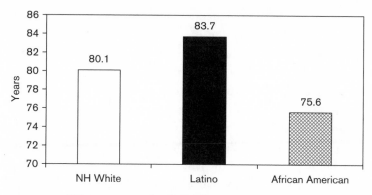

FIGURE 10. Life expectancy at birth, California, 2010–2012. Source: Measure of America, Social Science Research Council, "A Portrait of California 2014–2015," 9 December 2014, A-Portrait-of-California_vF.pdf [downloaded 11 December 2015].

As a result of War on Poverty policy efforts, minority populations are the subject of special federal attention, and their perceived failure to thrive for the past fifty years has continued to power this policy. Whether the dysfunctions are attributed to external oppression or to internal rejection of individualist American values, dysfunctionality has been assumed for nearly all "minority" populations, with the exception of "model minority" Asian Americans. As data have become increasingly available on Latino behavior and health, however, it has become abundantly clear that, although the majority of Latinos do suffer from poor education and low income, most Latino populations nonetheless show a very strong adherence to the individualist American values and behaviors championed by new nativists regarding work, welfare, and the family. In addition, they exhibit extraordinary health behaviors and outcomes. As a result, a small body of scholars are coming to the conclusion that the urban underclass model does not fit the Latino populations found almost everywhere in the United States.[40]

Half the babies born in California now are Latino and will be raised in Latino families. It should be a priority to understand how those babies' parents, with little education, low income, and generally poor access to health care, are able to achieve such outstanding health outcomes. The accomplishments of these Latino babies—how they survive infancy, how well they perform in school, the types of jobs they seek, the businesses they create, the strength of the families they establish, their voting patterns, their support for the arts—eventually will become the statistical norm for the state.

Understanding Latino social dynamics in health, family, employment, business development, and education is a key to understanding the future of California. Yet they cannot be understood through the lens of a minority dysfunction model. Even though Washington continues to define Latinos as a "minority" group, their actual behaviors and health status do not fit the model of a "minority" as defined by the prevailing theoretical model. And clearly, Latinos do not reject the new nativist definition of "American" in terms of adherence to individualist values. In his 2010 book, Murray could not figure out how to transfer the new nativist values of hard work and personal responsibility to what he saw as decaying white American neighborhoods, but the Latino immigration wave of 1965 to 1990 is providing a solution to that problem.

FOUR

Latinos Define Latinos

1975–1990

> We [the bank] understand there is an incredibly important group of people in Los Angeles, New York. We have to become much smarter about talking to these people.... We know that [these] consumers are different. We have to market differently.... We are no longer in denial.

FROM 1849 TO 1965, Anglo-Saxonist nativists attempted to define nearly every aspect of Latino existence, from language use, areas of residence, educational opportunities, and career options. From 1965 to 1975, activist Latinos of the Chicano generation rejected those definitions, but institutional America paid little heed. In fact, from Washington, DC, official America defined Latinos anew, this time as an "underclass minority," a definition still used in the early twenty-first century, and one that has been employed by new nativists claiming that Latinos reject American values. But between 1975 and 1990, a new definition began to take shape: Latinos began to define Latinos. The late twentieth-century wave of immigrant Latinos provided a new point of departure for defining Latino culture—not, as in the Chicano era, in relation to white or mainstream culture, but on its own terms.

As Latinos began to define Latinos, various business interests—notably in radio, television, food, beverages, and banking—became aware of the growth of the Latino market and of these emerging new definitions. Wanting to capture a share of the large and growing Latino market, these businesses reoriented themselves to offer new products and services, and advertising that would resonate with the new Latino definitions and images. Some were Latino-owned businesses, and others were not; but irrespective of ownership, they pursued the emerging Latino market by doing business differently.

Grocery stores owned by Latinos have served the Latino market in Los Angeles since at least the 1850s.[1] Prior to World War II, most people in California bought their groceries at small, specialized neighborhood stores: the butcher shop, the bakery, the green grocer, and so on. In the postwar era, supermarkets sprang up, offering under one roof most everything needed for home consumption, and drove many of the small neighborhood specialty stores out of business. In Latino neighborhoods, the days of the typical Latino mom-and-pop store likewise seemed to be numbered. Some Latino-owned stores, trying to keep pace with the changing industry, expanded from corner stores to small supermarkets, then acquired a second and a third store, to create small chains of stores. Yet as quickly as they evolved, the grocery industry always seemed to be one or two steps ahead of the Latino-owned store, favoring ever larger, more efficient supermarkets and regional chains of such supermarkets over small, independently owned, two-or-three-store chains (fig. 11).

In contrast to these national trends, however, a specialized niche emerged in South Central Los Angeles. After the Watts riots of 1965, many big chains closed their stores in this and other inner-city areas; therefore, from 1965 to 1985, small independent grocers became virtually the only grocery sources for these areas. Yet even though they had a near monopoly on the local market in these urban areas, Latino grocers were increasingly at a financial disadvantage. Because they ordered in relatively small volume, their suppliers demanded cash payment, whereas credit was extended to the larger chains. Furthermore, smaller Latino-neighborhood stores often did not receive their shipments in time to participate in the industry's weekly specials. The small independents serving largely Latino areas of Southern California frequently were not even notified of special promotions, much less invited to participate. All these practices meant that the independents had to charge higher prices than the large chains, which had in any case abandoned the urban core. The increasingly Latino population of inner-city Southern California was paying more money, yet had fewer product and store choices. The area's independent grocers sought to change these policies and provide better conditions for the Latino consumer and grocer alike. The Mexican American Grocers Association (MAGA) brought together the small, independent grocers serving the barrios of Southern California to push, prod, and threaten to sue the

ANUNCIOS.

ABARROTES.

Por Mayor y Menor:

Francisco de P. Rodriguez,

TIENE el honor de participar al respetable público de esta ciudad y condado, que ha traspasado el almacen de abarrotes conocido con el nombre de

"LOS GARCIAS,"

situado en las casas de D. Juan Temple, calle Principal—y habiendolo surtido con una variedad de artículos que acaba de traer de San Francisco, ofrece venderlos a precios sumamente cómodos. El surtido en su almacen es como sigue :—

FIGURE 11. Advertisement for Latino-owned grocery store in Los Angeles, 1857. Source: *El Clamor Público,* 5 September 1857, p. 3.

large distributors and chains until they offered the same advantages to the independents serving Latino communities as they did to the larger chains serving non-Latino areas. MAGA leadership felt that, as a matter of equal opportunity, the Latino consumer should be as well served as the non-Latino consumer.

A funny thing happened on the way to civil rights and equal opportunity: the Latino market exploded in size. Based on firm belief in the market economy, MAGA expanded its objectives from advocating equal access to credit and shipments to applying marketing principles to the Latino market. MAGA member stores rode the growing wave of Latino grocery purchases to an unprecedented level of sales; the food product preferences of the increasingly immigrant Latino families became the basis of profitability for these stores.[2]

These increased food expenditures were made possible in part by rising Latino incomes. Latino disposable income in the United States grew during the period 1975 to 1990, to reach $207.5 billion in 1990, nearly three-fourths of the gross domestic product (GDP) of Mexico, which was $266 billion during the same period.[3] By 2001, in fact, US Latino buying power—$452.4 billion—had become nearly as large as the entire GDP of Mexico. It was something of a shock to the Food Marketing Institute to discover, in 1993, that salsa now outsold catsup and tortillas outsold white bread in the United States, in dollar value amounts.[4]

This changing consumer base was taken seriously by Von's, a large supermarket chain in Southern California. That company's president and CEO, Bill Davila, prided himself on being in touch with customers; indeed, during the 1980s he personally invited customers into his stores in English-language radio ads. Being Latino himself sensitized him to the rapid changes in the chain's customer base. In 1986, according to MAGA, Davila surprised the industry by featuring his own voice in a Spanish-language radio commercial. But he did more. He visited supermarkets in Mexico and small independent chains in California, invested in research, and in 1988 opened a subchain, Tianguis, a fifteen-store group located in heavily Latino areas, which emphasized Latino products and services. The very name reflected an insider's knowledge of Latino shopping habits: *tianguís,* a word of Náhuatl origin, denotes the small weekly open-air farmers' markets of Mexico. The aroma of freshly made tortillas and *bolillos* (small bread rolls) filled the air. A large, colorful selection of vegetables such as *nopales* (a type of edible cactus) and *jícama* (a root vegetable), and fruits such as *chirimoya* and *membrillo,* uncommon in the big chain supermarkets, spilled out of bins. Meat was cut in ways rarely found in non-Latino areas. Products imported from Mexico and Central America—soap, soup stocks, preserves, candies—were available in great quantity. On Friday and Saturday evenings, strolling mariachi bands and trios played. Tianguis elevated the shopping experience to a new level for the previously ignored Latino customer, and its success blew the small independents out of the water.

A competing chain, Fiesta, opened its own specialty supermarkets, seeking a competitive advantage in the growing Latino market. The battle between these two giants took its toll on the independents. Unable to compete in the areas of volume, price, and amenities, some independents moved to underserved areas; others simply went out of business. MAGA's leadership wryly commented that their efforts to bring corporate America to the barrios had succeeded beyond their wildest dreams; Mrs. Gomez now had access to low prices and special promotions, but Latinos' own independent grocery stores had paid the price.[5]

The demographics of the twenty-five years from 1965 to 1990 changed the course of California social history, and did so in such a quiet way that the transition was not noticed at first. It all came down to the fact that, increasingly, the mothers giving birth in hospital delivery rooms, and their newborn babies, were Latino. At the beginning of this period, California's Latino population was still a small minority. At 3.5 million in 1975, it was barely 16% of the state's total population. In just fifteen years, however, by 1990, it had doubled in size, growing to over 7.8 million, more than 25% of the state's population.[6] Everything followed from that.

The Latino immigration boom of the 1970s and 1980s did not come out of nowhere. Most immigrants had been involved in the bracero program, which from 1942 to 1964 had brought hundreds of thousands of Latinos to work in agribusiness, providing essential labor for the industry that has, at times, generated more of California's economy than all of Hollywood. When they changed status from bracero to immigrant, these farmworkers were able to bring their wives and children to the US. Central Americans fleeing civil strife augmented immigrant numbers. For the first time since the 1930s, Latino barrios in East Los Angeles, east San José, Fresno, and Oakland saw significant numbers of immigrant Latinos establishing households in areas Latinos had initially settled, in some cases, as long ago as 1769.

An immediate effect of immigrant Latino-driven growth was that California's Latino population became, overall, more "immigrant" in its composition. After the massive deportations of the 1930s, immigrants constituted only a small part of the Latino population. As shown in figure 12, less than 25% of the state's Latinos were immigrants in 1970.[7] The arrival of hundreds of thousands, then millions, of Latino immigrants, however, caused a shift in that population's composition.

Latino immigrant presence was amplified by two features that made it loom larger than mere numbers would indicate. First, immigrant Latinos were nearly always young adults, between fifteen and thirty years of age; few children or middle-aged adults, and almost no elderly Latinos, immigrated. Young adulthood is a very important age in social dynamics, at which people begin to form families and create households. Second, immigrant Latina women, compared to US-born Latinas, non-Hispanic whites,

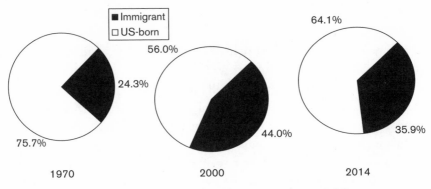

FIGURE 12. Immigrant and US-born portions of Latino population, California, 1970, 2000, and 2014. Source: IPUMS-USA, University of Minnesota, http://www.ipums.org.

and African Americans, had comparatively higher fertility rates. Among the US-born Latina population, fertility had dropped to replacement level—that is, the number of births equaled the number of deaths—and little net growth by natural increase occurred. Immigrant Latinas, on the other hand, have a fertility level somewhat above replacement; that is, there are more births than deaths, resulting in natural increase. As a result, there has been net population growth among Latinos, even though the immigrant portion of the population has been decreasing. After reaching 44% in 2000, by 2014, only 36% of the state's 15 million Latinos were immigrants (fig. 12).

In 1975, 83,638 Latino babies were born in California, constituting about one-fourth (26.5%) of all babies born in the state. In 1990, 229,244 Latino babies were born, almost 39% of all births (fig. 13). In 1975, by contrast, non-Hispanic white births predominated in California, representing nearly two-thirds (61.3%) of all babies born that year. By 1990, they accounted for less than half (43.7%) of all births, slightly more than Latinos (39%). The African American percentage remained nearly constant during this period at less than one-tenth of all births, dropping slightly from 8.9% in 1975 to 8.1% in 1990. The Asian/Pacific Islander percentage grew from 3.0% to 9.1%.[8] Latino births subsequently increased to over half of all births in the state (50.5%), passing that milestone in 2004, and remained around 50% from then to 2013. In less than twenty years (1985 to 2004), Latino births went from a minority to over half of all births, while non-Hispanic white births dropped from a majority to a minority, about one-third of all births (32.4%).

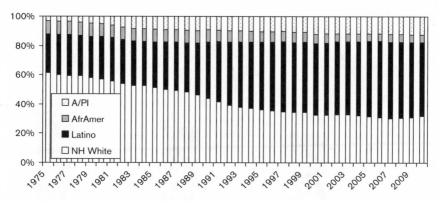

FIGURE 13. Composition of births by year, California, 1975–2010. Sources: 1975–1989, CA DOF, 1999; 1990–1999, CA DOF, 2001; 2000–2001, California Center for Health Statistics, *Birth Records—Years 1994, 1999, 2000, 2001* (Sacramento: CA DHS, 2002), http://www .applications,dhs.gov/vsq/default,asp [originally accessed 25 October 2002; dead link; printout stored at CESLAC]; 2002–2005, CA DHS, VSC-2005-0204.pdf, table 2–4, http:// www.cdph.ca.gov/data/statistics/documents/vsc-2005-0204.pdf [accessed 3 August 2016]; 2006–2010, VSC-2010-0204.pdf, table 2–4, http://www.cdph.ca.gov/data/statistics /documents/vsc-2010-0204.pdf [accessed 3 August 2016].

IMMIGRANT LATINO BEHAVIORS

The growing immigrant Latino population created a cultural environment woven with thicker strands of "typically Latino immigrant" behaviors and attitudes. If Latinos, overall, presented a paradox to the minority model of behavior, immigrant Latinos heightened and emphasized this paradox. Despite having lower levels of education and income, the immigrants exhibited even higher rates of labor force participation and family formation, and lower rates of welfare use, than did US-born Latinos. This can be seen in the marked differences between US-born and immigrant Latino patterns of behavior in the period 1990 to 2014.

A key tenet of the urban underclass theoretical model is that low educational levels and low income lead, almost inevitably, to socially undesirable behaviors. Yet while Latinos have consistently had both low incomes and low education, they do not demonstrate "typical" dysfunctional behavior. Immigrant Latinos had, and continue to have, far lower educational levels than US-born Latinos. From 1990 to 2014, immigrant Latinos were about half as likely as US-born Latinos to have graduated from high school (fig. 14). In 1990, almost three-fourths of US-born Latino adults had graduated from high school, and by 2014, over 86% had done so. In contrast, little more than

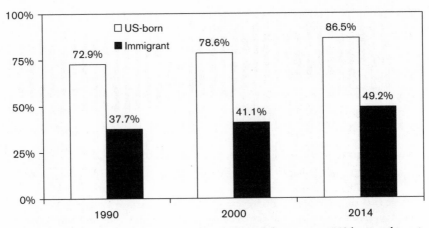

FIGURE 14. Percent of Latino high school graduates, adults 25+ years, US-born and immigrant, California, 1990–2014. Source: IPUMS-USA, University of Minnesota, http://www.ipums.org.

one-third of immigrant Latino adults in 1990 had graduated from high school, and by 2014, less than half had done so. Yet this lower educational level did not translate into socially undesirable behaviors.

Another key tenet of the urban underclass model is that poverty leads to dysfunctional behavior, such as labor force desertion, welfare dependency, and health-harming behaviors. Overall, Latinos have had higher poverty levels than any other group, and immigrant Latinos have had even higher poverty levels than US-born Latinos. In 1990, immigrant Latino households were nearly twice as likely as US-born Latino households to have incomes below poverty levels (fig. 15). While that discrepancy had lessened slightly by 2014, the pattern remained the same: immigrant Latino households were still more likely to be below poverty level compared to US-born Latinos.

Clearly, immigrant Latino households enjoyed far less income and education than US-born Latino households. Yet these greater risk factors did not necessarily translate into dysfunctional "urban underclass" behaviors. In fact, immigrant Latinos showed far stronger social behaviors than US-born Latinos with higher educations and higher incomes. This Latino social paradox was heightened by immigrant Latino behaviors. For example, despite their high poverty and low education levels, Latino males consistently had a higher rate of labor force participation than non-Hispanic white, African American, and Asian/Pacific Islander males, for the seventy-five-year period from 1940 to 2015 (fig. 3). Immigrant Latino males have had an

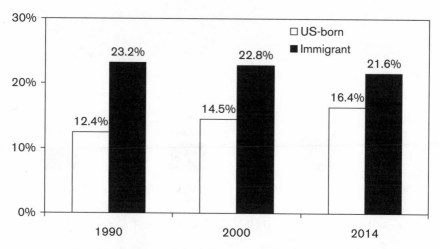

FIGURE 15. Percent of Latino adults below poverty level, US-born and immigrant, California, 1990–2014. Source: IPUMS-USA, University of Minnesota, http://www .ipums.org.

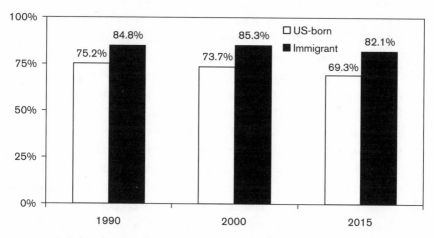

FIGURE 16. Labor force participation, Latino male 16+ years, US-born and immigrant, California, 1990–2015. Source: 1990, IPUMS-USA, University of Minnesota, http://www. ipums.org; 2000–2015, Schink custom analysis, data from Flood et al., IPUMS CPS (2015).

even higher rate of labor force participation than US-born Latino males. Federal data from 1990, 2000, and 2015, for example, show that while US-born Latino males had labor force participation rates varying from 69% to 75%, immigrant Latino males had even higher rates, between 82% and 85% (fig. 16).

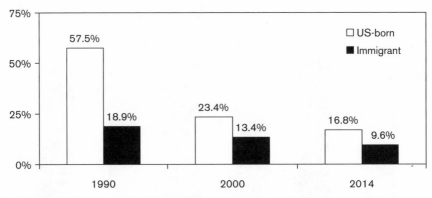

FIGURE 17. Latino adult public assistance to poverty ratio, US-born and immigrant, California, 1990–2014. Source: IPUMS-USA, University of Minnesota, http://www .ipums.org.

Nor, in general, have Latinos exhibited the greater use of welfare predicted by the urban underclass model for groups with such low levels of education and income. Immigrant Latinos, with lower education and income levels than US-born Latinos, demonstrated even lower levels of welfare use. Because welfare is means-tested—that is, one must demonstrate low income in order to be eligible—its use can be measured as a percentage of all those who live in poverty. By this metric, immigrant Latinos between 1990 and 2014 consistently showed a lower welfare use rate than that of US-born Latinos (fig. 17).

Nor have these higher risk factors for the immigrant Latino population led to disastrous health outcomes. Continuing the trend seen in work ethic and family formation, immigrant Latinos, even though faced with the greater risk factors of lower income and education than US-born Latinos, have enjoyed even better health. Infant mortality rates provide one indicator of this unexpected differential. During the forty-one-year period from 1970 to 2011, Latinos had an infant mortality rate virtually identical to that of non-Hispanic whites, and far lower than that of African Americans (fig. 9). Immigrant Latina mothers, with far lower education and less access to pre-natal care than US-born Latinas, fared even better. In 2013, immigrant Latinas had a lower infant mortality rate (4.54 deaths per 1,000 live births) than US-born Latinas (5.42 deaths per 1,000 live births)—this immigrant Latina rate was even lower than that of non-Hispanic whites (5.06 deaths per 1,000 live births) (fig. 18).

Therefore, not only were immigrants a growing portion of the Latino adult population in the period from 1975 to 1990, but they also strengthened

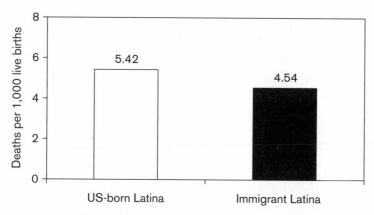

FIGURE 18. Infant mortality, immigrant Latina and US-born Latina, United States, 2013. Source: T.J. Mathews, M.F. MacDorman, and M.E. Thoma, "Infant Mortality Statistics from the 2013 Period Linked Birth/Infant Death Data Set," *National Vital Statistics Reports*, vol. 64, no. 9 (Hyattsville, MD: National Center for Health Statistics, 2015), p. 14, table 1.

patterns of behavior already typical of Latino populations, behaviors that contradicted the dire predictions of the urban underclass model. In short, immigrant Latinos displayed even more strongly the paradoxical Latino patterns of behavior described in chapter 3. These strong immigrant Latino behaviors also challenged the claims of the new nativists, who use adherence to individualist values such as work ethic, independence from welfare use, and family formation to measure a group's "American-ness." By these measures, it is actually Latino immigrants who adhere most strongly to the new nativists' definition of American, even more than non-Hispanic white populations do.

Spanish Language Use

Older US-born Latinos remember when public use of Spanish was actively discouraged, and few US-born Latinos of that generation are able to speak Spanish fluently. By the mid-twentieth century, Spanish appeared to be headed into the same disuse as other languages originally spoken by immigrants to the US, such as Italian, Greek, Swedish, or German. The abandonment of Spanish by Latinos in the postwar period was so extensive that in 1988, Mario Barrera lamented that the "'struggle of cultural survival' . . . is rapidly being lost." He suggested as a countermeasure the establishment of politically distinct "ethnic autonomous regions" where young Latinos could pursue their distinctive "music, art, literature, food [and] styles of dress."[9]

The wave of immigration in 1965–1990 changed that, perhaps permanently. As the immigrant presence increased from less than one out of every four Latinos in 1970 to nearly one out of every two in 1990, Spanish became the preferred language of half the Latino population.[10] Among immigrant Latinos aged forty to forty-nine years, 76.6% primarily spoke Spanish. By comparison, US-born Latinos of the same age were nearly completely English-dominant; only 12.8% spoke Spanish to any extent. Moreover, comfortable with their culture, immigrant Latinos did not exhibit the anguish of the Chicano generation about what "real" Latinos would do. Eating a hamburger was not seen as an act of cultural genocide. Speaking Spanish was not an act of cultural defiance. Listening to music in Spanish was not a political choice.

Because of their young-adult age and comparatively higher fertility, immigrant Latinos increasingly became the population segment who created families and settled down. Their focus was intensely domestic. They bought or rented houses and fixed them up, furnished them, purchased food regularly, clothed their children, gave them toys, saw them off to school, and dealt with the problems of teenagers. Their hopes, dreams, and fears for their families became the norm for young families in their neighborhoods. In 1998, one United Way focus group participant described her perspective as "Queremos superarnos, queremos tener una casa, queremos tener un buen trabajo, queremos que nuestros hijos vayan a la universidad" (We want to better ourselves, we want to have a house, we want to have a good job, we want our children to go to college).[11] They pursued their dreams, often dreaming in Spanish and using Mexican and Latin American cultural references in making those dreams come true.

BUSINESS AND THE LATINO MARKET

As with the grocery industry, other businesses that catered to the needs of these young immigrant-headed families began to see their bottom lines improved by overall trends in Latino purchasing decisions. By 1990, most industries in California were at least thinking about marketing products and services to Latinos. As businesses moved to accept the Latino market, they often had to modify their products and services to better suit the Latino market's tastes, desires, and demands.

By 1990, the annual Mexican American Grocers Association conference had attracted a following among Latinos working in large food and beverage corporations. Corporations in various aspects of the food and beverage industry—soft drinks, fresh produce, processed meats, snack foods, breakfast cereals, soups, and detergents—and others sent their Latino executives to the conference, held each winter in Palm Springs. Many of these Latino executives shared frustrations about their corporations' indifference to growing Latino markets. By 1992, these informal "gripe sessions" had tipped MAGA leadership to the fact that all was not well with Latino executives in corporate America. MAGA's chief executive officer asked the Center for the Study of Latino Health and Culture (CESLAC) at UCLA to undertake a qualitative research project to help them understand how American corporations were approaching the burgeoning Latino market.

Latino Market Denial

Although the study was not quantitative, nearly all the participating Latino executives reported at least once in their careers chafing under the situation we came to label "Latino market denial," which is the collective conclusion made by other, usually non-Latino, executives in their corporations that a viable Latino market simply did not exist. As one participant in the study observed, "Twenty percent of corporations are not going to do anything [in the Latino market], no matter what statistics we present. They've already made their minds up.... Presentations are exciting [but] often fall on deaf ear [sic]."[12]

The most virulent form of Latino market denial was physical rejection: when faced with the prospect of a growing Latino customer base, in a few instances corporations would actually take steps to keep Latinos away from their stores, out of fear of driving away the "good" customers. "When people don't know the first thing about the Hispanic market, they believe [that] 'If we advertise in Spanish, we're advertising to a group of illegal people'; and they have to consider, 'What do other people think of us? What impression does this make on other people who don't like illegals?'"[13] More often, however, the rejection was psychological. Some corporate executives, succumbing to the media-driven stereotypes of Latinos, feared the Latino customer base. "You're trying to convince people who come to L.A., stay in Bel Air, and don't dare get east of downtown [to the Latino neighborhoods]. They're afraid for their lives. They think, 'If I go out there, I'm going to get shot; people will carjack me.'"[14] Many of our respondents' non-Latino colleagues had grown up with the typical stereotypes of Latinos presented for decades on nightly news programs. Convinced that the urban underclass model of social dysfunction applied to Latinos, those colleagues made decisions involving billions of dollars based on these stereotypes. "It's extremely difficult to get the top ten to twenty VPs to accept that this is a vital, growing segment; it has money; they're not all welfare-living, drug-taking, baby-having heathens. But that's really what some think of us."[15]

A less intense form of Latino market denial involved minimizing, in which a business did not believe that the Latino market was important to the company's bottom line. "Business is emotional, to a certain extent. . . . A business decision may be made on the assumption that a Hispanic consumer is on welfare, and it may not ever be pulled out [and examined rationally]."[16] Believing that the Latino market was not important, these companies continued the practice of not giving priority to Latino market research, thereby stunting the growth of the knowledge base needed to engage that customer base. "[Hispanic marketing] takes a back seat to regular product development, regular product marketing, a new-item introduction. All those things come before you get to Hispanic marketing as a focus. So, in terms of focus, it's a very low priority."[17]

Latino Market Confusion

Some Latino executives saw that their companies had moved out of Latino market denial but had not yet been able to productively engage with this population. They described confusion, dithering, vacillation. "Many companies jumped on the wagon and said, 'I don't know what we're going to do, but we've got to do something. And fast.'"[18] These corporations could see that the Latino market had potential but did not know how to engage it. As the Latino market took off in the 1980s, a few "gazelle" corporations—those that spring quickly to the head of a herd—became quite profitable by successfully engaging with it. Those still in the confusion stage heard of these success stories but could not figure out how to achieve similar results. At times, companies would spend money on a few research projects, but without any strategic planning. Some jumped into ill-advised activities that burned cash but produced few tangible results. Some Latino executives felt that the public failure of some noted Latino marketing attempts poisoned the well for their own efforts. "A lot of companies are looking to make a buck. What they find is that the investment can be extensive, and the return is long-term, not short-term. The difficulty is to get people to continuously make the effort. Those who have deeper pockets reap it. Others who do it [Latino marketing] haphazardly have created problems in the marketplace."[19]

Companies moving out of the confusion stage entered the contemplation phase; although they saw the Latino market as viable, they realized that they were woefully unprepared to engage with it. Latino executives of companies in the contemplation phase felt it was their job to shepherd their colleagues through to full acceptance. They could best do this, they reported, by providing information that their colleagues needed to make decisions. Despite being rational businessmen working in large, rational corporations, they described a surprising amount of "emotional hand-holding," helping their colleagues overcome stereotypes and fears.

> [The ones] who run these businesses are people ... [who] get their experience on Latinos from the media. . . . Our job is really hard, to break down the stereotypes and biases. . . . Not only does this guy "know" that, he feels in his heart that these people are bad news. . . . You need to feed in [Latino market] numbers on one side, and on the other are the emotional things you have to work on.[20]

Latino Market Acceptance

But an increasing number of Latino executives reported that their companies had come to accept the Latino market. These organizations realized they must be competitive in that segment to survive in the new California. The sheer growth in population numbers and purchasing power had won over these companies. In most Latino-committed businesses, at least one senior executive, or one business unit—usually the sales unit, initially—had led the way. The "CEO worked in ... Latin America ... [and] always had an appreciation for the Latino culture. He knew what he wanted. . . . [It's not just] a matter of information. It's a matter of *attitude in key positions*, [executives] who have lived it and understand it."[21]

A small number of Latino executives worked for companies that had decided to be the dominant presence in their industry in Latino markets. Such a position required a significant investment, and these Latino executives described their companies as enthusiastically making such commitments, not only in marketing—finding Latino ad agencies, cultivating Latino product endorsers, buying time on Spanish-language television and radio—but also in product-line development. Latino markets were simply not receptive to some products: sauerkraut, for example. "Everyone else, of course, thinks the same thing, so you have to differentiate yourself from the competitors. . . . Other companies are spending more just to catch up with us. As the pie gets bigger, if we don't spend more, our slice of pie gets smaller. If we want to outdistance the competitors, then we have to spend faster than the pie is growing."[22] While companies in the denial or confusion stages might shrink from redefining their core business, companies in the acceptance stage make full investments in redefining their product and service lines.

The greatest form of acceptance was affiliation with the Latino market; a company determined that its future was tied to the Latino market. No longer a foreign, unknown "them," the Latino market was seen as, and more importantly felt to be, part of the larger community in which the company functions. Affiliation was achieved only when top-level executives felt comfortable with the Latino market. The top executive did not necessarily have to be Latino, but did have to have significant experience with Latino markets. In international corporations, a Latin American posting often provided that connection. Such executives usually hired Latino vice presidents so that those making decisions would have a "feel" for the market and its tastes. One focus group participant noted, "[The] top cookie [in this bank] grew up in Mexico, grew up in [a banking corporation], always knew that South America was [the bank president's] favorite place." Another observed, "A lot of Latinos in the bank [are] doing extremely well."[23] The Latino executive respondents were nearly unanimous in estimating that only a small proportion of corporations had moved to the full acceptance and competitive stages.

As the young-adult demographic in the state became increasingly Latino, from 1975 to 1990, the musical tastes of young-adult Latinos increasingly came to reflect the tastes of immigrant Latinos. Perhaps it was inevitable that a growing consumer base with an increasing discretionary income would support its local musical industry. A new musical genre, developed in California, swept the Southwest and had a "blowback" effect in Mexico. Although Latino consumers had a wide array of musical options available to them—classic mariachi, *norteña* music from northern Mexico, and standard Latin American pop music—many rural immigrants were partial to the danceable music played by brass bands in village squares back home. The city of Zacatecas in Mexico takes credit for developing this style, called *banda,* which features a lively polka beat and a bouncing tuba bass line. Bands in California took that basic style, updated it with electronic instruments, and called it *techno-banda.* Banda music was itself a social phenomenon, an indigenously developed alternative to the *cholo* "gangbanger" ethos of baggy pants and lowriders. Banda youth did not glamorize violence or get involved in the spiraling rounds of gang killings and paybacks that characterized the cholo life. As banda clubs sprang up all over the state, Latino youths embraced the traditional culture that inspired their music. They danced *la quebradita,* a Latino update of Country Western–style dancing. Even banda clothes reflected the style's Mexican rural origins; both men and women wore tight Levis and Mexican cowboy boots, hats, and belt buckles. The men also wore a vestigial riding crop. It being California, there was also a characteristic vehicle: a pickup truck, with a coiled lasso hung over the rearview mirror.

In 1992, few FM stations in Los Angeles played Latino music. Heftel Music had just acquired an FM signal and wanted to carve out a niche. On a hunch by the musical programmer, who had been an undocumented Latino immigrant himself, the station was the first to pick up the new techno-banda format and play it, along with more traditional banda songs, round the clock. KLAX tapped a consumer vein that had been ignored until then, and in a matter of months, it became the number-one station in Los Angeles.[24] Other radio stations in Southern California were not long in noticing the banda bandwagon, and three other FM stations soon changed to a banda playlist. After twelve consecutive quarters as the number-one station, KLAX finally lost its top ranking, becoming merely one of the top five stations. The new number-one station was KLVE (pronounced *K-love*), a Spanish-language station playing Latin American pop music. But the radio industry had learned its lesson; by the early 1990s, 110 stations were focusing their programming on the 10 million Latinos in the state.[25]

Latino cultural dynamics influenced the television industry as well. The two major Spanish-language chains in Southern California, Univision and Telemundo, saw their quarterly ratings increase in this period. By the early 1990s, the growth in immigrant Latino viewership had catapulted Univision's six o'clock news program into the lead, and fifteen television stations were transmitting in Spanish throughout California.[26] Likewise, print media were affected by the increase in Spanish-language readership. The number of new newspapers, magazines, journals, and other publications grew threefold in this fourteen-year period. Between 1975 and 1979, Latino publishers in the state started a total of twenty-one publications. Between 1980 and 1984, this number grew by 50%, to thirty-four new publications. In the next five years, the number of new publications doubled, to fifty-eight new print publications.[27] I recall that even the *Los Angeles Times* mulled over the idea of printing a Spanish-language edition of its daily coverage.

Latinos were not merely the consumers but also increasingly the manufacturers, distributors, and sellers of products California needed. Initially, Latino-owned businesses in California were few in number, barely 28,166 in 1972. They tended to be small in size; only 24% had employees, and their average gross receipts were $46,230.[28] Facing common problems of access to capital and business know-how, Latino businesses shared contacts and knowledge in Hispanic Chambers of Commerce. The Latin Business Association (LBA)—established in Los Angeles in 1974 with only seven members, mainly in the printing business, and no budget—became the largest Latino business interest group in the state in the 1990s.[29] Like the Mexican American Grocers Association, its original focus was on civil rights. The LBA helped its members become officially designated Minority-Owned Businesses, so they could qualify for set-aside contracting. The LBA also lobbied city, county, and state governmental entities to contract with Latino businesses.

The explosion of interest in the growing Latino market added new dimensions to the LBA agenda: to assist its members in better serving the needs of the expanding Latino consumer base and to assist non-Latino corporations in their pursuit of Latino market share. LBA's annual conference developed a significant marketing focus. Figure 19 shows the growth in Latino businesses from 28,166 in 1972, to 249,717 in 1992, to 815,304 in 2012. While the Latino population tripled between 1970 and 2014, Latino-owned businesses soared by an additional order of magnitude, increasing almost thirty-fold between 1972 and 2012.

By 2002, the LBA had forty-two thousand members in Southern California, with average annual sales and receipts of around a million dollars. Nearly one out of every five LBA members had average annual sales and receipts of more than $5 million. The LBA itself grew tremendously and by 2002 had achieved an annual budget of over $3 million, with twelve full-time employees.[30]

US-BORN LATINOS RESPOND TO IMMIGRANTS

Immigrant Latinos made the speaking of Spanish more commonplace. Billboards began to advertise food, beverages, and durable goods in Spanish. The buses that crisscrossed Southern California started carrying ads in Spanish. Both construction workers in East Los Angeles and movie stars in

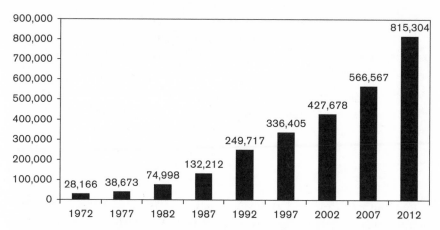

FIGURE 19. Latino-owned businesses, California, 1972–2012. Sources: 1972, US DOC, *1972 Survey of Minority-Owned Business Enterprises: Minority-Owned Businesses; Spanish Origin* (Washington, DC: US DOC, 1975), p. 84, table 2; 1977, US DOC, *1977 Survey of Minority-Owned Business Enterprises: Minority-Owned Businesses; Spanish Origin* (Washington, DC: US DOC, 1980), p. 61, table 2; 1982, US DOC, *1982 Survey of Minority-Owned Business Enterprises: Minority-Owned Businesses; Hispanic* (Washington, DC: US DOC, 1986), p. 43, table 2; 1987, US DOC, 1991, p. 20, table 1 and table 14; 1992, US DOC 1996, table 4 and table 14; 1997, US Department of Commerce, *Summary, 1997 Economic Census: Survey of Minority-Owned Business Enterprises* (Washington, DC: US Department of Commerce, 2001), p. 31, table 2, https://www.census.gov/prod/ec97/e97cs-7.pdf [accessed 2 August 2016]; 2002–2007, US Department of Commerce, *Hispanic-Owned Firms: 2002; 2002 Economic Census; Survey of Business Owners* (Washington, DC: US Department of Commerce, 2006), p. 5, table 2, https://www.census.gov/prod/ec02/sbo200cshisp.pdf [accessed 2 August 2016], and US Census Bureau, *Survey of Business Owners (SBO)—Hispanic-Owned Firms: 2007,* Table C, http://www.census.gov/library/publications/2007/econ/2007-sbo-hispanic .html [accessed 2 August 2016]; 2012, US Census Bureau, *Los Angeles County a Microcosm of Nation's Diverse Collection of Business Owners, Census Bureau Reports,* Release Number CB15–209, http://www.census.gov/newsroom/press-releases/2015/cb15–209.html [accessed 2 August 2016].

Beverly Hills could be stuck in traffic behind ads in Spanish for diapers, long-distance service, and legal representation. Immigrant Latinos also created new nodes of civil society. Still enthralled by the soccer they had played at home, they created youth soccer leagues for their children. Nostalgic for home, they formed hometown associations: *clubes jaliscences, clubes zacatecanos, clubes michoacanos.* The clubs often sponsored youth sports leagues in soccer, baseball, and basketball. Annual dinners, increasingly held at the better hotels in Southern California, awarded scholarships to college students and crowned "Miss Zacatecas" or "Miss Jalisco." These immigrant Latinos did not see themselves as consciously trying to create anything new or different; they were simply trying to establish themselves and their families. They saw themselves primarily as homemakers and breadwinners, doing what they felt was necessary and appropriate for their young families. But in doing so in greatly increased numbers, they changed the face of the state. They had arrived in such great numbers that their presence affected nearly every facet of California life. One segment of the state's population in particular whom they changed was US-born Latinos.

Retro-assimilators

One group of US-born Latinos, characterized as "retro-assimilators," felt comfortable in the new cultural conditions.[31] Although these Latinos had been born and raised in the United States and were quite familiar with Atlantic American cultural cues, they nonetheless felt they were part of the immigrant-led cultural revolution.

US-born Latinos are, almost by definition, English-dominant speakers. Typically, a US-born child of immigrant Latino parents will learn to speak Spanish in the home before starting the formal educational process. Once in kindergarten, however, by and large his or her formal education is conducted in English. Even if the child retains some Spanish, its acquisition usually does not advance along with that of English. Only in a few cases do bilingual programs exist that are strong enough to create true bilingualism. High school–level Spanish then typically presents the first opportunity for many US-born Latinos to study the language formally; but by the time they are learning to say a simple sentence such as "Hola, me llamo José" (Hi, my name is José) in Spanish, they are learning physics, calculus, and chemistry in English. In earlier decades, when Spanish-language radio and television did not exist and few people they interacted with as adults spoke Spanish, there was little reinforcement for developing Spanish-language skills. Now, however, the growth of Spanish-language media detailed above, and of the Spanish-speaking adult population, has provided reinforcement for speaking the language.

During the period 1975 to 1990, many US-born Latino young adults engaged in linguistic retro-assimilation; that is, they became increasingly engaged in a Spanish-speaking world, as opposed to leaving it. Whereas the ability to speak Spanish had been discouraged in earlier generations, with the growth of a Spanish-language environment, it acquired a certain cachet. CESLAC focus groups conducted among English-dominant US-born

Latinos brought some of these feelings to the surface. A number of participants, English-dominant Latinos who retro-assimilated as college students, remarked:

PERSON 1: Things have much, like, more meaning in Spanish.
PERSON 2: Yeah. Most things sound so much prettier.
PERSON 1: It's more of a passionate language.[32]

Use of the Spanish language was also described as adding emphasis to a spoken comment: "I always want to tell her [girlfriend] something [in Spanish], just because I know it will be stronger, what I'm trying to get across, in Spanish. Yeah, [things sound] so much meaner, like when they yell at you."[33]

A cultural retro-assimilation became linked to this language reacquisition. Part of this occurred by cultural osmosis; in listening to Spanish-language radio, one picked up knowledge about the artists and musical genres, as well as news of Latino California and Latin America. Watching Spanish-language television, one learned about events in Mexico and Latin America, and was presented with a different media treatment of Latinos. While English-language media tended to concentrate on depictions of Latinos as illegal immigrants, gangbangers, or welfare mothers, Spanish-language news media treated Latinos as a larger, whole community, with school bands, soccer leagues, musicians visiting town, human-interest stories, Latino businesses, and politics. Formal knowledge constituted another part of this cultural retro-assimilation. While Chicano studies programs, established a generation earlier, had been treated by campus administrators as politicized, marginal activities, US-born Latino students increased their enrollment, learning about Latino history, literature, music, theater, and Latino-focused social sciences. One focus group participant reminisced, "My dad was born and raised here in the U.S. . . . I lost the ability to speak Spanish from fourth grade to high school. [In college] I learned what being Chicano meant, and Mexican-American culture and the mariachi and banda [music]."[34]

Retro-assimilated US-born Latinos, with their ability in Spanish and greater knowledge of Latino California, served as a bridge between California's institutions and organizations and the burgeoning Latino adult population. Leading-edge private businesses hired these young adults, who could tell them about the tastes and desires of this growing market. "I was . . . born in the U.S. . . . Once I discovered that [in college], I just fell in love with the fact that, wow! I could speak Spanish, so there was a connection there [with other Latinos]."[35]

Proud, but Confused

Not all Latinos, of course, experienced retro-assimilation. CESLAC also held focus groups with US-born Latinos who did not speak Spanish to any functional degree, to elicit their reactions to the growing influence of the immigrant Latino population. They described a more confused picture.

Older US-born Latinos described growing up not being able to speak Spanish. This was nothing remarkable in the period prior to 1975, when the vast majority of Latinos were US-born and English-dominant, and immigrant Latinos were comparatively rare. The growth of the Spanish-language environment in from 1975 through 1990, however, created language confusion for them, because of the assumption made by many immigrant Latinos that a person who "looks Latino" should be able to speak Spanish. One focus group participant complained, "Now I have somebody who comes [into the store] and speaks Spanish to me and makes me feel, 'Oh, you can't even speak your own language.' But that wasn't my language. My language was English."[36] She went on to describe an exchange she found herself engaging in more and more, as the store's clientele became increasingly immigrant Latino-based. "They'll say, 'Well, how come you don't speak Spanish? You're a Mexican, aren't you?' And I just tell them, 'But I was born here.'"[37] Growth of this Spanish-language environment also has led some non-Hispanic whites to assume that someone who "looks Latino" must be able to speak Spanish. "When I go to Mexico, they [Mexicans] speak to me in English. When I'm here, they [non-Hispanic whites] speak to me in Spanish."[38]

When a Latino is not able to engage in a Spanish-language environment, informal cultural osmosis from that environment does not occur. Latinos who do not continue their education in college often are limited to what they learned about Latinos in high school, which is still a very small part of the state's high school curriculum. "Out here in the LAUSD [Los Angeles Unified School District], they don't teach you about Hispanic heritage at all. It's mostly all [Atlantic-]American heritage."[39] Latinos who are not comfortable in Spanish miss out on the flow of information about musical events, theater, health tips, and corporate Latino initiatives expressed by Spanish-language ads prepared by Macy's, Nordstrom's, Sears, J. C. Penney, and other large national chains. They are limited instead to Atlantic American presentations of Latinos in English-language programming, which largely have not changed from the images of 1940: Latinos as gang members, undocumented immigrants, and welfare mothers. "Well, we have mixed images. Like when you ... [watch TV, the] first thing on the news: *cholos,* you know, or killings. That's negative.... And then we have that [Latino elected official] doing drugs, and then, first thing, they put him in the news."[40] Latinos not fluent in Spanish had become accustomed to Atlantic American definitions of Latinos. When faced with the sudden presence of Latino-derived definitions, they were confused. Which image was the "real Latino"?

US-born Latinos in these focus groups described, with a twinge of envy, observing immigrant Latinos moving into their communities with high levels of energy, dedication, and self-esteem. "Immigrant ... students who come here are so eager to learn.... They're so outgoing ... so self-oriented. You know their initiative is there.... They're doing better than the second- and third-generation Mexican-American."[41] Poorly educated second- and third-generation respondents described themselves as having lost some of their initiative, in a sense internalizing the discouragement they had received from their schools. "The Chicanos are the ones that are saying, 'Oh, it's not good to go to college. Who are they, and why are they [immigrants] trying to be better than me?'"[42] US-born Latinos, especially in the focus groups with less-educated participants, described feelings of frustration, or feeling that somehow they were no longer sufficiently Latino. "[Immigrant Latinos], well, they're making me feel like, you know, I'm not a Mexican."[43] Their confusion was compounded because, during the era from 1940 to 1965, they had been told in numerous ways that they were not completely American, either. "In high school I didn't look like all the other Mexican girls, and I hated that 'cause I wanted to be able to identify with ... the other Mexican girls ... but I couldn't identify with white girls either."[44] The major difference was that, by the end of the 1990s, Latinos did not have to use nativist Atlantic American definitions of Latinos as the only standard; they could also use immigrant-driven definitions. Retro-assimilators did this easily. The confused US-born, who did not speak Spanish and did not know the worlds of formal and informal culture, felt caught in a state of limbo: not able to retro-assimilate, not accepted by the Atlantic American world, and feeling vaguely caught up in Latino-derived cultural forces they could not understand.

The key to their uneasiness was a transformation in Latino identity dynamics. Nativist Atlantic Americans no longer were the sole suppliers of images and definitions. Increasingly, Latinos, especially immigrant Latinos, were supplying alternative definitions and images, in very unconscious, apolitical ways. Immigrant Latinos in our focus groups described understanding why US-born Latinos would be ignorant of the Spanish language, of Latin American history, or of their feelings of identity. "These [Mexican American] folks, that they are complaining about us [immigrant Latinos] now, were some of the very ones that were punished for speaking Spanish, or their parents were punished for speaking Spanish.... When I used to travel here [to the United States] as a young kid ... being Mexican was a bad thing."[45] Although they had not lived through the period in which Atlantic American definitions predominated, they were sensitive to the fact that those older US-born Latinos had undergone a different experience. "The American-born Latino lived a different reality than we would like to live, than I would like to live. The reality was that being Latino mean[t] you had to hide the Latino aspects of your life."[46]

The conversion of braceros to permanent immigrants, just at the moment when the non-Hispanic white "baby bust" began, created the conditions both for a tremendous Latino population growth and for an expansion of Latino cultural choices. The market choices of millions of Spanish-dominant immigrants and their Spanish-familiar children created a new language and cultural environment that offered new personal opportunities and challenges to US-born Latinos. Far from disappearing, Spanish became the preferred language in media for a majority of Latinos. Far from dwindling into numerical insignificance, Latino populations grew and came to dominate urban schools and neighborhoods. While this growth did not result in "identity politics" among Latinos, it did among a good many alarmed non-Hispanic white voters, as will be described in chapter 5. Instead, it reflected the mundane, daily choices made by parents, children, relatives, friends, and neighbors as they went about the quotidian business of raising children, running a household, going to work, establishing a business, enjoying weekends, finding spiritual solace, and reminiscing about earlier days. The major difference was that these families now were largely composed of immigrant Latinos. By sheer force of numbers and economic importance, immigrant Latinos forced the state's business community to take these wants, dreams, and fears into account as they developed products and services to sell to them. Increasingly, immigrant Latinos and their choices determined which businesses would live and which would die in the state's marketplace. Although they were not aware of it, and although it had not yet been made an issue, immigrant Latino behavior directly challenged the new nativist definition of what is American.

Far from rejecting the individualist values of the work ethic, independence from welfare, and family formation, immigrant Latinos believed in those values, and acted on them, even more than the non-Hispanic white population.

Immigrant Latinos, however, did not form a monolithic bloc. Immigrants from Central America, South America, and the Caribbean entered the mix from 1975 to 1990. And even though the vast majority of immigrant Latinos still came from Mexico, there was considerable diversity among these Mexican immigrants. They came from urban as well as rural areas; from the heavily Hispanicized northern states of Sonora, Chihuahuha, and Coahuila, as well as from still largely indigenous southern states such as Oaxaca and Chiapas. These regional diversities were reflected in radio programs, musical choices, even the jokes used by Spanish-language disc jockeys. But unlike the wave of immigrants in the early twentieth century, these Latino immigrants could live most of their lives responding to Latino definitions of Latinos, rather than to Atlantic American ones. Those new definitions created by immigrants also had a profound effect on US-born Latinos, one hard to ignore. Some felt empowered to explore their "Latino side" and reveled in the opportunities to live large portions of their lives within Latino cultural con-structions. Others felt confused by it, at times a bit resentful that they were considered not sufficiently American by Atlantic Americans but also not sufficiently Latino by immigrant Latinos. Whatever the individual reaction, the dominant dynamic had been put into place: Latinos were defining Latinos.

Times of Crisis

PROPOSITION 187 AND AFTER, 1990–2000

> I was about twelve years old then [1994], just before the Proposition
> 187 vote. For weeks, on the rock stations that I listened to then, the
> DJs were saying horrible things about Latinos and immigrants,
> and I felt so bad. Then, one day, I was in a theater in Westwood [an
> upscale non-Hispanic white section of Los Angeles], when an ad
> for Coca Cola or something started, and there was Gloria Estefan
> on the screen; and I was thinking, "Please, God, don't let her sing
> in Spanish. I would be mortified." And sure enough, she sang in
> Spanish, and I felt like the whole theater was watching me. Me, I
> felt ashamed to be Latina. That's how bad it was.
>
> —C. HAYES-BAUTISTA, 2003

EVERY WAVE OF URBAN TURMOIL to hit the country during the late
1960s swept more and more whites out of urban areas, leaving behind an
increasingly African American population to become the urban majority in
most US cities. But this urban population, too, soon experienced change. By
1990, much of the black middle class also had fled the declining urban cores,
taking with them their capital, skills, and businesses. In many American cities, such as Detroit and Newark, the fleeing black middle class found no buyers for their properties and simply walked away from them, leaving block after
block of uninhabited, derelict buildings. Nearly 80% of Detroit's urban white
population had left the cities, and less than half the remaining adult population was in the labor force.[1] By 1990, inner-city America appeared to be a
nearly terminal case. But in Southern California, there was life stirring in the
urban wasteland. There were people willing to move into areas abandoned by
both the non-Hispanic white and the black middle class; there were people
willing to move into ghettos, willing to put "sweat equity" into restoring
houses and refurbishing businesses. These people were immigrant Latinos.

Yet, after planting seeds of new development and bringing Southern
California's cities back from the brink of social and economic death, the

Latino community was punished by the passage of Proposition 187, the elimination of affirmative action, and the abolition of bilingual education. These were indeed times of crisis for California's Latinos.

THE LOS ANGELES RIOTS

As recently as the mid-1960s, Latinos in the Los Angeles region, like African Americans, had been legally restricted to home ownership only in specific areas. In the case of Latinos, these areas were centered in East Los Angeles and the northern San Fernando Valley. Those who could not afford to buy houses crowded into large rental complexes just west of the downtown core. With the repeal of restrictive covenants, however, areas previously inhabited only by non-Hispanic whites changed. The Watts riots of 1965 panicked white home owners, who felt their properties were "too close" to African American enclaves. Fearful that their property values would be hurt by areas that had become too volatile, white home owners in the center of Los Angeles County—Compton, Hawthorne, Inglewood, Fox Hills—sold their houses and fled to its outer perimeter. Often they sold to the newly affluent African American middle class, who were themselves seeking to flee the disorder of crumbling inner-city areas.

As black middle-class flight from the inner city accelerated in the late 1970s and throughout the 1980s, rather than leaving behind hundreds of blocks of deserted, unproductive properties, as had happened in Detroit, Newark, and other cities, departing African American homeowners in Los Angeles County found buyers who were willing to move into previously all-black ghettoes: Latino immigrants seeking their own piece of the American dream. So the immigrants poured out of rental housing, into areas shunned by more middle-class buyers. The immigrant Latino population slowly moved outward from the downtown area, filling in the vacuum left by the fleeing black middle class in areas such as South Central Los Angeles. Latino immigrants did not hesitate to buy in Watts, Compton, Inglewood, and other areas deemed undesirable by non-Hispanic whites and middle-class African Americans. And as they moved into what, for two to three decades, had been inner-city ghettos, they renewed life in Southern California's portion of urban America.

When abandoned property became derelict, no tax revenue was produced; when immigrants bought houses, they paid property taxes, thus providing a

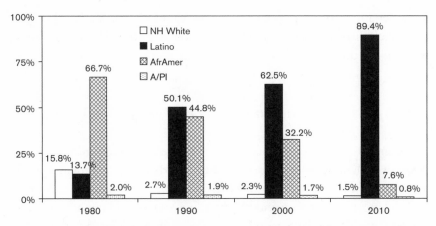

FIGURE 20. South Central Los Angeles ethnic composition, 1980, 1990, 2000, and 2010. Sources: 1980–1990, David E. Hayes-Bautista, Werner Schink, and Maria Hayes-Bautista, "Latinos and the 1992 Los Angeles Riots: A Behavioral Sciences Perspective," *Hispanic Journal of Behavioral Sciences* 15 (1993), p. 431; 2000, US Bureau of the Census, *Census 2000 Summary File 1 (SF1): 100 Percent Data*, map TM-P001H; 2010, Steven Ruggles, Katie Genadek, Ronald Goeken, Josiah Gorver, and Matthew Sobek, Integrated Public Use Microdata Series: Version 6.0 [machine-readable database] (Minneapolis: University of Minnesota, 2015).

revenue base for city services. In addition, the houses were rehabilitated and remodeled. Although War on Poverty and Housing and Urban Development (HUD) programs had largely failed in their goal of urban renewal, immigrant Latinos, with their own private capital, painfully accumulated from low-wage jobs, rehabilitated wide swaths of formerly declining properties in South Central Los Angeles. Beginning in the early 1980s, families returned to South Central Los Angeles. Laughter was again heard in the parks, tricycles littered the sidewalk, chiming ice cream trucks appeared, and sidewalk taco stands brought life back to the streets. Enterprising Latino businesspeople bought abandoned businesses, un-boarded the windows, and stocked the shelves. Commerce revived.

South Central Los Angeles quickly became Latinized. In 1980, two-thirds of that area's population were African American (66.7%), and only 13.7% were Latino. In only ten years, by 1990, Latinos were the majority population (50.1%), and African Americans a slight minority (44.8%) (fig. 20). Although almost no one noticed, the 1990 census showed that the African American population had become a minority in previously all-black areas such as Watts, Compton, and South Central. Continuing the trend in 2000, Latinos made up nearly two-thirds of the population of South Central (62.5%), and

African Americans only one-third (32.2%). By 2010, Latinos comprised almost 90% of those communities' population, with African Americans less than 8%.

During the 1970s and 1980s, when the manufacturing regions of the northeastern United States were declining, California's economy seemed charmed. While unemployment soared in the rest of the country, California's unemployment rate was far below the national average, and jobs were still being created. Aerospace provided high-wage, high-benefit jobs for the state's highly trained workforce. But when the Soviet Union fell apart, and America no longer needed to maintain a huge arsenal, defense spending was extensively cut, practically overnight. California was hit especially hard because the state had enjoyed a disproportionate amount of defense spending on its military aviation and aerospace industries. As the aerospace industry imploded, many manufacturers went out of business or were acquired by others; hundreds of thousands of jobs were lost, while thousands of remaining jobs were downgraded and shuffled to new areas. For the first time since World War II, the state's economy was in worse shape than the national economy; unemployment was higher, jobs were lost at a higher rate, and bankruptcies were being declared at an alarming rate.

For nearly 140 years, California had been a magnet for in-migrants from the rest of the country. In the golden years after World War II, cheap housing and plentiful jobs had provided an irresistible attraction for the millions who moved in from Minnesota, Iowa, Illinois, Pennsylvania, and Ohio. But in 1991, the Department of Finance announced the unthinkable: more non-Hispanic whites were moving out of the state than moving in. For the first time in nearly 150 years, the state could be losing population overall.[2]

Southern California's social fabric unraveled even further during the spring of 1992, when long-simmering passions exploded in an uprising that recalled the "long hot summers" of the late 1960s. Recession and white flight had taken their toll on Los Angeles's inner city, but no one was prepared for what would happen on April 29, 1992, when white police officers on trial for the beating of African American motorist Rodney King were declared not guilty. The verdict stunned the remaining African American community of South Central Los Angeles and initiated a week of outrage and violence.

From the corner of Florence and Western Avenues, just west of the Latino enclave of Huntington Park, members of the African American community poured into the streets, voicing their disbelief that the infamous videotape of King's beating had not been enough to convict the police officers of brutality.

The crowd grew, and its mood turned ugly. Members of the crowd began shouting at passing cars, then banging with their fists on car fenders.

Bricks were thrown; shop windows shattered. A shop was torched, then another—and suddenly it was Watts, 1965, all over again. As flames jumped from shop to shop, hand-lettered signs provided an eerie reminder of the long, hot summers: "Burn, baby, burn." For the first two days, burned-out shops were brazenly looted by rioters as an expression of contempt and anger. By the third day, however, the riot's dynamics began to change. As household food supplies ran low, the partly looted shops represented the only possible opportunity for survival. Residents of the area—since the late 1980s, predominantly immigrant Latinos—began darting furtively into burned shops to pick over the remaining stock. Far from demonstrating their solidarity with those protesting the not-guilty verdict, these hungry families had to cope with the breakdown of civil order, even if only to establish some order in their own lives. Yet television camera crews broadcast images of Latino looters with their arms full of diapers and milk cartons, and made little distinction between them and the original rioters; the *National Review* ran a cover photograph of a Latino lugging an eight-pack of soft drinks across a parking lot.[3]

As the bulk of the area's residents, Latinos in fact were the primary victims of the Rodney King verdict crowd violence. About one-third of those who died in the riots were Latino, largely the victims of crowd-driven violence. As Latino and Korean immigrants had been virtually the only entrepreneurs brave enough to risk their capital to restore commerce to the area, about 40% of the stores burned or damaged were Latino-owned.[4]

Glenn Spencer was an older non-Hispanic white whose first job had been in the aerospace industry. Raised and educated in Los Angeles public schools and universities, he had been fretting for some time about the growing Latino population. He felt as if his state was being taken away from him. As he later recounted, these television images of Latinos scuttling away with their arms full of groceries were an epiphany to him. "I was stunned and thought, 'Oh my God, there are so many of them and they are so out of control.'" As he saw it, non-Hispanic white America was losing control of its borders, and he jumped to the conclusion that the major cause of the riots was undocumented Latino immigrants. He felt it was his duty to awaken America to the danger, by whatever means necessary. Latinos had to be stopped.[5]

Yet in the Latino barrios of Huntington Park, East Los Angeles, Pacoima, San Fernando, and Wilmington, there had been little or no looting. On the third day of the riots, a number of Latino leaders gathered in East Los Angeles and congratulated the Latino community of the city for not taking part in the riots. Mayor Tom Bradley appointed the 1984 Los Angeles Olympics Games czar, Peter Ueberroth, to lead a hastily convened committee called Rebuild LA (RLA) to assess the damage and recommend action. Latinos, however, were largely overlooked in the appointments to RLA.

I was asked to help write an alternative report for an ad hoc group of Latino leaders, the Latino Coalition for a New Los Angeles, to provide the Latino perspective we feared would be left out of the RLA document. Under the leadership of David Lizárraga, executive director of the East Los Angeles Community Union (TELACU) in East Los Angeles, the coalition met weekly to pore over data I had been extracting from the recently released 1990 census files and to discuss what these data meant to the assembled coalition members.

Census tract by census tract, I walked coalition members through the new South Central Los Angeles, looking at a new topic each week: labor force participation, education levels, unemployment, welfare use, family formation, language patterns, nativity, poverty, and the like. We analyzed how immigrant Latino populations differed from other inner-city populations living in the same census tracts. A pattern quickly emerged: while Latinos in the South Central and Pico Union areas had far less education and lived in far greater poverty than their non-Latino neighbors, they nevertheless had the strongest labor force participation rates of any group in the county,[6] and they were far more likely to have households composed of a married couple with children.[7] Immigrant Latinos throughout Los Angeles County were also far less likely to use welfare.[8] My analysis was a revelation to some Latino leaders.

Moreover, presidential candidate Bill Clinton's visit to Los Angeles changed their mind about how to tackle the poverty issue. Clinton had toured the burned-out areas of the city, then declared that the destruction was the result of an urban underclass that had taken root there, a population that bore virtually no relationship to the rest of the American population. "People . . . are looting [in Los Angeles] because they are not part of the system at all anymore. . . . They do not share our values, and their children are growing up in a culture alien from ours, without family, without neighborhood, without church, without support."[9] Unknowingly, Clinton was repeating the new nativist definition of minorities as un-American because they supposedly rejected individualist values such as a strong work ethic, independence from welfare, and the formation of stable families.

Faced with this reiteration of the classic minority dysfunction equation, coalition members almost unanimously decided to demonstrate how Latino strengths, as documented by census data, could be used as a force to rebuild the city. Job creation was one area in which Latinos could help. The Ueberroth group had argued that the county needed thirty thousand new jobs and had lobbied for tax breaks for businesses willing to relocate into the affected areas. The Latino Coalition argued for a new, more cost-efficient use of federal aid funds, having estimated that, out of approximately 103,000 Latino-owned firms in the county, there were 18,800 prosperous enough to have paid employees. If these locally owned firms each had access to investment capital, to grow enough in sales to employ two additional persons, more than 37,000 new jobs would be created, quite a few more than the Ueberroth commission had recommended. The Latino Coalition report recommended that RLA broker investment in Latino-owned firms already functioning in Los Angeles County rather than trying to convince businesses to relocate from the suburbs to the inner city. Although the recommendation went unheeded, it was a major breakthrough in policy thinking: the Latino community saw itself using its strengths to help rebuild the city. In early 1993, the coalition released its report, *Latinos and the Future of Los Angeles.* Perhaps too far ahead of its time, it showed that in many areas pinpointed by RLA as needing attention—job growth, health services, employment, welfare—Latino patterns of behavior could provide the spark to rebuild Los Angeles into the city of the future.

PROPOSITION 187

One week after the riots, with the smell of burned buildings still in the air, the *Los Angeles Times* probed the mood of Angelenos in the aftermath of the country's worst race rioting in decades.[10] They found it to be somber, pessimistic, wary. Nearly all Angeleno respondents—non-Hispanic whites, Latinos, and African Americans (Asians were not polled)—cited pressing problems that needed resolution. Racial tensions, unemployment, the economy, gangs, and violence were the top-ranked concerns. Immigration, curiously, was not in the picture; it was mentioned by just 1% of the sample. In a follow-up poll six months later, the *Times* confirmed the residents' concerns.[11] Even though now suddenly qualified as "illegal," immigration still was mentioned by only 3% of the sample. Despite this, Governor Pete

Wilson's reelection problems changed that perception radically; his campaign managed to convince a majority of Californians that Latinos were indeed the problem.

Wilson had been a popular and moderate governor up to that point. The *Los Angeles Times* showed that in 1991 he had an approval rating of 52%. But many things in the state went terribly wrong on his watch. First there was a recession, then the riots, even earthquakes and firestorms; under Governor Wilson's stewardship, everything seemed to have gone wrong. His approval ratings plummeted, reaching a low point of 28% five months after the Los Angeles riots.[12] How could he run for reelection in 1994, with numbers so low?

A political consultant, holding focus groups for a governor in trouble, mentioned the nativist theme that had recurred in California for nearly 150 years: the presence of foreign, un-American Latinos in the state, with the phrase "undocumented immigrant" used as code for Latinos in general. Instantly, a focus group of non-Hispanic whites lit up. They denounced "illegal immigrants" for ruining the state, claiming that they took away jobs, crowded schools and hospitals, sucked up government expenditures fueled by tax dollars, overused welfare, increased crime rates, rioted, and broke into stores. The new nativist urban underclass minority theoretical model apparently had been internalized by these respondents, for they described these dysfunctional behaviors as being "un-American." Perhaps, even more ominously, the undocumented represented to them a rejection of individualist American values. As waves of invective poured out, the consultant realized he had found the governor's "red-meat" issue. Wilson jumped on the anti-immigrant bandwagon. As his campaign manager later described it, Wilson's style was to "pound an issue until it registers"; and thanks to his efforts to "beat the immigration drums," illegal immigration rose from not registering as a policy issue in 1992 to becoming the number-one policy issue by 1994.[13]

Glenn Spencer provided Governor Wilson with an engine to pull that wagon: a state initiative that would bar undocumented immigrants from using almost any public health or education service. This rather loosely worded initiative would require teachers and social service workers to deny services to anyone who "appeared to be illegal" or to be the children of illegal aliens. This would involve expelling suspected students from public schools and denying prenatal care to undocumented pregnant women. Spencer's group gathered the forty thousand signatures required to put the initiative on the ballot in record time and began churning out inflammatory campaign literature blaming undocumented immigrants for nearly all of California's woes. One such piece addressed to the California taxpayer was titled simply "OUR BORDERS ARE OUT OF CONTROL." It went on to charge that "every 4 hours, four to five thousand illegal aliens cross our southern border into California virtually unimpeded." The flyer concluded that close to 1 million undocumented immigrants crossed the border every year and would go on to appear on the state's welfare, public education, and criminal justice rolls, "funded by *our* tax dollars."[14]

Governor Wilson came out publicly in support of the new ballot initiative, henceforth to be known as Proposition 187. His poll numbers moved up, as the state's electorate found Latino immigrants a visible scapegoat for all the recent problems. When asked by the *Los Angeles Times* to list the burning issues facing the state, Angelenos now ranked immigration in the top three, along with gangs/crime and unemployment. Wilson was still in trouble, as his overall approval was only 39%, but Republicans liked his message; 66% of Republicans approved of the way he was handling events.[15]

Supporters of Proposition 187 crafted a nativist image of a state drowning in a wave of undocumented immigrants from Mexico. Commentators frequently mentioned on television that up to half of all Latinos in Los Angeles County were "probably" undocumented immigrants. Spencer's pro-187 group poured fuel on the fire by charging that "over 2/3 of births in county hospitals are to illegal aliens."[16] Even Senator Dianne Feinstein (D-CA), fighting a close reelection campaign against novice Republican Michael Huffington, capitalized on the nativist "drowning in immigrants" theme when she approved a televised cinema verité–style scare ad to show her tough stance on illegal immigration.[17] The ad featured a narrator announcing in a loud, voice-of-doom tone, "And they keep coming! Two thousand each night" crossing the border from Mexico, presumably to live in California.

No public figure ever disputed the pro-187 campaign's rhetoric, and many voters went to the polls fully convinced that millions and millions of illegal immigrants from Mexico were crossing the border and signing up immediately for welfare. Magazine covers depicted an America being invaded by dreaded foreigners.[18] Yet if two thousand or more Mexican immigrants indeed were crossing the border every night, as Senator Feinstein's ads stated, there would have been, by 1994, nearly 9 million undocumented Mexican immigrants in California alone. The California Coalition for Immigration Reform's figure of five thousand border crossings a night would have resulted in 21.9 million undocumented Mexican immigrants in the state. Although these numbers were clearly impossible, many Californians were left with the impression that, at that time, from 10 to 20 million undocumented immigrant Latinos resided in a state of 27.8 million people.

Once worried potential voters were convinced that this large number of undocumented Latinos was living in the state, their next conclusion was that any Latino must be, ipso facto, an undocumented immigrant. Distinctions between US-born Latinos, documented immigrant Latinos, and undocumented immigrant Latinos became lost in the popular discourse. Then another round of nativist accusations against "immigrant Latinos" began. Because of their allegedly large numbers, Latinos now were said to be responsible for water shortages during California's periodic droughts, for clogged freeways, for overcrowded schools. In this new nativist view, Latinos in general came to be blamed for everything from firestorms to high taxes. Perhaps the most apocalyptic vision was supplied in 1995 by Voice of Citizens Together: "As illegal aliens flood in, schools are overwhelmed, wages fall, and *English becomes an unknown language in this city.* Seeing this, *Americans are fleeing Los Angeles,* leaving a collapsing real estate market and declining tax base behind them. We are importing poverty and exporting jobs."[19]

On election night in November 1994, Proposition 187 was passed by an overwhelming majority. Governor Wilson was reelected by a comfortable margin, and Senator Feinstein squeaked by her opponent. Nativist immigrant-bashing had worked—for a while. Yet although Proposition 187 had passed overwhelmingly, a careful reading of voting patterns provided a hint of the polarization to come. The measure passed easily among the non-Hispanic white electorate, with 59% approval; and in 1994, the state's electorate was overwhelmingly non-Hispanic white. But Latino voters, who were US citizens and theoretically not the target of the measure, had overwhelmingly (78%) rejected the measure. It marked the first time the Latino vote had been so decisively for or against any state issue. The measure was also rejected, albeit by smaller margins, by the African American (56%) and Asian/Pacific Islander (54%) electorates (fig. 21).

THE REALITY BEHIND THE IMAGE

Ironically, the same quadruple whammy of recession, riots, earthquake, and wildfires that had convinced many non-Hispanic whites to leave the state also had led many Latinos to pack their bags. For all the cries of "they keep coming," Latino movement into the state had already slowed tremendously

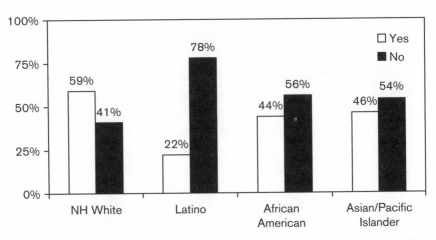

FIGURE 21. How each group voted on Proposition 187, California, 1994. Source: Daniel M. Weintraub, "Crime, Immigration Issues Helped Wilson, Poll Finds," *Los Angeles Times,* 9 November 1994, p. A1.

by the mid-1990s.[20] The peak period for Latino in-migration was 1982 to 1986, when an annual average of 182,575 Latinos moved into the state permanently; this figure does not include Latinos who moved through the state en route to another destination. In fact, anti-immigrant rhetoric to the contrary, estimates from the California Department of Finance show that Latino immigration to the state not only slowed tremendously during the late 1980s but had virtually stopped by 1993. In 1994 and 1995, as television ads warned of millions flooding into the state each year, California actually lost Latino population. During those two years, more Latinos—around twelve thousand—left the state each year than entered it to stay. By the late nineties (1997–1999), Latinos were moving into the state at an annual average of 89,401, less than half the peak from the eighties (fig. 22).

Another nativist pro-187 television ad panned over a classroom full of dark-skinned, apparently Latino grade-school children, while a voice-over claimed that undocumented immigrant children were causing school crowding. This charge was repeated in print ads. Voice of Citizens Together charged that as a result of illegal aliens flooding in, schools were overcrowded, and "Southern California has the lowest school ranking and the poorest educated young people in the U.S. . . . . California taxpayers will *no longer be willing to pay taxes* if we are forced against our will to pay for *lawbreaking invaders.*"[21] In 1994, Latino school-age children were predominantly US citizens, having been born in the United States. Data from the census show that 91.1% of

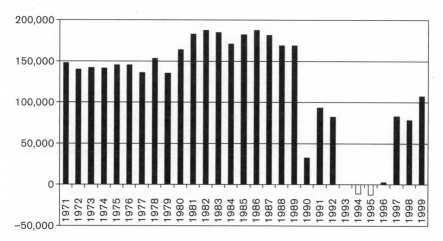

FIGURE 22. Annual residual Latino in-migration to California, 1971–1999. Sources: 1970–1989, CA DOF, "Race/Ethnic Population Projections," 1999; 1990–1999, CA DOF, "Race/Ethnic Population Estimates," 2001.

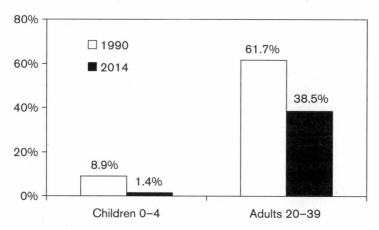

FIGURE 23. Percent immigrant among Latinos ages 0–4 and 20–39, Los Angeles County, 1990 and 2014. Source: IPUMS-USA, University of Minnesota, http://www.ipums.org.

Latino children four years old or younger residing in Los Angeles County in 1990—who comprised the five- to ten-year-old group at the time Proposition 187 passed—were US-born. Only 8.9% were immigrants (fig. 23), and, of course, not all of those would have been undocumented immigrants. These trends continued to 2014, so that 98.6% of Latino children ages four or younger were US-born (only 1.4% were immigrant).

We do not have reliable census data about the immigration status of the relatively few immigrant children in 2014; but even if we assume that all of the 1.4% were undocumented, more than ninety-eight out of every one hundred Latino children still would have been either US citizens or legal permanent residents. The paltry two undocumented children per hundred certainly could not be the cause of school overcrowding, much less the other problems laid at their door. Yet although Latino school-age children were overwhelmingly US-born citizens, they did usually have immigrant parents. A little over 60% of Latinos of child-bearing age (ages twenty to thirty-nine) were immigrants in 1990, but even this proportion had dropped to less than 40% by 2014. One further note is in order. While Voice of Citizens Together constantly raised concerns about overcrowded schools in Los Angeles, the fact is that Los Angeles Unified School District enrollment in 1994 was actually 2.7% lower than it had been in 1969, when LAUSD enrollments had peaked at 650,324, afterward declining sharply, to 534,712 by 1981. Starting in 1982, LAUSD enrollments recovered somewhat, but by 1995 were still short of their 1969 peak.[22] Schools *were* overcrowded, but that was the result of LAUSD's decision to close some schools during the 1970s rather than the result of a sudden influx of vast numbers of undocumented children.

I had noticed that estimates of undocumented immigration prepared in 1992 by the Los Angeles County Board of Supervisors for the year 1990 were quite a bit lower than the figures being shown repeatedly on television.[23] I wanted to create a new, independent estimate, using the newly released 1990 census Public Use Microdata Samples (PUMS) to see which "ballpark" estimate was most consistent with the census data. Therefore, I compared and evaluated different estimates of the Latino undocumented population, based on 1990 census data, for a report on the immigrant Latino profile in Los Angeles County.[24] Figure 24 provides the different estimates used at the time. For comparison, the 1990 census counted 3.3 million Latinos, *both* US-born and immigrant, in Los Angeles County.

The California Coalition for Immigration Reform (CCIR) figure of over 6 million undocumented Latinos would have meant, first, that *every single Latino* would have been an undocumented immigrant, and second, that the census had undercounted by 100%. Neither of these assumptions is viable. For Senator Feinstein's claim of 2.711 million to be true, eight out of every ten Latinos would have had to be undocumented. Voice of Citizens Together claimed that 20% of Southern California's population consisted of undocumented immigrants. Applying that figure to 1990 census data would mean

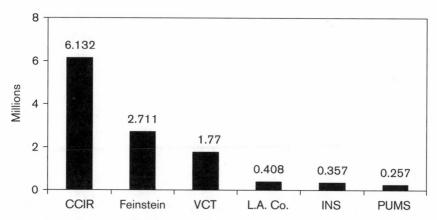

FIGURE 24. Comparative estimates of undocumented immigrant population in Los Angeles County, 1990. Sources: David E. Hayes-Bautista, Werner Schink, and Gregory Rodriguez, "Latino Immigrants in Los Angeles: A Portrait from the 1990 Census" (Los Angeles: Alta California Policy Research Center, 1994); California Coalition for Immigration Reform, "Our Borders Are Out of Control" (Huntington Beach, CA, n.d.); Voice of Citizens Together, "Why Los Angeles County Is Broke," advertisement, *Los Angeles Daily News*, 16 July 1995, p. 9.

there were 1.77 million undocumented Latinos in the county. Only if literally every immigrant Latino were undocumented could that figure have been valid.

Official estimates showed all these claims to be hyperbolic. The Los Angeles County study, based in large part on 1980 census data, estimated 0.408 million undocumented immigrants.[25] The INS estimate, based on visa issuances, estimated visa overstays, and "Entry without Inspection," provided an estimate of 0.357 million.[26] My own 1990 census PUMS estimate, based on response patterns to the 1990 census on birthplace, naturalization status, and year of entry, provided the lowest estimate, at 0.257 million.[27] Although the "official" estimates did not completely agree, they were far closer to one another than they were to the lurid, highly publicized estimates of anti-immigrant groups, which were based on guesses and suppositions but very little data. So, in fact, the actual number of undocumented immigrant Latinos was *not* in the tens of millions, even though many California voters had the impression that it was.

In 1992, the Los Angeles County Board of Supervisors went further. They commissioned their Urban Research Section to estimate not just the number of undocumented and other immigrants, but also the costs of providing county-funded services to them. They were also asked to estimate the tax base generated by that population. In summary, the county report estimated that for every dollar in county-funded services provided to an undocumented person, that person paid $4.56 in taxes.[28] Accusations to the contrary, undocumented immigrants were not costing more than they paid in taxes; rather, they paid far more in taxes than they used in county-funded services.

THE EFFECT ON LATINOS

After California's electorate overwhelmingly had passed Proposition 187, some discontent was voiced that it was not being implemented with sufficient rigor. At the same time, various civil rights organizations blocked every attempt by Governor Wilson to initiate implementation. Four months after the passage of the proposition, a *Los Angeles Times* reporter was interviewing an older, non-Hispanic white resident of Orange County about the state's strict tobacco laws. From complaining about unfairness to smokers, she suddenly veered to a nativist accusation about what was really bothering her: "Everyone in the country [*sic*] voted for Proposition 187 . . . the law against the Mexicans . . . and they still have those kids in the schools."[29] Her comment illustrated the mind-set of many of Proposition 187's most ardent supporters, and confirmed the worst fears of the Latino voters who had rejected it: her concern was not with undocumented immigrants, but with Latinos in general. She apparently expected that most, if not all, Latino children would have left the region's schools after the passage of Proposition 187. The fact that, in Los Angeles County, at least 91.1% of those children were US citizens evidently had not registered with her (fig. 23).

Pollster Mervin Field, pondering the many polls he conducted before and after the vote, confirmed that the passion was not about immigration so much as it was about Latino population growth and culture in general, and their impact on daily life in the state. "How can you stop culture? How can you stop people from speaking the Spanish language or posting signs in Spanish? Here was a way to stop it—at the ballot box."[30]

About six years after the passage of Proposition 187, the United Way of Greater Los Angeles asked CESLAC to help prepare a "Latino Report Card" to provide some metrics on Latino participation in Southern California society. We accordingly conducted focus groups among various groups of Latinos, and the participants' comments revealed smoldering resentment. Each set of participants—US-born Latinos, immigrants, blue-collar workers, businesspeople, and political figures—described, in varying detail, the effects of Proposition 187 on the Latino community. Although most Latino immigrants in that debate were not undocumented, they nonetheless felt the very wide net cast by political advertisements and political debates during the period of "immigrant-bashing," which was perceived by legal permanent residents as having been aimed at them. "El gobierno sí nos ha marginado en ese aspecto, al latino, porque nos ha puesto en un status diferente a los demás, aunque estemos legalmente aquí" (The government certainly has marginalized us, the Latinos, in this respect because it has placed us in a different status from everyone else, even though we are here legally).[31]

US-born Latinos likewise felt they were targets of Proposition 187. Even though they were not illegal immigrants—in fact, were not immigrants at all, but US citizens, by birth—they perceived the policy debate to be about Latino presence in society rather than merely the presence of undocumented immigrants. "I think that ... [Proposition 187 was] telling us that we no longer belonged here."[32] They remembered picking up code words, or "dog whistle terms"; for example, *illegal* or *undocumented* was a code word for "immigrant." *Immigrant,* in turn, was a code word for "Latino." "It's just like they say, 'Immigrant is always Mexican,' you know. If you're Mexican, you're an 'immigrant.'"[33] When the word *undocumented* was used, the other words were often implied. "You sense that there's a race card, that, 'Oh, it's because they're undocumented; you know, it's taxing our whole structure.' So, therefore, they don't like it. There is no 'Latino' mentioned."[34] These negative effects were described as attempts to thwart the growth of Latino influence. "Están poniendo muchas leyes que están truncando a que el latino pueda superarse" (They are passing many laws that are cutting Latinos off from bettering themselves).[35] A number of participants in the various United Way study's focus groups—immigrant, US-born, high school educated, college educated—described the situation in great, macro-level detail and saw recent public policy decisions as barriers that would impede Latino access to education and decision-making power.

The survey demonstrated the lasting hurt to US-born Latinos. Nearly two-thirds (62.0%) of US-born Latinos surveyed felt that "most Latinos are suspected of being illegal immigrants." A similar percentage of immigrant Latinos (60.7%) felt themselves the targets of lingering suspicions engendered by such polarizing debates. Nearly all Latinos had come to recognize that they themselves were the real target of Proposition 187, not illegal immigrants, however many (or few) of them there might have been.[36]

Reelected, Governor Wilson was riding a crest of popularity. His eyes now set on a run for the presidency, he decided to burnish his conservative credentials by announcing his intention to eliminate affirmative action programs, an action that polls indicated a majority of non-Hispanic white voters supported. At that time, an initiative had already been placed on the statewide ballot that would eliminate all affirmative action programs in California. Called the "Civil Rights Initiative," it forbade the state to provide any advantage to any person due to race, ethnicity, or gender. Even before this measure passed, the governor convinced the Regents of the University of California to pass university-only measures (SP1 and SP2) that eliminated the use of affirmative-action admissions and simultaneously raised the bar for admission by mandating that a certain percentage of students must be admitted on the basis of grade-point average (GPA), test scores, and other such "objective" criteria alone.

The ballot measure, Proposition 209, passed, but a trend was becoming visible in voting patterns that worried its backers. As with Proposition 187, the initiative was popular among the non-Hispanic white electorate, winning by an even larger margin (63%) than Proposition 187 had. But the polarization of the rest of the electorate was also even clearer than in the 187 vote: 76% of Latino voters, 74% of the African American vote, and 61% of Asian/Pacific Islander voters rejected the measure.[37] These "wedge issues" were prying the state's population apart; while they were welcomed by much of the non-Hispanic white electorate, they were alienating Latinos and other minorities. And the latter groups, especially Latinos, were fast growing in numbers.

Republicans became increasingly nervous about this trend and, for this and other reasons, did not endorse Governor Wilson's presidential aspirations. Still, feeling that immigrant-bashing and affirmative action elimination would get the job done, he campaigned in the Republican presidential primary. Wilson's wedge issues did not translate nationally, and his campaign ended in a resounding defeat in the Republican primary. He spent the rest of his term in state office trying to implement portions of Proposition 187. After his tenure ended, most of the measure was eventually declared unconstitutional. By 1996, his political fortunes had waned; the Republican National Convention pointedly did not offer him a role in its convention, feeling he was too divisive and alienating to the growing number of Latino voters.

Meanwhile, Ron Unz, a high-tech entrepreneur, had become convinced that bilingual education programs were handicapping immigrant children by preventing them from mastering English quickly enough. Using his personal wealth, he sponsored another initiative for the California ballot, Proposition 227, intended to banish bilingual education from the state. Unlike Propositions 187 and 209, the newly proposed Proposition 227 did attract a few high-profile Latinos to the campaign. Polls indicated that Latino parents supported the idea that their children should learn English, so Unz was confident that he had the support of the Latino electorate. As with the other initiatives, Proposition 227 was passed overwhelmingly by the state's electorate, which—unlike the general population—was still overwhelmingly non-Hispanic white. But Latino voters nonetheless voted against it by a very wide margin. African American and Asian/Pacific Islanders also voted against it, albeit by narrower margins. The polarization of the electorate along ethnic lines was continuing.

Unz was right about one thing: Latinos do support, very strongly, the idea that their children should learn English. This trend can be seen in any poll taken over the last twenty years. In a 1990 poll I conducted along with Aída Hurtado, Robert Valdez, and Anthony C. R. Hernández, Latino parents overwhelmingly agreed that their children should learn English.[38] In a 2000 reprise of that poll for the United Way, modified for circumstances ten years further on but exploring the same issues, I observed the same trend.[39] Basically, nearly all Latino parents consistently understand the value to their children of mastering the English language.

Mark Barabak, a *Los Angeles Times* reporter covering the Proposition 227 campaign, noted that while Latinos supported the idea of their children learning English, they were nevertheless wary of the tone of the debate. Again and again, he discovered that if the campaign took an anti-Latino tone, Latinos would turn against it.[40] Some ardent Proposition 227 supporters indeed did inject anti-Latino tones into the public debate, and Latino voters came to perceive it as just another anti-Latino measure, not an educational imperative. In the end, they voted massively against it, continuing the trend of polarized voting.

Although perhaps well intentioned—and there was considerable debate about Unz's intentions—this proposition missed a chance to build on the nearly universal parental desire, irrespective of ethnicity, for California's children to become bilingual. Data from the United Way of Greater Los Angeles survey demonstrate a nearly universal desire for children to speak

English *and* Spanish.[41] It is not surprising that 96% of US-born Latino parents and 98% of immigrant Latino parents wanted their children to speak Spanish as well as English. But 87% of non-Hispanic white parents and 88% of African American parents also wanted their children to be able to speak Spanish. In retrospect, a far better measure could have been prepared that would have brought together parents who wanted their children to be fluent in both Spanish and English, as well as non-parents afraid that Latino children were not becoming sufficiently fluent in English. This could have been a "win-win" situation. Instead, it became another wedge driven into the electorate.

THE POLITICAL GIANT AWAKENS

Noting, in 1997, that more than 80% of newly registered Latino voters in the state were affiliating with the Democratic Party, Republican strategist Stu Spencer took his party to the woodshed. He felt that unless Republicans made an effort to heal the rift created by these divisive issues, the party could be committing political suicide in a state so markedly moving toward minority-majority status. At this event, a former Wilson advisor remarked, "We walked over the sleeping giant on our way to [Wilson's] reelection in 1994, but in the process, we woke it up."[42] Indeed they had. The feelings of rejection and marginalization caused by Propositions 187, 209, and 227 created a Latino backlash. US-born Latinos of voting age were not immigrants; nor were they always fluent in Spanish. Yet they perceived that these initiatives were not really about immigrants, but instead were nativist reactions to the large Latino presence in the state. "[Proposition] 187 woke us up to ourselves as a community, and it made us aware that, yeah, we do contribute socially, economically, politically, and everything else to this community."[43]

In the United Way focus groups CESLAC conducted with Latino businesspeople and professionals, they perceived that these measures were reactions to the recent surge in Latino presence in the state. "We're in the middle of what I think is a historical transition in southern California and in California. Never have you seen, in the history of the planet, a European majority of an industrialized country become a minority. And we're right there, like the 'barbarians at the gate,' man. And we're still growing economically."[44] In these participants' experiences, supporters of the initiatives were not willing to accept the demographic and social changes that were sweeping the state. "For some people, I think, they're in denial about the changes that are happening because they are so drastic and so they're coming up so fast."[45]

Some of the more politically involved focus group members interpreted the initiatives as a power play, part of a contest over who would decide the future of the state. "People don't give up power gladly. And power is not given; it is taken. Notwithstanding the fact that we have a tradition in this country of peaceful transitions of power, we are witness to an unpeaceful transition in the form of Prop 187, etc."[46] After tasting economic and political power, US-born Latinos, in particular, were not willing to be thrust back to the margins of society, as they had been while growing up in postwar America. "I think the power structure . . . [is] trying to retain what used to be, which is where the Latinos—mostly Mexicans—were properly humble and properly downtrodden and accepted their lives."[47]

Furthermore, rather than distancing themselves from the publicly reviled "undocumented" immigrant Latinos, many Chicano-era groups instead rallied around them, providing valuable legal and political support to a population with whom they had not interacted much before. MALDEF, for example, was instrumental in securing injunctions against blatantly unconstitutional portions of the measures. The Southwest Voters Registration Project increased its efforts to register new voters and encourage participation. The Latino Coalition for a Healthy California, a reprise of the 1970s National Chicano Health Organization, offered to find legal advice for health providers who preferred to practice civil disobedience by providing needed medical services to undocumented patients rather than to comply with the provisions of Proposition 187. The Mexican American Grocers Association held fund-raisers for candidates who opposed the measures. "So, as it happens, there are certain issues like 187 that awakes [sic] a few other souls and decides [sic] that they want to make a difference."[48]

Each focus group conducted for United Way expressed the opinion that Proposition 187 was a watershed moment. It forced the Latino community to define its role in society, rather than allow itself to be, once again, defined by others, especially by nativists. This self-definition took place in the face of strident opposition. "I think, after Proposition 187 . . . there was—I felt here, within the church, we started banding together, Latinos. And we had some groups get together and talk about what we need to do in our community."[49] In responding to questions about the initiatives, focus group participants recounted weaving tighter strands of community. In much the same way that the World War II experience had marked a generation of non-Hispanic

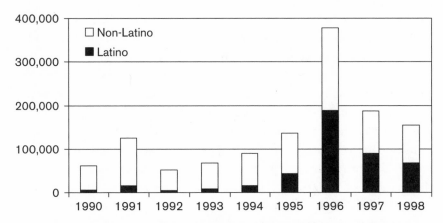

FIGURE 25. Annual number of immigrants naturalizing, California, 1990–1998. Source: Immigration and Naturalization Service (INS), *Statistical Yearbook of the Immigration and Naturalization Service, 1990* (Washington, DC: US Government Printing Office, 1991); INS, *Statistical Yearbook* (1992–1999).

whites, five years of anti-Latino invective also marked this generation of Latinos. "I saw a change around the time [of Proposition 187] ... where Hispanics started to get together and to kind of band together and, I think, to make a better [life] for themselves."[50]

Historically, most immigrant Latinos, especially from Mexico, had been reluctant to become naturalized US citizens because of their desire to eventually return to Mexico for good, to retire to a house and property they owned there. In 1990, 5,671 Latinos living in California became naturalized US citizens; they represented only 9.2% of the 61,736 immigrants from around the world who became US citizens in the state that year (fig. 25). Before 1994, only around 8,500 Latinos became naturalized citizens every year. But spurred by the negative imagery of the Proposition 187 debates, those numbers soared thereafter, reaching a peak of 188,627 in 1996, at which point immigrant Latinos were almost exactly half (49.9%) of all immigrants who naturalized that year.[51]

Not only were many more immigrant Latinos becoming naturalized, but also more were registering to vote. In the eight years from 1992 to 2000, the number of Latino registered voters increased 38.7%, from 1.4 million to 1.9 million.[52] They were joined by US-born Latinos in the registration process. Thanks to their anger at Governor Wilson, they were registering for the Democratic Party in proportions never previously seen. In a William C. Velásquez Institute survey of Latino registered voters conducted one month

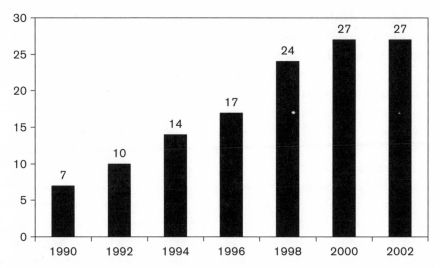

FIGURE 26. Number of Latino state legislators, California, 1990–2002. Source: Fernando Guerra, personal communication, 6 June 2003.

prior to the 2000 presidential election, 79.9% of respondents declared an affiliation with the Democrats, and only 12.0% with the Republicans.[53] The drumbeat of the negative political campaigns—Proposition 187, the elimination of affirmative action, the ending of bilingual education—had awakened the sleeping political giant as nothing had before. Yet some focus group participants wondered, wistfully, if this effect could have been achieved without wedging apart the state's electorate. "It is unfortunate, for example, that it takes Proposition 187 to get Latinos to become citizens, to get Latinos to go and vote. I'd like to find other ways, that [we] don't have to be attacked from outside the community."[54]

An almost inevitable result of the growth of the Latino population and the Latino electorate was an increase in Latino holders of elected office at the state level. This growth was spurred by another Republican move to curtail minority political power, the term limits initiative, originally designed to break the grip that Willie Brown, an African American assemblyman from San Francisco, had held on the state legislature for nearly twenty years. The measure did move Brown out of the state legislature, but it moved many other incumbents out of their comfortable sinecures as well, suddenly opening the way for an emerging generation of Latino candidates. Latino officeholders in the state legislature grew from seven in 1990 to twenty-seven in 2002 (fig. 26).[55]

There has also been a tremendous increase in the number of Latino local officials. As recently as 1990, cities with a majority Latino population rarely had Latino council members or mayors.[56] For example, the towns of Bell, Bell Gardens, Cudahy, Huntington Park, and South Gate were more than 90% Latino in 1990, yet that fact was not reflected in the composition of their municipal councils. By 2002, in four of the towns—Bell Gardens, Cudahy, Huntington Park, and South Gate—80 to 100% of the council members were Latino.[57]

Lieutenant Governor Cruz Bustamante, the first Latino to be elected speaker of the California State Assembly, in 1996, told an anecdote four years after his election that could well be repeated by many other Latino politicians. A newspaper reporter wanted to know if Bustamante, as newly elected speaker, was going to follow a "secret Latino political agenda." Wanting some good press, Bustamante replied that yes, absolutely, he had a secret Latino political agenda. The reporter asked him what that agenda consisted of. Ticking the points off on his fingers, Bustamante listed the topics on this secret Latino political agenda: good schools, safe streets, and good jobs for everyone. Disappointed at such a pedestrian agenda—certainly not the agenda for an ethnic political takeover—the reporter objected that, as such, it did not seem particularly Latino or very secret. In fact, it seemed very ordinary. Bustamante replied that such was indeed the case. The Latino agenda is California's agenda, and vice versa. As far as Bustamante was concerned, there was no difference.[58]

Early in the George W. Bush administration, the president addressed Latinos nationwide by radio, in Spanish, to commemorate the Cinco de Mayo. Some critics grumbled that his pronunciation left much to be desired, but that a sitting president would even attempt such a feat demonstrates how much Latino political fortunes had changed since the immigrant-bashing days of 1994.[59]

"IT'S OKAY TO BE LATINO NOW"

The nativist rhetoric of the 1920s, followed by the massive deportations of "Mexicans" in the 1930s—during which many Latino US citizens were also deported—had served to intimidate many Latinos who lived through that period, forcing them to bury their language and culture. As recounted in chapter 2, the children of deportation-era Latinos stated that the period from

1940 to 1965 was one in which being Latino was definitely not validated; some focus group participants even remembered feeling that they had had to hide their Latino side. Yet although attacks on Latinos in the 1990s were as vicious as they had been in the 1930s, the result was quite different. Rather than creating another generation of "silent Latinos," they galvanized a pride in being Latino, which in turn resulted in increased political participation and higher visibility. One focus group member recounted, "I think that . . . 187 woke up that sleeping giant . . . that was dormant, not only in the political aspect but in the social aspect, the education aspect, because they were telling us that we no longer belonged here . . . As a Latino community, as a whole, it woke up and said, 'Wait a minute!'"[60] Repeatedly, US-born Latino focus group members recalled the difference between being Latino as children in postwar America and being Latino in the late 1990s. Being Latino was once something to be hidden, but by the late 1990s, it was a validated experience. "You know, it's okay to be a Mexican. Now it's okay—[laughter]—but back in the forties and fifties, it was not. My mother raised me so that I wouldn't have to go through what she went through."[61]

Validation of being Latino came from within the group, not from outside. Indeed, the external barrage of negative imagery was a deliberate nativist effort to invalidate the American-ness of Latinos, which left Latinos little choice but to validate themselves. One participant expressed his feeling of validation in a quintessentially American way, pointing to the growing establishment of Latino-owned businesses, which he saw as the future of Los Angeles. "You go from here [downtown Los Angeles] all the way down to 120th [Street] . . . and it is thriving. You see stores, you see cafeterias, you see everything. And you see people on the streets, and you think, 'Wait a minute, this is the future of L.A., and it's an entrepreneurial spirit that's dynamic and resilient.'"[62]

The sea change in political representation created a corresponding high tide of Latino validation. While political conflicts were painful in the early 1990s, by 2002 politics was another area in which Latinos could point, with pride, to significant representational accomplishments. "It's a fact that we are now coming into positions of power, I think."[63] Although the road ahead might not be particularly smooth, focus group members expressed a sense of empowerment. "I believe very firmly that Latinos are going to be running this place."[64] That both Republicans and Democrats were now courting their vote was not lost on Latinos. "In fact, we're becoming the strongest political people you want to get on your side."[65]

The political arena provided one locus for eventual validation. Just as important, however, was corporate America's validation of the Latino consumer base. Interested in profiting from that base, businesses started to pay the attention to Latinos that many politicians had tried to deny them.

> What we have going for us now, that we've never had before, is the growing recognition, on the part of those people who have historically been biased against us, that we are an economic power and that we are a major source, potential or present, of revenue for them. And they want to do that. In order to do that, they have to find out what our needs, our wants, our preferences, our ways of doing business are.[66]

Although many US-born Latinos were not fluent in Spanish, advertising in that language nevertheless was a source of validation for them. Immigrant Latinos saw Spanish-language advertising as a recognition of their presence. A Latino executive of a Fortune 500 corporation reported how his company saw the issue: "We, as a company . . . have no choice but to do our business in Spanish. We have no choice but to do that if we wanted to retain the consumer market."[67] Spanish-language advertising also presented the public with more positive imagery of Latinos. In contrast to contemporary English-language news portrayals—gang members, welfare mothers, illegal immigrants—these new images treated Latinos as human beings with dreams and ambitions. "Businesses . . . say, 'Hey, we're making money out of the Latino community.' You see commercials now that you wouldn't see before, like [department store, fast-food outlet]; and not only are they doing the commercials, but they're doing it with, like, values and cultural traditions that are addressed in these commercials."[68]

Corporate efforts went far beyond merely Latino-oriented marketing. Adapting to specific Latino patterns of consumer taste, nimble businesses created completely new products more in tune with Latino self-images. These efforts have been quite successful. "I mean, it was nice for me to find a magazine, *Latina,* that I can buy, and I can actually read something in there and say, 'Oh yeah. okay.' No more *Glamour,* no more *Vogue,* no more *Housewives* [laughter]."[69] These new commercial images resonated with Latino aspirations, and the corporations that published them reaped financial rewards. The contrast with Proposition 187's images could not have been greater. Where once, thanks to the negative campaigns of the 1990s, being Latino had been a source of shame, it now became a source of pride and satisfaction. "When I was going to college, there was [*sic*] very few Latins [*sic*] . . . and now

I look at the colleges that I visit, or whatever, and you see a lot of Latinos, and that's beautiful."[70]

· · ·

The 1990s were times of crisis for Latinos in California. Immigrant Latinos, who had been largely responsible for the renovation of large swaths of inner-city Los Angeles, were poorly rewarded for their efforts: the passage of a string of initiatives meant, in part, to limit Latino participation in the state. Yet they stayed the course. Having made their investments in family and home, immigrant Latinos chose to protect them politically by taking the heretofore rare step of becoming naturalized US citizens, then registering and voting in extremely high numbers. US-born Latinos, by and large, did not shrink from immigrant Latinos, but joined with them to defend the Latino presence in the state from attack. In doing so, US-born and immigrant Latinos created a new political power base and are beginning to fill statewide offices. "You can be a Latino and keep doing that, and live here very successfully, as opposed to have to hide it or lose it."[71] Although Proposition 187 initially caused Latinos to feel uncomfortable in the public sphere, it also galvanized the community. Some nevertheless expressed regret that it had taken such a drastic, negative, and divisive action to create the subsequent positive reactions. Latinos did become citizens, they registered, they voted, and they changed the face of elected officialdom. Rather than shrinking from being Latino, they expressed pride in it, strength in it, and fulfillment in it. California will never be the same. "Now I can say, 'Yes, I'm a Mexican.' You know, it's okay now."[72]

SIX

Latinos Define "American"

2000–2020

> I think they [Latinos] want to be Americans, but . . . they want
> to be Americans on their own terms.

FOR YEARS AFTER THE EMOTIONAL campaign waged in 1994 to pass Proposition 187, Mexican American Legal Defense and Education Fund (MALDEF) attorneys had been hearing a low drumbeat, the sound of a negative public perception of Latinos. They overheard comments, made in various meetings and functions, reflecting the feeling that it must be true—as had been depicted in the television ads—that most Latinos were undocumented immigrants, that immigration from Mexico and Latin America was ruining the state, and that Latinos refused to become part of American society. MALDEF attorneys were astounded by the residual ill-will still expressed in many quarters, years after that measure had passed.

At about that same time, I was visited in Los Angeles by a former academic colleague from Berkeley. Much to my surprise, he told me he had voted in favor of Proposition 187. He was a bona fide red diaper baby whose father had been involved in numerous liberal causes during the Cold War period. He himself had been an early Peace Corps volunteer, serving in a severely underdeveloped country for two years, then marrying a health professional from Latin America. It seemed out of character to hear such a self-described political liberal say that he had voted in favor of 187. I asked why he had done so, and he proceeded to repeat the depictions in the various television ads that had run for months: the state was awash in millions of undocumented immigrants who increased crime rates, relied on welfare, and the like. He was concerned for the state and truly wanted to help "Save Our State"; hence his vote.

I shared with him data from my research on the relatively small numbers of undocumented Latino immigrants and the positive role that Latino immigrants played in society, and his eyebrows shot up. Why had no one shared any such data during the campaign? He had been shown only one side of the debate and had never been offered an alternative argument. His shoulders slumped; he felt he had been duped, and he wondered how many liberals like himself had been sold an image of Latinos that was not sustained by the data. How many of his friends, he wondered, were in his position regarding their perceptions of Proposition 187—and were now, as he labeled himself, "lapsed liberals"?

While the actual vote on the proposition receded into the past, the vivid images that had been broadcast for months remained, and were poisoning the political atmosphere. In 1997, Antonia Hernandez, MALDEF's then-president and CEO, decided to counter this negative tide with an alternative view of Latinos. She called together an advisory group of Latino business and communications leaders, who concluded that constantly televised negative images were responsible for much of the public's jaundiced view of the Latino community. Thus, a television message that presented a more positive view of Latinos and their role in the state was needed. The target audience for the spot was the "lapsed liberal," a non-Hispanic white who was not necessarily negative about Latinos but lacked a positive Latino image. But what should MALDEF say to such "lapsed liberals" about Latinos? MALDEF asked CESLAC to conduct the background research that would identify content for the message. We were invited into this process because we specialize in developing messages tailored to create awareness in Latino populations of topics ranging from elderly Latino enrollment in Medicare to the US origins of the Cinco de Mayo celebrations held every year. We applied our methods to discover how to create similar awareness in a non-Hispanic white population.

NON-HISPANIC WHITES DEFINE "AMERICAN"

We began by assembling focus groups from the target population of non-Hispanic white "lapsed liberals." The only selection criterion for participation in the focus group was that those selected not be overtly anti-Latino. Participants were told only that they would participate in developing a television commercial, a frequent activity in Los Angeles, where television show pilots and movies are routinely tested. We began by asking the groups to define what it means to be an American.

Perhaps reflecting the groups' liberal composition, participants were initially a little reluctant to provide a specific definition. "I hear over and over again that no one can say what 'American' is. . . . I don't think there is an American identity."[1] Over time, though, a range of opinions about the nature of American society and identity emerged. In all the groups, there was always a small core who refused to be pinned down on the nature of American identity. Those who did feel that there was a defined American society and identity also felt that it had changed over the past few decades. The participants themselves said they did not regret these changes in American society and identity, but felt that their parents, the World War II generation, were having difficulty accepting and adjusting to the changes. "Definitely, I think my parents' age [group], the senior citizens, they're just frustrated because their world is changing. It used to be, say, the community where my parents lived, [was] 99 percent English-speaking."[2] They described how their parents' generation had defined American according to Anglo-Saxonist norms, using race, language, and culture as indicators of American identity.

Yet they themselves had moved away form their parents' acceptance of Anglo-Saxonist conceptions of American identity, to embrace more of a "new nativist" definition of possession of the work ethic and personal responsibility values. For some participants, the classic "American dream," the desire to aspire to a level of well-being that is not possible elsewhere, was a central part of being an American. "But I say, definitely, part of American life is the sort of American Dream mentality. Like, you have this dream of what you want. You always want more. [It's an] individual-achievement mentality: 'I can get this if I work hard enough.'"[3] Part of this achievement is for oneself, but part is for one's children, to provide for them the opportunities one did not always have personally. "Yeah, working towards, 'Someday I can buy my own house, if I work hard. Someday, you know, I can send my kids to college. . . . I can have a decent car.'"[4] The desire to achieve, however, must be matched with actual accomplishment, in order to be truly American. "I would term that as the American culture: that wanting to get ahead, wanting an education, wanting to buy a house, a hard work ethic."[5] Individualism also has been an American trait for at least two centuries. These focus groups shared that image enthusiastically. "'American' means that I am an individual, I am unique, I am different."[6] This individualism, the ability to define oneself and one's own life, was seen as a particularly American virtue, even if sometimes carried to the extreme of going against the majority. "American is: 'If I want to go on, I will go.'"[7]

Once the focus groups had defined their views of what was "American" in terms of the values of the work ethic and personal responsibility, we gradually and subtly turned their attention to Latinos. The bottom-line question was: Are Latinos Americans? The non-Hispanic white participants proved to be extremely confused about Latinos as Americans, and tended to revert to Anglo-Saxonist defintions of "American" based on culture and language when describing Latinos. Their primary dilemma was: How could Latinos be Latino and be American at the same time? In their view, if Latinos still retained some sense of emotional commitment to Mexico or other countries of origin, this might interfere with their loyalties to America. "It's hard for us to identify with how you can have two homelands. . . . How can you love America and still love Mexico? . . . I love it here [in America]; and if you're going to be a citizen, don't you want to love it, too?"[8]

They expressed concern that a continuing desire by Latinos to maintain their culture might cause some harm to American society. "If you are going to be Mexican first and American second, what is that going to do?"[9] Such a cultural continuity, they feared, might threaten the cohesion of American society. "What is the common identity that we are going to have that's going to keep us from falling to pieces?"[10] In the worst case, they expressed fear that a continued emotional attraction to things Mexican might lead to the physical collapse of American society, such as happened in the former Yugoslavia, by that point torn apart by civil war and ethnic cleansing. "Look at what happened to Yugoslavia. Do we want the balkanization of America?"[11] At base, their fear was that Latinos might not be willing to fight this country's wars if they were waged in Mexico or Latin America. "If we went to war— like, if we went to war with Cuba—a Mexican might have some affiliation or ties to Cuba because of the whole Latino-bonding thing and . . . [I would wonder] whose side are you on?"[12] At the same time, the depth of the emotions, particularly the fears, expressed left no doubt that the non-Hispanic white participants were quickly able to move beyond the fact that Latinos were facilitating these focus group sessions. Their greatest concern was, can Latinos truly be Americans if they feel a bond to things Latino?

US-BORN LATINOS AS AMERICANS

After hearing the concerns of the non-Hispanic white "lapsed liberals" focus groups, we felt it important to assemble some Latino focus groups to discover if they saw themselves as Americans. US-born Latinos usually did not hesitate to describe themselves as Americans. "I love being an American."[13] Some described "American" as a transcendent identity that could, and should, bridge over other group identities, including Latino. "I definitely do [feel American], and I think that's very positive. . . . The problem is that a lot of people . . . are always identifying themselves as one thing or another, but we are all Americans, you know."[14] More affluent respondents who had traveled outside the United States had discovered that, even if other, non-Hispanic white Americans viewed them as not quite American, overseas they felt more American than anything else. "I had the experience of being able to live out of the country for a long time. . . . I felt foreign when I left. . . . Once you leave this country, you realize that you're not a foreigner [here]."[15]

Some Latinos in the focus groups traced their families' presence in what is now the United States to the original de Oñate expedition to New Mexico in 1598, twenty-two years before the Pilgrims landed at Plymouth.[16] With their ancestors antedating nearly every other population segment in this country except American Indians, these Latinos said proudly that they, too, were part and parcel of the American landscape. "One of the things about Hispanics is that, as Americans, some of us have been here for a long time. We're part of this land."[17]

The fact that many non-Hispanic white Americans might not see Latinos as Americans grieved some, for they wanted to be seen, and appreciated, as Americans. "When I see the word 'American' . . . that's who we are. . . . It needs to be engraved [sic] to the other ethnic groups out there that that's who we really are, and they need to accept that."[18] But although they accepted the term, they often felt that they were excluded from that identity by others, usually non-Hispanic whites. The exclusion process was a lifelong experience, but was described as occurring particularly in late adolescence and early adulthood. Respondents remembered naively assuming, during their childhoods, that they were simple, unhyphenated Americans. "Other people impose artificial separation. . . . As a child, you identify yourself as an American first. Later on, you start learning you are different, kind of Hispanic."[19] In late childhood or early adolescence, they became aware that some elements in their daily experience were not part of the "American" experience. Classes in American history that left out Latino experiences were cited as an early example of feeling excluded from the term "American." "Part of it happens when you take history classes, and you learn about the Pilgrims, and you think that is not part of *your* family that came over on the Mayflower."[20]

As they emerged into adulthood, this sense of exclusion from an "American" identity continued. One respondent recounted his sense of loss of childhood certainties that he was simply "American."

> Before college, I never questioned my identity. We lived in a Mexican community, and we did everything that everyone around us did, so the issue of identity never bothered me. Until we got to college. Excuse my language, all hell breaks loose, and you are being thrown all these terms . . . of . . . who you are. And then you ask yourself, "Wait. Wasn't I American to begin with?"[21]

A few described how, over time, they had developed a reluctance to apply the term "American" to themselves, as the process of exclusion continued. This reluctance was more the product of being excluded than of their own active rejection of the term, or things, American. "We are not racist. We want to be part of it. We don't want to separate ourselves; they separate us."[22]

In popular discourse about immigrants, the net is often cast very wide, jumbling nearly all Latinos together, irrespective of whether or not they were born in the United States. Claims about the undesirability of undocumented immigrants sometimes are generalized to all Latino immigrants, then to all Latinos. A letter to the editor of the *Los Angeles Times Magazine* in 2001 illustrates how quickly and effortlessly the distinctions between undocumented Latino immigrants and all Latinos can be overlooked. "You can call me a racist or anything else you want. . . . Mexicans don't have the right to force their values, standards and way of doing things down our throats in our own country. In fact, illegal aliens don't have the right to be here at all."[23] The widespread immigrant-bashing of the early 1990s was felt by US-born Latinos to be an extreme example of excluding them from the category "American." "In the late seventies, early eighties, we became the enemy again, the target."[24] The negative images and heightened political rhetoric of those times gave the final push to some respondents, who admitted feeling they did not belong any longer. One participant showed the depth of her feelings when she mocked "typical" statements she sarcastically attributed to supporters of the various 1990s initiatives. "We gave them too much opportunity, we're opening too many doors for them. Stop them! Cut their health care, everything! Make it impossible for them to succeed!"[25] Such immigrant-bashing was often interpreted by US-born Latinos as being directed at them, and they resented it. One participant alluded to his own experiences with the Anglo-Saxonist view when said he felt "distanced" from the term "American," although he would prefer to use it. "A lot of people, when they think of

Americans, they equate that with Anglo-Americans. So it is sometimes very difficult to call yourself Americans . . . because you have been distanced from that word."[26] Having been excluded for so long, some respondents were reluctant to use the term because the struggle to be included had become too painful. "I just wanted to say [that] when the word 'American' comes up, I don't feel like an American. I feel, sometimes, I'm treated as second class. . . . The label 'American'—it's like it doesn't fit me."[27]

✳ US-born Latinos, therefore, usually felt that they were American; but as they grew up, they felt pushed aside, excluded from this identity by Anglo-Saxonist definitions and not accepted by non-Hispanic whites as truly American. Yet when members of this group travel abroad, it is clear to them they are Americans. ✳

IMMIGRANT LATINOS AS AMERICANS

People have been moving from the interior of Mexico to California for nearly 250 years, as explained in more detail in chapter 7. Between 1821 and 1848, when California was part of Mexico, they were simply Mexican citizens moving from one part of Mexico to another and living among their fellow citizens. After 1848, however, migrants following the same paths suddenly were faced with entering a foreign country; and ever since then, people moving from Mexico to California have been made acutely aware of their Mexican-ness, often more so than when they were in Mexico. "Según ellos, nosotros somos diferentes a ellos; costumbres latinas son diferentes" (According to them [non-Hispanic whites], we are different from them; Latino customs are different).[28] Yet the dream that had brought many of these focus group respondents to California included putting down roots, marrying, buying a house, and raising a family. It was, in fact, a reprise of the classic American dream, which echoed the same new nativist values described by the non-Hispanic white respondents. "Así como uno viene del extranjero . . . y el sueño de uno de formar familia, de educar a los hijos, comprar casa—ese es uno de los sueños fundamentales" (When one comes from a foreign country . . . and one's dream of starting a family, of bringing up one's children, buying a house—that is one of the fundamental dreams).[29]

Their usual trajectory was to go from feeling they were strangers and foreigners to finally feeling an emotional attachment to the United States and engagement with their new identity as Americans. Over time, they engaged in activities that helped to anchor them in the daily life of their communities in the United States. These could range from finding stable employment to learning English, which helped them begin to feel part of a larger community. "¿La actividad cuando ya sentí que era parte de este pais? Pues, aprender el inglés y trabajar" (The activity when I felt I was part of this country? Well, learning English and working).[30] Other such activities could be as mundane as participating in a child's schooling, helping a neighbor, or paying taxes.

> Incluso, fuí voluntaria de la escuela por un año, y me sentí muy satisfecha poder ayudar y poder servir a los niños (Also, I was a volunteer at the school for a year, and I felt really satisfied that I could help and serve the children). . . . Participar en actividades comunitarias (Participating in community activities). . . . Pagar impuestos (Paying taxes).[31]

Voting was routinely described as the culminating activity signaling that they had dedicated their lives to the United States. "Cuando dí un voto allí y me dieron un sticker y que pude ir a la urna, dije, 'Ya soy parte del poder'" (When I cast my vote there, and they gave me a sticker, and I could go to the ballot box, I said, "Now I am part of the powers-that-be").[32]

In increasing numbers, Latino immigrants have begun to become naturalized US citizens. In the past there was considerable reluctance to do so, but the Immigration Reform and Control Act of 1986, which facilitated the amnesty and naturalization process, and the Proposition 187 debate, which was often perceived as challenging the roots they had put down, spurred more and more Latino immigrants to become naturalized citizens. "Cuando la tomé la residencia . . . yo tambien me considero . . . ciudadana americana. No sería ciudadana hispanoamericana" (When I became a resident . . . I also considered myself . . . an American citizen. I would not be a Hispanic-American citizen).[33]

Latino immigrants from Mexico and El Salvador remarked that after they had been in the United States about a decade, when they returned to their countries of origin, they begin to realize that they were no longer purely Mexican or Salvadoran. They had developed some new habits of the heart. They felt that they were American, and they felt a surge of pride when they saw the American flag. The focus group facilitator asked one group how the members felt when they saw the US flag in the MALDEF television advertisement:

FACILITATOR: Una vez me dijeron que sienten un poquito de tristeza y confusión. ¿Me pueden decir que es lo que sienten con la bandera [de los Estados Unidos]? (They told once me that you feel a little sadness and confusion. Can you tell me what it is you feel when you see the [US] flag?)

GROUP MEMBER: Cuando uno mira, le da a uno alegría. (When a person sees it, it gives him joy.)

FACILITATOR: ¿Les faltó ver la bandera de México y El Salvador en este comercial? (Did you miss seeing the Mexican and Salvadoran flags in this commercial?)

GROUP MEMBER: ¡No!

GROUP MEMBER: ¡No!

GROUP MEMBER: ¡No!

GROUP MEMBER: ¡No hay necesidad! . . . Nosotros no somos de aquí, pero la sentimos así, como también los niños, nuestros hijos, han de sentir la alegría de la bandera. (It's not necessary! . . . We are not from here, but we feel as if we were, just as the children, our children, must feel the joy of the flag.)[34]

Whereas years earlier they had felt that they were immigrants and foreigners, by the time they became naturalized citizens, they described a deep emotional attachment to the United States. In essence, they had finished the transfer of their loyalties from their country of origin to the United States, and now considered this country to be their adopted homeland. "Entonces ésta es una segunda patria" (So this is a second homeland).[35]

In spite of being the direct targets of the anti-immigrant campaigns of the 1990s, immigrant focus group respondents expressed little resentment about the treatment they had received. Rather, they wanted other Americans to learn to accept them as fellow Americans.

Para demostrar que nosotros también estamos aquí, y que luchamos con ellos, y que hacemos cosas con ellos (To let them know that we are here, too, and that we fight alongside them, and that we do things together with them). . . . Que lo tienen que aceptar (They have to accept that). . . . Les guste o no les guste (Whether they like it or not).[36]

More information about how Latinos see their attachment to this country was revealed by a survey for the United Way of Greater Los Angeles, which CESLAC was asked to conduct between 1999 and 2000. I asked a sample of US-born and immigrant Latinos in Los Angeles to respond to the assertion "I am proud to be an American." The question was intentionally provocative, designed to polarize the respondents. I did not want respondents to be vague about their feelings, so I included the qualifier "proud." Figure 27 provides the patterns of response, from agreeing somewhat to agreeing strongly.

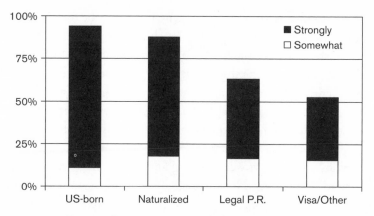

FIGURE 27. Percent of Latinos agreeing with the statement "I am proud to be an American," Los Angeles County, 2000. Source: CESLAC Social Attitudes Survey, population-based survey conducted by telephone by the UCLA Survey Research Center, Juarez and Associates, and CESLAC, under the direction of David E. Hayes-Bautista and Paul Hsu, 2000; SPSS files stored at CESLAC.

US-born Latinos were nearly unanimous: 94% replied "yes" to the question, with 83% agreeing strongly—and this after nearly a decade of Latino-bashing in the popular press and the public scourging of Proposition 187. Immigrant Latino responses to the question largely reflected the emotional investment individuals had made in the United States. Naturalized citizens answered almost as positively as US-born Latinos had: 88% replied "yes," with 70% agreeing strongly. Legal permanent residents, who had been in the United States a shorter period of time than the naturalized citizens, were understandably less likely to answer in the affirmative, yet nearly two-thirds of them (64%) also responded "yes." The most ambivalent group included those immigrant Latinos on visas and having other temporary statuses; only half (53%) responded positively. By way of comparison, when asked the same question, 97% of non-Hispanic whites and 96% of African Americans also agreed that they were proud to be Americans.[37]

An earlier study, the California Identity Project, designed to understand how Latinos constructed their social identity, provided further information on American identity formation among Latinos. The phenomenon of Latino identity change and continuity from one generation to the next interested us especially, so we oversampled second- and third-generation US-born Latinos, including more of them than would be encountered in a strictly population-based sample, so that we could better see their responses. This way, we could see changes in how Latinos viewed themselves from the immigrant Latino (first generation) to the US-born Latino child (second generation, adult at the time of the study), to the US-born Latino grandchild (third generation, also adult at the time of the study). Although the study was conducted more than a decade ago, the general pattern is still valid today. We gathered responses from a statewide sample of 1,086 adult Latino heads of household (average age, thirty-eight years) who had been asked to identify themselves using descriptors such as "Democrat" or "blue-collar worker." Included in the list of possible descriptors were "immigrant," "foreigner," "American," "US citizen," and "US native." Not surprisingly, most of the immigrant Latinos saw themselves as "immigrants" or "foreigners." Seventy-seven percent of first-generation Latinos still called themselves immigrants, and more than 63% still called themselves foreigners. But by the second generation, the sense of being an immigrant or foreign had dropped substantially; only 18% of this group called themselves immigrants, and 13% called themselves foreigners. By the third generation, these terms had nearly disappeared from Latino self-identity; only 4% of third-generation US-born Latinos called themselves immigrants or foreigners. They no longer saw themselves as being separate from other Americans. In 1990, only 18% of immigrant Latinos described themselves as Americans. Their children, however, saw themselves as part and parcel of the American landscape, describing themselves as "US natives," "US citizens," and "Americans." In the second generation, 85% described themselves as US citizens, 76% as US natives, and 74% simply as Americans. By the third generation, 90% described themselves as US citizens, 84% as US natives, and 83% as unhyphenated Americans.[38]

The results of ten years of surveys and specially commissioned focus groups pointed to one conclusion: Latinos feel that they are Americans. The longer Latinos are in the United States, the more likely it is that they will consider themselves to be American. As more immigrant Latinos have become naturalized in the last decade, a much higher percentage of this community considers itself American sooner, as the 2000 United Way data confirm. Yet their emotional connection to America was not perceived clearly by even the most sympathetic non-Hispanic whites, the "lapsed liberals," in our focus groups. As the MALDEF advisory group pored over the research, dissected non-Hispanic white concerns, and felt stung by Latino frustration over exclusion, we decided on the advertisement's core message: Latinos are Americans, like anyone else.

MALDEF asked Hector and Norma Orcí, the principals of La Agencia de Orcí, one of the largest Latino advertising agencies in the country, to help craft a message that could provide a more positive, healthy, productive, and realistic image of Latinos. They agreed and immediately committed key agency staff members to the project. Two staffers, given in-depth briefings on the focus group findings, developed a series of storyboards for presentation to the community advisory committee. Once the message was agreed on, all the necessary work for shooting and broadcasting a commercial began: writing the script; getting permission to film on location around Los Angeles; finding volunteer actors; editing the film; layering in the voice-over narration, music, and optical effects; and raising funds to buy prime-time broadcast hours from the major television stations. Then, between February and April 1998, Southern California viewers of news-commentary programs and upper-end sports events such as golf and tennis saw a thirty-second commercial that caught many of them off guard: "A message from Hispanic Americans." While an off-screen narrator reassured listeners that Latinos shared the same goals, dreams, and problems as everyone else, a number of images flashed across the screen:

—two white-coated Latinos peering through a microscope
—a business-suited Latino presenting at a meeting
—a Latino construction contractor on the job with his workers
—a gaggle of multi-hued children sliding down playground equipment
—a multicultural neighborhood birthday piñata party
—a group of young Latino children wearing anti-drug T-shirts
—Latinos washing out and painting over graffiti
—a grainy television news archive shot of a Latino soldier wounded in action
—a Latino soldier returning home to his family
—a Latino Cub Scout and a Latino Boy Scout
—a multicultural group of children playing baseball
—a young Latino couple buying a house
—a diversified group of students graduating from college

The closing shot showed a ten-year-old boy saluting the American flag, as the announcer signed off with "America. It's home. For everybody."

MALDEF's office received scores of calls about the television spot. The ad, some callers said, went by so fast that they were a little confused. Was MALDEF trying to sell them something? If so, it wasn't clear what the product was. Was it presenting a position on another proposition about immigrants? Latinos were among the callers, enthusiastic about what they had just seen. Was this a motivational, inspirational message for Latino immigrants? If so, was it available in Spanish? Was it going to be shown on Univision or Telemundo, the Spanish-language networks? MALDEF asked us at CESLAC to hold another round of focus groups to evaluate the public service announcement and provide suggestions for a follow-up campaign. We convened groups of non-Hispanic whites and Latinos, both US-born and immigrant, in the Agencia de Orcí's focus group facilities.

NON-HISPANIC WHITE REACTIONS

First we convened groups of non-Hispanic whites, most of whom had not seen the commercial on television. To commence our sessions with these groups, we showed the ad to them twice in succession, then asked them to discuss how it made them feel. Initially, the emotional responses were uniformly positive. The ad's high production values showed and set the desired emotional tone. The short commercial gave an unprecedented message of hope, unlike ads for Proposition 187 campaign in 1994, which had been designed to make people feel uneasy and upset about Latino presence in the state, so as to stampede them into supporting the measure. "I think initially I was, like, 'What is it selling?' but at the end I was, like, 'Oh, I had hope. That was good.'"[39] The combination of high production values, soothing voice-over narration, and soft but peppy salsa background music created a feel-good atmosphere. "It threw me off. I actually felt good about it."[40] The images of Latinos doing things that non-Hispanic whites also did—working, playing, celebrating, buying houses, graduating, fighting the country's wars—provided an unusual sense of commonality. "You look at this, and you're saying, 'Yeah, they look like us; they are doing the same things we do; they are appreciating the things we appreciate.'"[41]

But then the serpent appeared in the garden. As the non-Hispanic white respondents reflected a little, they began to notice discrepancies between the commercial and what they "knew" about Latinos, especially their perception that Latinos are not middle class at all. ["Is this what you would call middle-class Latinos?"[42] Their daily images of Latinos were not of middle-class persons with whom they had a lot in common, but of a different class of people, who probably did not have much in common with them. "It's a nice, pretty picture, but it's not what we read about all the time in the *L.A. Times.*"[43] A few respondents, after reflecting on these discrepancies, began to reject the commercial. "I got this sense of looking for the Latinos in the picture, and I couldn't find them."[44] [Rather than perceiving that Latinos could be scientists, teachers, builders, and soldiers, they reverted back to what they "knew" Latinos did: menial labor, poorly remunerated.] "The people that connect with your conceptual center are the Latinos you see, that bus dishes, nannies, who do the car wash."[45]

One respondent provided a partial analysis of the genesis of this discrepancy, blaming previous policy debates for creating an image of Latinos as not belonging to the middle class. "In political culture, we don't talk about the middle-class Hispanic. We talk about the barrios and gangs and the violent, the people who don't have opportunities."[46] As the focus group respondents talked about their sources of information about Latinos, they described having very limited input, which perhaps had led them to feel that a commercial depicting middle-class Latinos was unusual. "I actually have no information, so I don't have any way of knowing what Latinos want or say. I mean, I don't live in a very integrated world. I don't really have many [Latino] social contacts."[47] Up to this point in their lives, they had not seen a Latino middle class.

In the non-Hispanic white focus groups conducted prior to and after the release of the MALDEF commercial, our focus group facilitator noticed that the participants kept developing a particular line of thought related to a perceived lack of Latino accomplishment and consequent inability to be considered "American" according to new nativist definitions. [After participants had articulated that a key element of the American dream was the desire to accomplish more, to better oneself, they admitted they were not sure that Latinos really wanted to progress, particularly into the middle class.] These non-Hispanic white participants, all of whom lived in California, certainly had noticed that Latinos were hard workers. "They do the jobs that nobody else does. And you know what, I wouldn't want to hire anyone else, because they are hard-working; they take pride, whether they are a dishwasher or a turkey carver. In California, the restaurant industry would die without

Latinos."[48] They also recounted personal experiences with Latino labor: gardeners, nannies, mechanics, odd-job workers. "My son had a babysitter, a Mexican lady. Gosh, I love her to death. She doesn't speak very good English."[49] Yet, for all the admiration they expressed about Latinos' strong work ethic, in their eyes all this hard work did not seem to get Latinos anywhere. It seemed to them as if Latinos were perpetually mired in poverty, in spite of working hard. "When you think of the Mexican Spanish, you think of the barrios, of lower class."[50] The participants speculated that this lack of upward mobility, in spite of their hard work, might be an indication that Latinos lacked higher aspirations. "They [Latino parents] are giving mixed messages. On one level, 'My kid is important; I will work one hundred hours, and I will be responsible for them.' On the other is, 'I can't verbalize anything beyond that.'"[51]

An important part of being American, from the new nativist perspective, was having aspirations to improve one's lot: getting an education, buying a house, improving oneself. When the focus group participants watched televised news at night, however, what they saw was a lack of Latino upward mobility. The pictures they described were, repeatedly, of Latino low-income workers, gang members, school dropouts, and poverty. "One thing I see prevalent among the Latino parents, especially in this community, is sort of a hopelessness, like, 'We are stuck here and there is no getting out of this' . . . and I see the same thing translated to their kids."[52] Participants conceded that virtually all immigrant groups are poor when they arrive in the US, including their own ancestors. But modern Latino immigrants and their children seemed not to be moving up, and this concerned them. This apparent lack of achievement was bothersome for the non-Hispanic white participants; they felt that it could be un-American. "If they [Latinos] express, 'No, I'm stuck in a barrio, I can't get out,' then they [Anglos] don't like that; it's not in line with their American Dream."[53] Rarely did the participants describe Latinos who had achieved. If anything, after some discussion among themselves, they expressed a sudden awareness of not seeing Latino achievement. "If you had a hundred Latinos, maybe five to ten would be in that [middle-class] category. . . . [They] are the exception, more invisible."[54] And if most Latinos were not achieving, given that the United States offered opportunity to everyone, might it not be possible, they mused, that Latinos were not, or did not want to be, or possibly could not be, American?

Because MALDEF had received so many calls from Latinos asking that the commercial be run on Spanish-language television, focus groups were also held with Latinos to explore that possibility. We held separate groups, in English for US-born Latinos and in Spanish for immigrant Latinos. As with the non-Hispanic white groups, the participants only knew that they were testing a television commercial. We showed the video twice, once without sound, to ask what message they thought the images were trying to convey, and once with sound, to get their reactions to the voice-over and music.

The US-born, in particular, generally did not watch Spanish-language television; hence, they had seen only English-language televised news images of Latinos. When shown this ad, they were overwhelmed by the simple fact of positive images of Latinos. "It was, like, wow! They are actually portraying people graduating and people happy and working, and these are all Latinos. I thought that was really cool, and I felt really proud."[55] After nearly a decade of deliberately negative portrayals of Latinos by the pro-Proposition 187 campaign, US-born Latinos described a feeling of emotional catharsis when presented with a positive image created for mainstream television. "Initially, I felt kind of like I wanted to cry, but not because I was sad, but because it was the first time I had seen a collection of so many positive things."[56] The US-born groups spent considerable time describing how validating it felt to see positive Latino images. They also consistently commented on the absence of such imagery from English-language television. Most often mentioned was the news media's treatment of Latinos. "I felt good, like some people said, that they knew it existed; but I was surprised to see it on TV, you know, because in the news you don't see that."[57]

Those immigrant Latinos who had learned English (which most of them eventually do) also watched English-language news, and they also noticed the prevalent negative imagery, which in the Spanish-language television news at least was balanced by portrayals of the rest of the Latino community, such as human interest stories, political events, business news, and entertainment. "Todo le echan al latino. Mira al latino, como está destruyendo" (They blame everything on Latinos. Look at the Latino, how he's destroying [things]).[58] As Latino respondents reflected further, they remarked on this lack of positive imagery for Latinos in general television programming. "Images are so powerful, and so far I can't think of one TV program that portrays positive images of Latinos."[59] Even commercial advertisements managed to present a less-than-flattering portrait of Latinos. For example, popular in the late 1990s was a commercial for a fast-food chain that used a talking Chihuahua dog to ask for Mexican-style food. "You can have something like this [MALDEF spot], versus us being [depicted as] gang members, prostitutes, and being sex symbols, or jumping the border, or being a Chihuahua. This is ridiculous; this is 1998, and we are still categorized as that, and we are going to become the majority in California."[60]

Although non-Hispanic white respondents were thrown off by not seeing the sorts of Latino images they were familiar with, Latino respondents, both US-born and immigrant, saw nothing out of the ordinary in the images provided. "There were a lot of images that were familiar to me."[61] Even English-dominant US-born Latinos who no longer lived in barrios could relate to these images, for they saw them in their daily lives. Whereas the non-Hispanic whites could not imagine that immigrants might possibly live as portrayed in the commercial, immigrant Latinos had no problem identifying themselves in its various images. The facilitator asked one focus group of immigrants if the people in the spot seemed authentic to them.

FACILITATOR: ¿La gente que vieron, es gente real? (The people you saw, are they real people?)

GROUP MEMBER: ¡Sí! (Yes!) [multiple responses]

GROUP MEMBER: Son personas como nosotros. (They are people like us)

GROUP MEMBER: Casos de la vida real. (Examples of real life)

They contrasted the negative images shown on English-language television with the ones provided in the ad, and felt the latter far better reflected their community. "Nuestra comunidad es más como ésta" (Our community is more like this).[62] Emotional connection to the positive images was very strong for the immigrants. "Se siente como si uno fuera parte de la vida de ahí" (One feels as if one were part of the life [shown] there).[63] In contrast to the bewilderment expressed by the non-Hispanic white respondents at the differences between the commercial's images of Latinos and those they were familiar with, Latino respondents said that the ad provided an accurate representation of their everyday life. The images that were so disconcerting for non-Hispanic white respondents were quotidian for Latinos. "What I remember about the ad is that it is almost colloquial, in that it's like everyday, like the events that happen in the course of a normal day for people. . . . This is ... what happens in our homes, our parks, our churches, our neighbor-hoods. ... Really, what I liked about it was its everyday kind of quality."[64] Immigrants, who loomed so large in the negative depictions of a California on the road to wrack and ruin, likewise felt that these images were simply a reflection of their daily life.

The dissonance described by the non-Hispanic white focus group members is a product of media and policy attention focused almost exclusively on the recently arrived immigrant. Immigrant Latinos, like most immigrants to the United States, generally arrive with few financial resources and start at the bottom of the socioeconomic ladder. They take the least desirable jobs—busing tables, selling oranges on freeway on-ramps, and working as nannies. Over time, most immigrants work their way out of poverty, learn English, and eventually become homeowners. But this movement up the socioeconomic ladder is rarely recognized by English-language media and policy shapers. Television news prefers dramatic images, catastrophes, immigrants dying forgotten in boxcars in Iowa. It is, therefore, not surprising that many people feel Latinos are not moving up, and so they ask if Latinos really have what it takes to be Americans.

BELMONT HIGH SCHOOL, CLASS OF 1989

In the 1950s, California's public education system was one of the wonders of the country, consistently ranking in the top five in the United States. By the 1990s, however, it had fallen nearly to the bottom of the US rankings by almost every measure. Some districts managed to function, and some functioned well, but on the rock bottom were some of the large urban districts, which seemed to be in chaos. The Los Angeles Unified School District (LAUSD) seemed to lag so far behind other school districts in the state that its then-superintendent, Ramon Cortines, called it the most dysfunctional school district in America.[65]

In June 1999, Robert Lopez, a young reporter covering the urban beat at the *Los Angeles Times*, wondered what had happened to his classmates from the Belmont High class of 1989. Was he, he wondered, the only one of his class to have become a modest success? Was his story unique? Had most of his classmates fallen prey to drugs, gangs, pressures to drop out, and teen pregnancy? He convinced his editor to use the *Times*'s surveying capabilities to find out what his classmates were doing with their lives ten years after graduation. After nearly five months of polling—including tracking one classmate down to an Indian reservation in Arizona—the survey was complete. What the reporter saw in the results both surprised and did not surprise him.

More than two-thirds of his classmates were Latinos, nearly all of them either immigrants or the children of immigrants, primarily from Mexico and El Salvador. Very few of their parents had graduated from high school, and they themselves had spent four years at the most dysfunctional school in the most dysfunctional school district in a state ranked near the bottom nationally in education. It sounded like a formula for a vicious circle—a poster school for the urban underclass—if ever there was one. Yet the data from the survey showed that the class of 1989, especially the Latino population, was solidly middle class, only ten years after their senior year, in spite of all they had had to contend with at Belmont High.[66]

The Latinos in the class of '89 had greatly improved on their parents' educational levels. While only a little more than one third (39%) of their parents had graduated from high school, a great majority of the Latinos in the class of '89 (85%) had. More than three-fourths (77%) had gone on to study at college, and over one-fourth (28%) had received a bachelor's degree. The magnitude of this increase in educational attainment under such dysfunctional conditions is best appreciated when we realize that in California, a virtually identical percentage of non-Hispanic white adults aged twenty-five and older (27.9%) also earned a bachelor's degree in 1990, but they came from families with far greater income, far higher parental educational levels, and generally superior mastery of English.[67]

Nor was Robert Lopez alone in achieving a middle-class job. The great majority of his Latino classmates (87%) were active members of the workforce, and over three-fourths (80%) worked in either white-collar or managerial positions. Almost half (45%) earned $40,000 or more per year, while still relatively early in their careers; at the time, the college graduates would have been in the workforce only about five years. Despite their youth, many Latinos of the class of '89 had not copied the television sit-com formula of eternal dating without commitment, but instead demonstrated a typically Latino pattern of marrying and having children. Nearly half (47%) were married, and slightly more than half of those couples (58%) already had children. It is unlikely that their low-income, poorly educated parents could have given them much help in buying a house, but just over a third (34%) were already homeowners, even so early in their careers. If improvement in life is a cornerstone of the American dream, Belmont's 1989 Latino graduates were thoroughly American. Virtually unanimously (94%), they believed they had much better opportunities in life than their parents had had. While still getting their professional feet under them, three-quarters of them (75%) already had improved on their parents' economic situation, while 19% were on a par with their parents' achievement but looking to move ahead eventually.[68]

The fact that some of his classmates now belonged to the middle class did not surprise Lopez. He had kept in contact with a few high school friends, and they had risen together. What did surprise him was that nearly *all* his classmates had moved up into the middle class. What might they all have accomplished, he wondered, if they had gone to a good high school, one that had had enough books, teachers, and space for everyone?

"AMERICAN" AS DEFINED BY LATINOS

Data from the previously mentioned 1990 California Identity Project (CIP) provide some clues as to how the "average American" of California will likely describe himself or herself by 2040.[69] We have seen that while first-generation immigrant Latinos are not likely to call themselves simply "Americans," their second- and third-generation US-born children and grandchildren almost unanimously see themselves as "American," with no modifiers added, rather than describing themselves as "hyphenated Americans." This sense of being American is a major change over the three generations of Latinos. It is equally important to note, however, that there were some descriptors that were as likely to be chosen by first-generation immigrants as by third-generation US-born Latinos. These seem to be consistent elements in the self-perception of these Latino Americans, passed unchanged from one generation to the next.

The family orientation of Latino populations in 2014 has become a marketing cliché. Yet seventy-four years of census data, from 1940 to 2014, confirm it, so there is some basis to this marketing shortcut. In the CIP survey, nearly all Latinos, in all three generations, identified themselves as members of a family. Ninety-one percent of the first generation, 96% of the second generation, and 95% of the third generation chose this descriptor. Unwittingly, they were supporting Braudel's contention that families "provide the geology beneath history";[70] in other words, that the basic "ways of being and doing" are learned first in the family, and those constructs then are used to create larger social organizations.

Although Latinos often have difficulty defining Latino culture, they are very likely to describe themselves as having been formed by it. Eighty-eight percent of first-generation respondents described themselves as being "Hispanic," as did 83% of second-generation and 83% of third-generation Latinos. Despite assertions that Latinos are largely becoming Protestant, data from the 1990 study, confirmed by a United Way study in 2000, showed that this movement was fairly minor. Most Latinos, in all three generations, defined themselves as Catholic: 79% in the first generation, 74% in the second, and 77% in the third.[71]

One element of social identity, however, did change significantly over the three generations. Eighty-seven percent of the first generation, 79% of the second generation, and 65% of the third generation called themselves "Spanish-speaking."[72] Although there was a significant decline over the three generations, this change needs to be taken in the context of the official discouragement of Spanish-language ability and lack of Spanish-language media during the lives of the third-generation respondents from 1940 to 1970. The fact that, despite that history, almost two-thirds of third-generation US-born Latinos regarded themselves as Spanish-speaking shows the tenacity of this language use.

From the surveys and focus group work, it is clear that Latinos, particularly those born in the United States, see themselves as Americans, are proud to be Americans, and identify with the American dream. These Americans, however, differ from Atlantic Americans in certain fundamental ways. They form strong family networks; they speak Spanish in addition to English; and they feel comfortable with the mores and values they learned at home. But they are Americans and resent any implication that they are not.

CONVERGING DEFINITIONS OF "AMERICAN"

By the end of each MALDEF focus-group session, the non-Hispanic white participants began to reflect on how much the definition of "American" has shifted from a strict Anglo-Saxonist focus on language, culture, and race to a more nuanced concept based on new nativist values of work and personal responsibility—one possibly expansive enough to include Latinos whose lives were still anchored in the Latino cultural experience. The participants wondered if their newly expanded definition of "American" might be a product of living in Southern California, with its diverse, multi-ethnic population. Today's California provides an opportunity to glimpse what American identity may become as the twenty-first century progresses. "For someone living in Los Angeles, it [American] seems more blurred for us than it is for somebody in the Plain[s] states, Idaho, or Iowa."[73] It is this very "blurriness" that likely provides a glimpse into the future of American identity.

Whoever aspires to be an American, according these focus group discussions, has to demonstrate an emotional commitment to the country. There has to be no doubt as to whose side such a person would fight for. "If you say someone is assimilated, they may love the country they came from, but they also have that sense of 'I love America.'"[74] Although non-Hispanic white respondents did not know it at the time of their focus group sessions, Latinos agreed with that definition.

Baby boomer and generation X non-Hispanic whites recognized that their parents' generation had required immigrants to assimilate nearly completely in order to be considered American. "This is one of the things that drives [older] Americans crazy, because they feel that immigrants should drop their [previous] culture."[75] The respondents themselves, however, leaned toward acculturation rather than total assimilation. They thought Latino immigrants should not have to give up their original cultures completely, although they should have to learn to navigate the local host culture. "It doesn't mean necessarily losing your own culture, but coming and coexisting with the culture that exist[s] in a neighborhood."[76] In cases in which the majority of the local host culture might already be Latino, acculturation meant learning to navigate outside the Latino cultural shell. "I think assimilation does have to do with being involved with [a] different culture other than your own—not necessarily moving out of a culture that's purely Hispanic, but involved with the [other] culture."[77] Living in an environment where the top-rated radio and television stations were aimed at the Spanish-language market, these non-Hispanic white participants did not expect that Latinos would stop speaking Spanish, but they did expect that Latinos should learn enough English to facilitate communication. "Well, if you are coming to my country, the United States, our country, I think you should have to learn some English, enough to get by."[78] Again, they did not know it at the time, but Latinos agreed with them. Given the ubiquity of Spanish-language communication in Southern California, the non-Hispanic white respondents also accepted that their personal economic success likely would hinge on learning enough Spanish to communicate. "I definitely see that the schools are pushing bilingual education to Anglos. They're saying, 'You're not going to have a future in economics, in business, in teaching, et cetera, unless you know English and Spanish.'"[79] Once again, Latinos agreed with them.

Any person interested in the economic well-being of Southern California understands how vital the Latino market is to its economy. Not only have many radio and television stations targeted this population segment, but entire chains of grocery, clothing, and consumer electronics stores have staked their future on this market. Far from being a minority culture in danger of extinction, Latino culture is alive and well in this marketplace. The strength of the cultural dynamics that now drive such major market decisions impressed the non-Hispanic white respondents. "This group has a very strong culture."[80] Of course, the sheer size of the Latino population segment—nearly 8 million strong in Southern California—helps propel the cultural dynamics. Internal changes in Latino musical tastes, for example, keep entire genres of music profitable, such as rock *en español,* banda, and *romántica.* "They are large enough to be able to keep their culture."[81]

Although the non-Hispanic focus group members were not sure that Latinos were actually American, some eventually expressed the opinion that perhaps Latinos did want to become American. "I do think and feel very strongly that the Latinos want to be American."[82] They could see that immigrants were attracted to this country; and from what they could tell, the opportunities provided to them here were far greater than they could have encountered in their countries of origin. Thus, it seemed reasonable that Latinos might have a desire to become Americans.

It appeared, however, that Latinos would be Americans in ways that included retaining large portions of Latino culture. "They want to keep their culture, I do believe; but I also think that . . . many, if not most, Latino immigrants, they would want to be Americans."[83] There seemed to be ways of being and doing that were not associated with Atlantic American culture but were part of the Latino culture. "[They become American], but they want to keep those ways of behaving, those ways of expressing themselves that don't seem to be part . . . of [non-Hispanic] white culture."[84] On the basis of a universalist definition of American values as belief in equality, freedom, and democracy, Latinos consider themselves to be as American as anyone. And even from a new nativist perspective that defines "American" in terms of embracing individualist values—work ethic, independence from welfare, and family—Latinos act out those values to a higher degree than non-Hispanic whites. From the Anglo-Saxonist nativist perspective, however, Latinos continue to be seen as somehow "not American," to the extent that they do not conform to the nativists' white, Anglo-Saxon, Protestant, English-speaking definition of "American."

Given the sheer size of the Latino population and the ubiquity of Latino culture, Latinos may turn out to be Americans in the ways that they themselves want to develop, independent of non-Hispanic white desires. One respondent nicely summarized this idea about Latinos becoming Americans in a slightly different way: "They want to be American, as Latinos."[85] Latinos in the focus groups agreed with the non-Hispanic whites on this point. Indeed, Latinos today are defining what it is to be American.

SEVEN

Creating a Regional American Identity

I come from Texas. What a Texan views as American is very different from somebody here [in Los Angeles].

A SENIOR REPORTER FROM A large East Coast newspaper decided that for one of his last professional columns before retiring, he wanted to write about something that was new to him: Latinos. He traveled to Los Angeles, to the epicenter of Latino population growth, to embark on a series of interviews with a variety of Latinos. He arranged to have breakfast with me to provide himself with some background before getting started in L.A. During our breakfast at a glitzy Westwood restaurant noted for its popularity in the movie business, the reporter kept prodding me to define myself: was I primarily a Latino, or primarily an American? I frustrated him by refusing to state an unequivocal choice. He appeared to think I was evading the question. But I too felt frustrated: I could not explain to him in a way he could understand that, particularly for US-born Latinos, there is no difference between the two.

Suddenly, an analogy came to mind, a way of explaining my position so that he could grasp that the very asking of the question has already posited a false polarity. I replied, essentially, "You have to look at it like this. When you ask me that question, you're implying that Latino is not American, or that maybe it's un-American, and that's not it. Think of it like this: being Latino is not un-American. It's not being anti-American; it's like being . . . being . . . a Texan. It's a *distinctive* way of being American."

"Oh, I see." The reporter eased back into his chair, reflecting on this insight. The analogy was new to me too, having just flashed across my mind. Thinking out loud, I continued, "Look, you know how Texans are; they're different. With their accent and vocabulary, they talk differently; they walk differently in those cowboy boots; they wear those cowboy hats. They are very proud to be Texan. You know some Texans, don't you?"

"Yes," he replied, still pondering my comments.

"Well, would you ever ask a Texan to choose between being a Texan and an American? Of course not. For a Texan, that's a ridiculous question. Texans are Americans. They will refuse to separate the two. You won't find any more patriotic group than Texans. And that's the key. Texans aren't un-American or anti-American; they're Americans, but Texas style, and proudly so. Well, think of Latinos the same way. Sure, we're Latino. And we're American. It's that we're American, Latino style. It's not a choice between the two. Being Latino is like being a Texan; it's a *distinctive* way of being American."

The quintessential cultural icon of Texas is the cowboy, a figure nearly synonymous around the globe with America. Yet the evolution of the American cowboy provides a case study of how societies, cultures, and traditions blend, modifying themselves to suit local circumstances. It also provides a clue to the future role Latinos may play in American identity and society.

From the beginning, cattle raising was a key element in defining the identity of the region that came to be known as Texas. British colonists brought cattle with them to North America, as well as cattle-tending methods; farmers on foot, aided by herding dogs, prodding cattle to pasture by day and back to cowpens by night, became the norm in the Atlantic colonies.[1] On the Iberian Peninsula, however, a different form of cattle raising had developed. There, men on horseback drove herds of cattle from one open range to another. Once a year, herds would be separated and animals branded with a hot iron to establish ownership. This form of cattle tending was also established in the Americas, giving rise to many local variants: the *gaucho* in Argentina, the *huaso* in Chile, the *llanero* in Venezuela, and the *vaquero* (cowboy) in Mexico.[2] Vaqueros operated as far north as Texas, New Mexico, Arizona, and California.

In Texas, Mexican vaqueros adapted Iberian techniques and equipment to local conditions. They wore broad-brimmed hats to protect themselves from the burning sun and leather *chaparreras* to protect their clothing from spiky mesquite branches,[3] and they carried a rope called *la reata* that formed a noose called a *lazo*, with which to capture cattle on the open range.[4] The finest rope was made from *mecate* (hair from horses' tails), which they used to form a bitless bridle, called a *jáquima*, to begin the process of taming a wild *bronco*. Astride a trained *mesteño*, they herded cattle into a *corral*, roped one animal and stopped it in its tracks by quickly snubbing the rope around the saddle horn in a maneuver called *dale vuelta* (give it a turn), letting the horse's weight serve as an anchor.[5] After a *rodeo,* vaqueros celebrating with too much liquor would be picked up to spend a few days in the local *juzgado.*

When settlers from Virginia, Tennessee, and Kentucky moved to Texas during the 1820s, they quickly discovered that tending cattle on foot, British style, was not suitable for the sparsely vegetated, wide-open plains. In a feat of cultural borrowing, they quickly picked up the cattle-raising techniques and equipment developed by Iberians and Mexicans, far better suited to Texas conditions, and even adapted the Spanish terminology. They became cowboys, *buckaroos* (a mispronunciation of *vaqueros*), with ten-gallon hats adapted from the wide-brimmed Mexican sombrero, wearing *chaps* (*chaparreras*) to protect their clothing, using a *lariat* (*la reata*) to *lasso* (*lazo*) cattle. They used fine rope made out of horses' tails called *McCarthy* (*mecate*) to make *hackamore* bridles (*jáquima*) for the early stages of *bronc*-busting (*bronco*). Once astride a trained *mustang* (*mesteño*), they would rope a calf in the *corral* (corral) and stop it in midstride by snubbing one end of the rope around the saddle horn in a maneuver known as *dally roping* (*dale vuelta*). Using a Mexican saddle with a horn, they participated in *rodeos* (*rodeo*), and when they celebrated and got drunk, they sometimes would spend a night or two in the local *hoosegow* (*juzgado*). That most American of images—the cowboy on the lone prairie—was the product of the meeting and partial merging of Latino and Atlantic American civil societies and cultures. British cattle-raising techniques alone never would have given rise to the cowboy; the social and cultural mix created a regional culture and identity that today is distinctly Texan, yet wholly American. This cultural mixture became an unconscious part of the daily life and self-image of people—non-Hispanic whites, Latinos, African Americans, American Indians, and Asian Americans—living in the Texas region. The interaction between cultural groups created a distinctive regional identity.

For over 160 years, a similar type of cultural blending process also has been at work in California, creating the foundation for a future regional American identity. To understand that process at work, we need to develop a new way to view Latinos: neither as a dysfunctional minority nor as simply an immigrant group, but as creators of a civil society. Such a view allows us to better understand the continuity and change that are California's history and its future.

With Latinos already comprising more than half of all children born in California, it is statistically incorrect to refer to Latinos as a "minority." As seen in chapter 3, moreover, Latinos do not fit the definition of "dysfunctional minority" traditionally used in policymaking. In fact, Latino social behaviors statistically have been the strongest of any demographic group, and their health outcomes are surprisingly good. Some have tended to see Latinos as just another immigrant group and have suggested the Latino future will resemble that of Italian or other immigrant groups.[6] Yet the European immigrant experience is of limited value in understanding Latino social dynamics. To begin with, for most of the past 160 years, the majority of Latinos in California have been US-born. At times in the company of immigrant Latinos, at times by themselves without immigrant accompaniment, US-born Latinos have been making their lives in this state, and doing so in very Latino ways.

Latinos are not just a minority or immigrant group. To understand Latino paradoxes, we need to look into the thoughts and behaviors of Latinos, both those born in the United States and their immigrant relatives, over the past 250 years, to discern their possible future, as well as the influence of immigrants on them. We need to look for the "Latino habits of the heart" that have been passed from generation to generation, constituting the "stock of knowledge" that an individual Latino uses in her or his daily life.

LATINO CIVIL SOCIETY

As Robert Bellah notes, "Tocqueville ... speaks of ... 'habits of the heart'; notions, opinions and ideas that 'shape mental habits.'"[7] Civil society is, essentially, the world of daily life—the world of primary relations such as are found in family, friends, neighborhood, faith communities, small businesses, workplace networks, and voluntary associations—upon which rest the larger institutions of society, such as governmental and marketplace organizations.[8] Over conversations at the dinner table, through behavior modeled while performing household tasks, through silent example and spoken word, this primary network provides a place for daily conversations about the guiding values of life: the good and the bad, the desirable and the undesirable, the just and the unjust, the beautiful and the ugly, and so on. These countless family conversations also provide important first notions of self and a sense of the "we" in society. Family tales, lore, traditions, and practices provide the initial notions. The larger network of relatives, friends, neighbors, and parishioners provides additional ideas.[9]

Civil society is an ongoing human production. Experiences are shared between individuals in a primary group, and the accumulation of these experiences and their meanings gradually constitutes a "stock of knowl-edge."[10] This stock of knowledge is transmitted from generation to generation and made available to each individual in daily life. Almost unconsciously, an individual develops, within the primary web of social relationships, de Tocqueville's "habits of the heart," the unexamined mental and emotional framework that guides an individual to actions because they "feel right," not necessarily because a rational decision has been made.

The 15 million Latinos in California in 2015 present a seeming paradox.[11] In spite of generally low income and poor educational levels, they present social behaviors and a health profile equal to, or stronger than, groups with far better education and far higher incomes. These profiles cannot be attrib-uted to income and education or access to care. Yet another area is left for investigation: the moral discourse and mores that lie at the core of Latino daily life—in other words, Latino civil society, based on "habits of the Latino heart," emanating from processes and dynamics brought to California by Mexican colonists from 1769, and still functioning in the twenty-first century.

HEALTH INDICATORS FOR LATINO CIVIL SOCIETY

Fischer studied the arrival, persistence, continuity, and change of four differ-ent British "folkways" in specific regions of the US over a four-hundred-year period, showing how they gave rise to regional variations of Atlantic American culture in New England, the mid-Atlantic states, Virginia, and the Appalachian Mountains. His methodology traced continuities and changes in twenty-four particular folkways passed from generation to generation. These range from "speech ways" and "food ways" to "power ways" and "free-dom ways."[12] My research leads me to add one more to Fischer's list, an important folkway visible in every society and group: "healing ways." This additional category concerns what people in any given group do to maintain health and manage illness.

For more than forty years, I have researched Latino experiences in health care in California. The disease and behavioral areas I have researched are many: HIV/AIDS, diabetes, asthma, arthritis, infant morbidity and mortal-ity, breast cancer, osteoporosis, teen pregnancy, and youth risk behavior, with special attention to the issues of children, adolescents, immigrants, the eld-erly, and farmworkers. This research has allowed me to look deeply into

Latino values and daily behaviors concerning issues basic to the human condition, stripped of superfluous noise about identity politics, political correctness, or annual doses of ethnic pride. I have heard Latinos grappling with fundamental issues of human existence: illness, pain, suffering, and death; relief, hope, birth, and life. I have heard them describe their values, their culture, and their sense of moral development, in describing daily activities related to health. These activities and conversations provide a framework of cultural meaning that yields the strong health and social behaviors so at odds with the low income and low educational levels common in most Latino populations.

As I continue to research Latino health, I am convinced that these daily conversations, on seemingly mundane, unimportant topics, provide the cultural and intellectual resources for a strong, productive, harmonious California society for the twenty-first century: the habits of the Latino heart, with roots that go back hundreds, sometimes thousands, of years. Although the research that would objectively prove the influence of Latino civil society in this respect remains to be conducted, I nevertheless want to share some observations that have led me to recognize the persistence of that civil society.

In a class I teach at UCLA each winter to around 120 Latino pre-health professional students, I routinely ask the aspiring physicians, dentists, epidemiologists, biostatisticians, nurse practitioners, and health educators to describe the last pregnancy in their family. Usually they allude to a sister's or a close cousin's experience. I ask them what sorts of beliefs and behaviors these mostly urban Latina women engaged in when pregnant. A number are mentioned year after year: they should avoid chewing gum, avoid "cold" foods and drinks, and shun smoking and alcohol. Also mentioned, year after year, is the belief that pregnant Latina women should wear red underwear adorned with a safety pin. Their mothers and grandmothers feel this ensures the birth of a healthy baby.

The wearing of red material around the belly during pregnancy dates back to pre-Columbian times. Unlike Europeans, who saw a "man in moon," the indigenous Náhua of Mexico saw a rabbit in the full moon.[13] They believed that if a pregnant woman exposed her fetus to the rabbit-faced full moon, her child risked a harelip or other deformity. Náhua prenatal practices suggested that a pregnant woman could protect her baby from the deleterious effects of the moon by suspending an obsidian blade over her swollen belly, tied by a red string—red being one of the Náhua cardinal colors. This advice was passed from mother to daughter in Náhuatl or other Indian languages. After the arrival of the Spaniards, a metal blade was substituted for the obsidian, and the advice came to be passed from mother to daughter in Spanish. Once underwear was developed, the red string fell into disuse, replaced by a full set of red underwear; the blade, over time, was replaced by a metal key. This custom has been observed by anthropologists studying modern-day Mexican birth behaviors.[14]

In twenty-first-century California, a safety pin stuck through red underwear does the trick, and the advice now is passed from mother to daughter in the English language. When I ask if the female students actually believe what their mothers and grandmothers have told them, they usually laugh nervously and reply that while it does not make rational sense, they will indeed wear red underwear with a safety pin when they are pregnant. "Better safe than sorry," one student inevitably replies.

Diabetes is the *bête noire* of the Latino community, the major disease for which the Latino Epidemiological Paradox does not hold true. Latino mortality from diabetes is two to three times as high as the rate for non-Hispanic whites. Because of its intractability in the Latino community, I have conducted a number of studies of diabetes knowledge, beliefs, and behaviors, with both Latino and non-Hispanic white populations. In 1997, I conducted a population-based telephone survey of Latino and non-Hispanic white persons sixty-five years or older in Los Angeles County.[15] Among other things, we asked our respondents an open-ended question: what did they think caused a person to become diabetic? The response patterns, for immigrant Latino and non-Hispanic white elderly, shown in figure 28, again reveal the persistence of Latino civil society in the world of health beliefs. It surprised the study's funders, the Centers for Disease Control in Atlanta, to find that immigrant Latino elderly persons were about as likely as the non-Hispanic white elderly to mention the roles of heredity, diet, and being overweight as factors in the onset of diabetes. Yet, unlike their non-Hispanic white counterparts, the immigrant Latino elderly were nearly as likely to attribute the onset of diabetes to emotional factors as well: *susto, nervios,* and stress.

Susto (literally, "shock" or "startlement") is a classic Mexican folk disease, having its roots in indigenous Náhua beliefs about the relation of body and spirit. It is believed to be caused by an emotional trauma or sudden emotional shock, and is often cited by Latinos as the reason for the onset of diabetes in an adult. "Con el susto que me dieron cuando me volvieron a decir que tenía cancer, me asusté y me volvió a subir el azucar . . . precisamente porque me

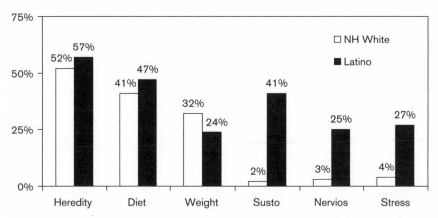

FIGURE 28. Perceived causes of diabetes, Latino immigrant and non-Hispanic white 65+ years, Los Angeles County, 1997. Source: CESLAC, Edward R. Roybal Institute for Applied Gerontology at California State University, Los Angeles, Roybal Immunization Consortium for Older Adults Survey, 1997; data stored at CESLAC.

asustaba" (Because of the fright [susto] they gave me when they told me again that I had cancer, I was frightened, and my sugar [levels] rose again . . . just because it had frightened me).[16] *Nervios* (nerves) and stress are two additional emotional causes of diabetes perceived by Latino respondents. The specific source of the emotional stress—susto, nervios, stress—is less important than the larger causal view, that an upset to a person's emotions can cause either the onset of diabetes, or, if one already has diabetes, an increase in blood sugar levels.

> Sí, es emocional, porque el diabetes pega de gusto, de susto, de tristeza; de todo pega el diabetes. . . . Entonces, si a usted le da gusto, le puede subir el diabetes, si tiene tristeza, puede subir el diabetes, si hace coraje . . . se sube . . . el diabetes. (Yes, it is emotional, because diabetes comes from an intense desire for something, from a fright, from sadness; diabetes comes from all of that. . . . So, if you really want something, diabetes can go up; if you are sad, diabetes can go up; if you get angry . . . diabetes . . . can go up).[17]

The Náhua believed that the link of *tonalli* (spirit) and body could be tenuous at times, and it could be endangered by proscribed activities such as drunkenness or inappropriate sexual intercourse. An emotional shock also could separate soul from body.[18] Bolton noted that indigenous descriptions of susto—shaking, debility, fainting, loss of consciousness, and anxiety—could also be descriptions of a diabetic suffering from hypoglycemia.[19] Although anthropologists have described susto as an illness that must be treated in its own right, none have cited it so far as a factor in the onset of diabetes.[20]

The existence of many folk cures for diabetes reflects a continuation of Latino civil society in the world of medicine. Perhaps the most commonly mentioned herbal cure is a nearly unshakable belief in the efficacy of nopal, a cactus found in Mexico.

> Cuando como nopales me baja [el nivel de azúcar], cantidad. ¡Cantidad! El nopal me ayuda cantidad. Hasta voy a buscar pastillas de nopal, que me dijeron que hay cápsulas de nopal. Porque cuando como nopales me baja. Cuando me sube, inmediatamente como nopales, y al otro día se me quita, me baja. (When I eat nopales, my [blood-sugar level] goes down a lot. A lot! Nopales help me a lot. I am even looking for nopal pills, because they told me that there are nopal pills. Because when I eat nopales, it goes down. When it goes up, I immediately eat nopales, and by the next day, it goes away, it goes down.)[21]

Nopal can be eaten raw, cooked, strained into a juice, or mixed into a "smoothie" in a blender. Although our surveys did not ask about the prevalence of nopal usage, its constant mention in focus groups and testimony from physicians managing Latino diabetics makes it another reminder of how deeply rooted Latino civil society remains in twenty-first-century California.

Another chronic condition, arthritis, is also routinely treated by Latinos with an astounding array of home remedies for pain: a tincture of alcohol and marijuana leaves, *ventosas* (cuppings), rattlesnake meat, uncontrolled *nostra* purchased in Tijuana pharmacies, and the like. Not surprisingly, we also have heard variations on an age-old Mexican humoral theory about the source of arthritis: a too-rapid change from warm to cold—such as throwing ice water on someone perspiring in the Mojave Desert, or moving too quickly from the summer heat into a cold meat locker—is believed to bring on the disease. But others described arthritis as being a result of *bilis* (bile), a humor supposedly produced when a person is emotionally angry or upset. A *bilioso*—an easily angered, type A personality—was described as being more susceptible to arthritis and other diseases.

> GROUP MEMBER: Another one [type of arthritis] is from your mind. . . .
> GROUP MEMBER: And one is people who get mad easily.
> FACILITATOR: Who get mad easily?
> GROUP MEMBER: Sí. Es muy bilioso (Yes. [One who] is a very angry personality).

GROUP MEMBER: It also is when you're angry and you hold it in.

GROUP MEMBER: Biliar (Biliary).

GROUP MEMBER: And nerves. Emotional, emotional.[22]

In many Latino respondents' views, these angry people expose themselves to adverse health outcomes, including arthritis, rheumatism, and other diseases.

GROUP MEMBER: Le pegó a mi suegra el reumatismo bilioso (My mother-in-law got bilious rheumatism).

FACILITATOR: ¿Bilioso? ¿Hay reumatismo bilioso? (Bilious? There's bilious rheumatism?)

GROUP MEMBER: Ese le vino de un susto. . . . Se puso amarillo . . . se enmoheció la coyuntura porque se le derramó la bilis (That happened to her because of a susto. . . . She turned yellow . . . her joints rusted because her bile spilled over).

GROUP MEMBER: Yo he sabido que sí derraman las bilis de un susto. De un susto hasta muda queda la gente (I've known that susto causes bile to spill over. People even have been struck mute due to a susto).[23]

These health beliefs have their origin in pre-Columbian Mexico. Furst described the Náhua belief that the somatic location of the tonalli was in the joints; an injury to the joint could cause an injury to a person's soul.[24] López Austin has examined medical manuscripts written in Náhuatl, and notes that the joints of the body—wrists, elbows, shoulders, knees, ankles, hips, and neck—were considered to be minor *centros anímicos,* or places where life-giving forces resided.[25] Although the Náhuatl manuscripts did not specifically state that anger would cause an arthritis flare-up, the relation between an angry state or personality (bilioso) and arthritis has been reported so consistently that I consider it as a primary indication of a pre-Columbian belief, related to Náhua concepts of the body and its relation to the universe.

Latino civil society is also present in the operating room. The late Dr. Ismael Nuño, chief of cardiac surgery at the Los Angeles County/University of Southern California Medical Center, talked extensively with his patients and their families about the possibility of death during a heart transplant. But when Dr. Nuño counseled Latino patients, their concern usually was not with possible mortality. Believing, as did the Náhuas, that the soul resides in the heart, Latino patients were more concerned about the transplant's effects on a person's character—kindness or meanness, astuteness, love and passion. Removing the diseased organ that contained one soul and replacing it with another, they thought, could be risky. They feared that a totally new person might awake from the operation, and they wondered if this person would recognize his or her family.[26] In our research on the relation between Latino culture and health, we have uncovered scores of similar examples that illustrate the persistence of a deeply rooted, fundamentally influential Latino civil society in the realm of health and illness. The growing Latino population has distinctive views on health and illness, life and death, which can be traced back centuries and which are alive and well in examination rooms in today's California.

They are part and parcel of the larger cultural dynamic that has been the experience of most of the western hemisphere. And by virtue of the size of the Latino population, they are becoming part of the daily experience of health and illness of the average person in California.

ORIGINS

This concept of "Latino civil society" should be used in viewing the past, present, and future roles of Latinos in California. Other definitions previously used to describe Latinos—a minority, a race, a linguistic group, a traditional society, or an urban underclass—are simply not useful, as Latinos defy those attempts to box them into a single category. According to the data presented in this book, clearly Latinos are more than a group practicing identity politics. Viewing Latinos as a civil society allows us a larger, more comprehensive, dynamic framework for viewing Latinos sui generis. But in order to see the future role of Latino civil society, we need first to appreciate its origins.

Iberian Overlay

For non-Latinos, perhaps the most recognizable and familiar elements of Latino civil society are the Iberian ones, for example, the use of the Spanish language and the practice of Catholic Christianity. The Iberian Peninsula was, and is, part and parcel of Western Christian civilization. Itself an amalgamation of disparate peoples (Iberians, Celts, Phoenicians, Romans, Goths, Arabs, Berbers, and Sephardic Jews) and religions (Catholicism, Islam, and

Judaism), Iberia was by 1492 a mosaic of languages, cultures, genetics, and politics, all tucked, sometimes none too tidily, under the tent of militarily triumphant Catholicism. Yet this amazing diversity was, officially at least, artificially reduced to an imposed homogeneity by the time it was brought to the Americas. Of the many languages and dialects spoken on the peninsula—Catalan, Euzkadi (Basque), and Portuguese, among others—only one, Castilian, the language originating in the region of Castile, was mandated, by the mid-sixteenth century, as the official language of the Spanish colonies.[27] This artificial linguistic uniformity has resulted, five hundred years later, in the relative linguistic unity that allows Argentine and Venezuelan *novelas* (televised soap operas) to find a lucrative audience also among the 55 million Latinos in the United States alone. Another key element of Latino civilization is, of course, Catholicism, which, although it is a unified religion, encompasses a wide variety of opinions about the experience of God, manifested in the multiple religious orders—Franciscans, Dominicans, Jesuits, and so on—that were given authority over different regions of Latin America. A further dimension of the Latin American experience was added by superimposing this artificially homogenized Iberian culture and language on the even more diverse indigenous societies of the Americas.

Indigenous Substrate

To understand the future regional identity of California, it is important to understand a major difference between the British and Spanish approaches to indigenous societies. While neither colonizer asked indigenous peoples what their desires might be, the British, and their Atlantic American descendants, generally saw Indians as an obstacle that should be removed as rapidly as possible. The Spanish Crown, however, saw Indians as potential subjects and potential Catholic converts—under certain restrictions, of course, but also deserving of certain protections. Thus, rather than establishing ever more remote reservations for Indians, the Spanish Crown sought to incorporate them into the regime. Yet the extent to which the various indigenous societies should, or should not, be influenced by the Europeans was often debated by the Spaniards. Some argued that the indigenous peoples should be assimilated as a source of labor and commerce, expecting that they should fully adopt Iberian ways of life. Others—for example, the first generation of evangelists—argued that corrupting Iberian influences should be kept away from Indians. They advocated the formation of Indian utopias, protected areas in which indigenous languages and traditions could flourish and into which the Spanish (except for missionaries) should not be allowed to intrude.

In the Americas, the tongue of Castile encountered hundreds of indigenous languages and dialects, and it did not always win out as the sole vehicle for communication. Many Indian languages, such as Náhuatl, actually gained in influence by being written down in the Roman alphabet and used in a wide variety of settings: religious instruction, theater, lawsuits, wills, music, and poetry. The early missionaries, in particular, were assiduous in learning native languages—especially Náhuatl, which they considered the lingua franca of Mesoamerica—and wrote grammars of eleven indigenous languages for use in translating religious materials.[28] Thanks to these linguistic efforts, the Castilian language for a time did not become predominant, and indigenous languages flourished. In a process lasting three centuries, Indians learned Spanish, but Europeans also learned indigenous terms for native plants, animals, foods, and social behaviors.

The Crown's Catholicism likewise confronted the diverse religious beliefs of the different indigenous societies. Some key Catholic beliefs—finding salvation in community, the importance of ritual, the sacramentality of life's events—proved to be critical points of convergence with indigenous traditions. This convergence and blending of European Catholic and indigenous spirituality can be seen, for example, in the reported apparition in 1531 of the Virgin of Guadalupe to the Náhuatl-speaking Indian Juan Diego (canonized by the church in 2002). Not coincidentally, the brown-skinned, Náhuatl-speaking Virgin Mary happened to appear at a spot where the Aztec goddess Tonantzin (Our Mother) had been worshipped for centuries.[29] For nearly three centuries, efforts to inculcate Western Catholicism into indigenous religious experience yielded a vigorous publishing industry in Náhuatl, producing narratives, plays, music, and poetry in that tongue, as well as in Castilian Spanish and Latin.

African Arrivals

Under Spanish rule, people also arrived from Africa. A few came as voluntary members of Spain's multiracial, multilingual armed forces. One west African, for instance, traveled to Seville, where he became a Christian and took the name Juan Garrido, then in 1503 crossed the Atlantic to Santo Domingo, where he helped "discover and pacify" the islands of San Juan de Buriqén de

Puerto Rico and Cuba. In 1519, he joined Hernán Cortés in the campaign against the Aztec Empire. Subsequently, Garrido introduced the cultivation of wheat to the Americas.[30] Most Africans, however, came as slaves, primarily from the west African regions of Angola, Bakongo, and Terra Nova. In Mexico, they usually became Christians; they formed families who were protected to an extent by Catholic canon law, and these publicly acknowledged family roles gave them an identity beyond being slaves.[31] During the colonial period, free Afro-Mexican males formed units of free-colored militia whose officers and enlisted men were all of African origin.[32] Along with food items and religious practices, these Afro-Mexicans also contributed musical rhythms such as the *fandango, bamba,* and *huapango.*[33]

Asian Settlers

In 1565, Miguel López de Legazpí sailed from Acapulco to Manila and back, thus initiating 250 years of travel and trade relations between Asia and Mexico.[34] During that period, an estimated forty to one hundred thousand Asians, mostly arriving via Acapulco, settled in Mexico. They were primarily Filipinos, Chinese, Japanese, Malays, and Moghuls, but smaller numbers came from virtually every region in Asia. Once in New Spain, they settled in three areas. In Acapulco, Asian immigrants and their offspring formed an Asian militia and served alongside Afro-Mexican and Spanish militias. In Mexico City, Asian immigrants dominated the barbershop trade. In Puebla, Asian immigrants participated in the ceramic industry.[35]

The formation of a mixed-race society in Spain's colonies in the Americas was facilitated by the epidemiology of the conquest, especially by smallpox, which was unwittingly unleashed on a population that had no related immune defenses. The ravages of epidemic *cocolixtli* (probably smallpox) took the lives of an estimated 95% of the indigenous population of Mexico over the course of the sixteenth century, reducing that population from an estimated 25.2 million to 1.1 million between 1519 and 1609.[36] By 1646, a mestizo population had emerged in the region from Mexico City to Chiapas and Yucatan. Of the nearly 2 million people counted, Europeans were the distinct minority, comprising less than 1% of all inhabitants of south-central New Spain; Africans outnumbered them by a ratio of more than two to one. Nearly a quarter (23.1%) of the population was of mixed race, in various combinations of Indian, African, European, and Asian. But even though their numbers had been greatly reduced by disease, the vast majority, 74.3%, were still of indigenous origin.[37] A new, diverse population—the mestizo, the offspring of Indian, African, Spaniard, and Asian—began to repopulate the country. Ultimately, the various waves of *cocolixtli* created an indigenous population vacuum in New Spain, filled by a growing mestizo population, and may be said to have created, by extension, the population dynamics of twenty-first-century California. Mestizo society was more than just a bridge, or mediator society, between the Spanish and Indian; it was a fusion of peoples from four continents. With apologies to Carlos Fuentes, I have coined the somewhat awkward but descriptive term "Indo-Afro-Oriento-Ibero-American" to refer to this mixed-race population.[38]

Meaning in mestizo society was created and sustained by two main sources: the formal, institutional church, and popular Catholicism, independent of, but linked to, the institutional church. Often called "popular religion" or "popular spirituality,"[39] Latino faith expressions are "those religious traditions which the majority of a people celebrate voluntarily, transmit from generation to generation . . . with the clergy, without them, or even in spite of them."[40] Of the two, more important to daily life was popular Catholicism, in which an unconscious welding of pre-Columbian and African moral discourses with pre-Tridentine Catholicism was largely unaffected by the search for individual perfection prompted in Europe by Martin Luther and John Calvin. Mestizo popular religion built on indigenous and African rituals, and on Iberian popular cults of saints. Reinforced only occasionally by the formal sacramental life of the institutional church, the mestizo worldview—what was desirable or undesirable, acceptable or unacceptable, beautiful or ugly, good or bad—was built up over centuries of everyday life. Nearly five hundred years of civil society in Mexico has been rooted in this worldview, or moral-spiritual matrix.

This demographic and cultural formation of mestizo society was repeated up and down Latin America. There were, naturally, regional variations, depending on the characteristics of the local indigenous society, and on genetics; some parts of Latin America have a larger indigenous genetic heritage, others more European or African heritage, and most have a soupçon of Asian, as well. Yet despite such local variations—in which one is not merely Mexican, but is a *poblano* from Puebla, a *jarocho* from Veracruz, a *tapatío* from Guadalajara, and so forth—the overarching presence of formal and informal Catholic religion provided a basis of continuity from region to region.

In his magisterial study of persistence, continuity, and change in four British folkways in modern American society, Fischer noted that, as they expanded across the North American continent, these regional British cultures interacted with each other, and with other distinctive cultural groups, such as American Indians, African Americans, and subsequent immigrant groups, evolving into seven regional American identities.

Working his way across the US, Fischer noticed that one region was very different from all the others: he briefly described the "Southern California" region—which he extended to include Nevada, Arizona, and New Mexico— as the meeting place of two British folkways, Highland southern and midland, with Hispanic culture. He also noted that speech patterns in this region combine Appalachian and midland speech "with many Hispanic expressions."[41] Apart from this brief note about speech ways, however, Fischer did not delve any further into this regional American identity.

My research indicates that twenty-first-century Latino civil society in California was constructed in three phases. The "charter group" phase (1769–1848) saw the arrival and implantation of Western society, in its Indo-Afro-Oriento-Ibero-American form, in California. In the "ethnogenesis" phase (1848–1869), the descendants of the charter group, together with new immigrants from Mexico and Central and South America, contested and negotiated a situation of being bilingual, bicultural citizens of the newly imposed institutions of the United States. During the "Latino civil society" phase (1869–present), the charter group's descendants, joined by those of six successive waves of immigration from Mexico, Central America, and South America, have had to continuously contest and renegotiate their place in America.

The Charter Group Phase (1769–1848)

The charter group that brought Western society to California spoke Spanish. The civilians and soldiers who laid the foundations of Latino civil society were largely of very humble origin, the lower ranks of Iberian colonial society: Indians, Africans, mestizos, and mulattoes. Most had been poor farmers and ranchers in northern Mexico, so poor that they volunteered to leave their hardscrabble holdings in Sonora, Sinaloa, and Culiacán to travel to the unknown frontier of Alta California for what they hoped would be a better life. From 1769 to 1781, the Spanish Crown recruited such groups of settlers in northern Mexico for California, a tightly organized first wave of population movement from the rest of Mexico to this state. While the purpose of the Crown in organizing this first wave of migration to California was to fend off Russian and British claims to this northern frontier of New Spain, the settlers themselves came to California hoping for a better life for themselves and their families.

Basilio Rosas and his family, part of the group who founded Los Angeles in 1781, provide an example of the racial mixture of the charter group. Rosas was born in Villa de Nombre de Dios in Durango, and was listed as an "Indio" (Indian) in the roll call of settlers.[42] By designating him an Indian, the list implied that he had been born into an indigenous community to indigenous parents, raised on indigenous foods, and taught to speak an indigenous language in addition to Spanish. At some point in his life, however, he had entered Western society by being baptized into the Catholic Church. On the Sundays that he attended mass, he would have become aware of some basic legends of Western culture: the fall of Adam and Eve, the wandering of the tribes of Israel, the nativity of the Messiah, and the cruelty of Roman centurions. He would have made his responses to the mass in Latin, repeating phrases in a language spoken by the creators of the Pax Romana nearly two thousand years earlier. His wife, María Manuela Calixta Hernández, was listed as a "Mulata" (mulatto woman). This implied that some of her ancestors had survived the middle passage from Africa to New Spain, had become members of Western society via baptism, had achieved freedom for themselves or their children, and had had offspring with either Iberian or Indian partners.[43] And so the mixed-race Rosas, and their even more mixed-race children—José Máximo, Carlos, Antonio Rosalino, José Marcelino, Juan Estéban, and María Josefa—shared their ancestors' Meso-American, African, and Iberian heritages, and were among the carriers of Western society to California. The *pueblos* (civilian settlements) and *presidios* (military bases) of Alta California were brought to life by this first wave of similarly racially mixed, Spanish-speaking, Catholic subjects of the Spanish Crown. They built houses, planted fields, and tended flocks and herds, their lives framed by the Ibero-Catholic version of Western civilization. They had children, who in turn had children.

Mexico gained independence from Spain in 1810–1821, and its new government sent a second wave of migration, recruited from Mexico City and

Guadalajara, to join the first wave of the charter group in California in 1834. Members of that 1834 Hijar-Padrés colony joined and expanded the society formed by the first wave, and these Mexican citizens went about their daily lives for another half-generation, until major political events intervened.

The Ethnogenesis Phase (1848–1869)

On the evening of February 1, 1848, approximately ten thousand charter group settlers and their descendants in California went to sleep as citizens of the Republic of Mexico. Over the previous eighty years, the life they had created for themselves in Alta California was simply a regional variant of Mexican society and identity. They spoke Spanish, ate the traditional foods of Mexico, and raised cattle in traditional Ibero-Mexican ways—and the adult males among them participated in both their local and the national government of Mexico—all with slight regional variations peculiar to California. They were Californios. When they awoke the next morning, however, they had become—putatively, at least—citizens of the United States of America, a country that held out to them both the promise of the universalist definition of "American," based the ideals of equality, freedom and democracy, and the Anglo-Saxonist definition that sought to deny them full membership as Americans because of their racial origin, religion, and language.

The Manifest Destiny that had prompted the clash of arms between Mexico and the US in the Mexican-American War had also just blasted the charter group into a new orbit. The Californios were no longer to construct meaning in their lives as part of Mexico, but instead would have to create that meaning as Latinos living in the US. The US acquisition and colonization of California caused profound ruptures and changes in the daily lives of both the conquered Spanish speakers and the conquering English speakers, yet considerable continuity persisted at the same time. The changes constructed by the charter group during the California Gold Rush and American Civil War form a case study in the field of ethnogenesis: the ongoing transformations of social identities catalyzed by the meeting of two or more cultural groups.

Ethnogenesis offers an alternative theoretical model to the more linear acculturation and assimilation models.[44] Following the lead of Singer's study of the transformation of African American culture and Sturtevant's demonstration of how Creek Indians turned themselves into Seminoles,[45] I here briefly sketch conclusions drawn from my demographic research on Latinos from 1848 to 1869, which have led me to use the model of ethnogenesis to better understand Latino agency in their situation of subaltern, conquered status in California in this period. Their situation as a conquered population was exacerbated by being mixed-race, Spanish-speaking Catholics confronted by a vast immigration of white, English-speaking Protestants and their institutions, the majority of whom subscribed to a greater or lesser degree of Anglo-Saxonist belief. The process of ethnogenesis offers a conceptual lens for understanding how Latinos transformed themselves under these conditions of racial discrimination and blatant attempts at economic marginalization, from Mexican citizens into their own version of full American citizens.[46]

This book began, in chapter 1, in the first days of the ethnogenesis phase, with José Antonio Carrillo rising to speak during the 1849 California Constitutional Convention to contest the assumption that he, as a former Mexican citizen, was not American. Chapter 1 illustrates how Latinos contested the Atlantic American nativist sentiment that sought to exclude them from American citizenship and identity, both on the institutional level of political campaigns and legislation, and on a more basic social level, for the next century and more. Even as Carrillo was speaking in 1849, however, tens of thousands of immigrants from Mexico, Central America, and South America were pouring into California, attracted by the chance of finding gold: a third wave of Spanish-speaking immigrants.

Along the Pacific coast, these new arrivals generally settled among the previously established Spanish-speaking population, mingling, trading, and worshipping with them in San Francisco, San José, Sacramento, Los Angeles, Santa Barbara, San Luis Obispo, Santa Cruz, and many smaller towns and settlements. As they ranged into the Gold Country, these Latino newcomers often stopped at nuclei founded by Spanish-speaking miners, which grew into towns and camps in the Sierra Nevada, such as Sonora, Hornitos, Jesus Maria, Melones, Vallecitos, Calaveras, Marmolitos, Banderitas, San Andreas, Lancha Plana, Rancho Amador, Greasertown, Spanish Flat, and Chile Gulch. As they lived and worked together, the Spanish speakers found partners, married, and had children. Far from disappearing—as traditional narratives of California history would have it—Latinos in fact grew in number. This is evidenced, for example, by the increase of the annual number of Latino babies born in Los Angeles, which tripled from two hundred in 1850 to six hundred in 1869.[47]

While the adults, both charter group descendants and recently arrived third-wave immigrants, struggled to learn English, their children picked it up easily, speaking it effortlessly in school while continuing to speak Spanish with their parents at home. Yet even as early as the Gold Rush, the adults were so surrounded by English that they incorporated some English words into their daily speech. The editor of a Spanish-language newspaper, reporting the wedding of an Atlantic American colleague, employed code-switching in his article, saying that he thanked his friend for giving him "una parte del 'wedding cake,'" assuming that his Spanish-speaking readers would know that phrase in English.[48] Newspapers were published in Spanish in California from 1851 on; but by 1859, at least one paper, *El Clamor Público* in Los Angeles, had added a page in English to help Latinos learn to read both English and Spanish.[49] The adults continued celebrating Mexican holidays they had known as children, such as Mexican Independence Day on the 16th of September and the Day of the Dead, or All Souls' Day.[50] Yet they and their children also incorporated new celebrations, such as the Fourth of July and Thanksgiving.[51] Navidad and Christmas naturally resonated with each other, and the new custom of Christmas trees was added to households that already enjoyed *guajolote de Navidad* (Christmas turkey).[52]

In spite of nativist grumbling about their "foreign" speech and customs, Latinos claimed their rights as American citizens. Their claim was sorely tested when the American Civil War broke out in 1861, followed by the invasion of Mexico in 1862 by Napoleon III of France, attempting to overthrow Mexico's democratically elected government. The majority of California's Latinos felt a primary loyalty to the universalist concepts of freedom, equality, and self-government, and supported both US president Lincoln and Mexican president Juárez in their parallel battles against slavery and monarchy. Latinos flocked to the colors: some to the United States Army, Navy, and Cavalry, to fight against slavery; others to the Mexican Army, fighting to preserve government of the people, by the people, and for the people in Mexico.[53]

The rebelling slave states enjoyed considerable military success in the early stages of the US Civil War, and by early summer 1862, they hoped that their self-proclaimed new government might be recognized by at least one European monarch. Napoleon III coyly hinted at recognizing the Confederate States of America as he sent his troops into Mexico to overthrow Juárez's government and replace it with a monarchy grateful to France. This, Napoleon hoped, would halt the spread of both US influence and the universalist American values of liberty and democratic self-government in the western hemisphere. Mexico's monarch then might make whatever arrangement he and his French patron might find useful with the Confederate

States of America, with which the projected Empire of Mexico would share a 1,500-mile border. This French invasion of Mexico pushed a fourth wave of immigration out of that country and into California, in 1862–1867, primarily political refugees: Mexican citizens unwilling, or unable, to pledge allegiance to a French-imposed monarch.

When news arrived in California on May 27, 1862, that the French had been stopped cold at the Battle of Puebla on May 5 and would not be able to assist the Confederate States of America, Latinos signaled their place as full citizens of the US by creating a new US holiday: the commemoration of Cinco de Mayo. This became an annual event, informing the world that Latinos supported Lincoln in the great Civil War, opposed slavery and supported freedom, opposed white supremacy and supported racial equality, and opposed elitist rule and supported democratic government.[54] By the end of the American Civil War and the French Intervention in Mexico, the transformation of California's Latinos from Mexican citizens into US citizens was essentially complete. They had provided ample demonstration of their support of the universalist ideals of equality, freedom, and democracy that undergirded America.

Latino Civil Society in California, 1869–2015

By the 1870s, the first cohort of children born to the charter group's descendants and to post-1848 immigrant parents had grown into bilingual, bicultural adulthood, and began to have their own children, the first cohort of third-generation Latinos born in California. In contrast to the widespread replacement of their natal languages by English among European immigrant groups arriving on the Atlantic coast in the same period, the Spanish language has thrived in California, alongside English, for over 160 years, ever since the ethnogenesis phase began. Today, the Latin Grammys for Latino music are hugely successful. Large chains of grocery stores devote themselves to providing specialty food products for the Latino market. Why has there been such a difference, 150 years later, between the fortunes of Serbian immigrant enclaves and Latino civil society, into which more than 50% of the babies in California are now being born? A major reason is that the Latinos of the charter group that established Western society in California in the eighteenth century, and their descendants, have been joined by successive waves of immigration from Mexico and Latin America, whose members consistently replenish their language patterns and other folkways.

My demographic research has identified four subsequent waves of immigration that arrived during the period 1869 to 2015. The builders, in 1890–1910, provided a lot of the muscle that developed California from a sparsely populated frontier to an urban, industrial economy during the Gilded Age. Refugees from the Mexican Revolution, in 1910–1930, fled the disruption that caused nearly a million deaths in Mexico. The braceros, in 1942–1964, originally were guest workers, not immigrants per se, who provided agricultural labor to California during the severe manpower shortage of World War II, to feed millions of US soldiers and factory workers. Finally, the immigration reform immigrants, in 1965–1990, were largely coterminous with the braceros, who were able to change their status to immigrants after US immigration laws were reformed in 1965, along with Central American refugees fleeing that region's civil wars in the 1980s.

In the 170 years between the incorporation of California into the US in 1848 and the writing of this update in 2016, these six waves of immigration from Mexico to the state have replenished Latino civil society's folkways roughly every twenty-five years. The members of these six waves, along with their children and grandchildren, have joined previously established Latinos in their defiance of being perceived as "not American." Latino civil society has provided not only place-names now world-famous—San Francisco, San José, San Diego, Los Angeles—but also patterns of daily behavior that have formed the core of social life for Latino babies born in the state for nearly 250 years. Temporarily overshadowed by a century of Atlantic American numerical dominance, Latino civil society once again provides a framework for behaviors that may come to be seen as "typical California behavior" by the middle of this century. Latino civil society will be at the center of a new regional American identity.

EIGHT

Latino Post-Millennials

LATINOS HAVE BEEN CONSTRUCTING a Latino civil society in California since 1769, when the charter group of settlers brought the Indo-Afro-Oriento-Ibero version of Western society to Alta California. For nearly 250 years since then, their descendants, augmented by successive waves of migration from Mexico and Central and South America, have created the bilingual, bicultural civil society extant in today's California. So far this book has analyzed the past seventy-five years (1940–2015) of this Latino civil society as it produced distinctive, and unexpected, patterns of work, family, health, and social behaviors. Since 2001, about half of the babies born in the state have been born to Latino families. As toddlers, young children, and adolescents, they have received their primary socialization in these families, in California's Latino civil society. In 2015, they are on the cusp of adulthood, about to engage in higher education, employment, business creation, and the formation of their own families. What kind of California society will these Latino young adults create by 2040? This chapter uses the framework of "generations research" to inform its attempts to glimpse into the near future. To illustrate the basic concepts of this type of research, I begin with a survey of the familiar baby boom generation, which in turn will help us understand the ways in which today's young Latinos likely will influence California during the rest of the twenty-first century.

GENERATIONS AND SOCIETY

The baby boom generation began to arrive in the US nine months after its soldiers returned home from World War II. After nearly thirty previous years of falling birth rates, suddenly many more babies were being born. At the peak of the baby boom in the late 1950s, nearly 4 million babies were born each year in the US, compared to just a little over 2 million in the 1920s and 1930s. The baby boomers' appearance motivated the country to invest in building an educational infrastructure for them; and as the boomers progressed through grade school, high school, and in many cases college, the country followed their antics, from Davy Crockett caps and hula hoops to psychedelic music. Baby boomers appeared to think and behave very differently from their parents, who had soldiered on during World War II without much questioning of the war or their society. Boomers seemed determined to remake America in their own image, and questioned war, authority, love, and peace.

Then, in 1965, the number of births per year started to fall, to nearly 3 million a year by the mid-1970s. Demographers gave these two birth events simple, demographically descriptive names: the "baby boom," followed by the "baby bust," the latter a generation that lived its life in the shadow of the baby boom. A 1991 novel gave that group a nickname, based on their social-psychological experience: *Generation X: Tales for an Accelerated Culture*.[1] And once the baby boomers became adults, beginning in the mid-1960s, they, in turn, had their babies, in what demographers called an "echo boom," as they were the demographic echo of the original baby boom. Once these "echo boomers" started to come of age, about the year 2000, they were dubbed the "millennials."

Baby boomers, generation Xers, millennials—when social researchers noticed that each generation had different values and behaviors, compared to the previous one, the field of "generations research" was created, in which researchers use generational grouping to track the values, attitudes, and behavior of a group of people closely linked in age over the course of their lives. Political polls, consumer surveys, and television viewing habits have become increasingly associated with the concept of generations research. In a 2015 report, for example, researchers from the Pew Research Center summarized the changes very simply: "Millennials are currently the least conservative generation. . . . Baby Boomers . . . express consistently or mostly conservative views."[2]

Researchers have been tracking the millennials since 2002, noting a fairly regular generational change in values and behaviors.[3] In their 2015 report on generations and research, the Pew researchers noted that each generation typically had a fifteen- to twenty-year span of membership, then mused about what might come after the millennial generation. They already had a name for it: the post-millennial generation. But they were unsure what would

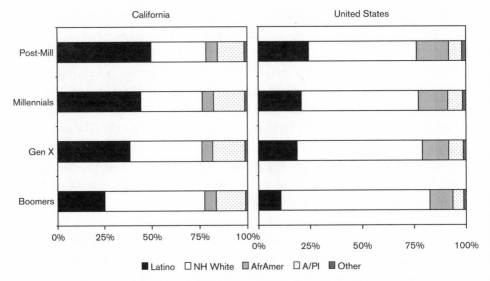

FIGURE 29. Race/ethnic composition by generation, for California and the United States, 2015. Source: Schink custom analysis, data from Flood et al., IPUMS CPS (2015).

distinguish post-millennials from millennials. The Pew report could see no "single indicator or an 'aha' moment that would mark the end of the Millennial generation."[4]

I, however, would like to offer just such an "aha" moment, one that has been the focus of my research for nearly forty years: the noticeable shift in the racial/ethnic composition of the generations born after the baby boom, which in California and other states has already given us the new generation: the Latino post-millennial generation. Figure 29 shows these four generations in California, each one disaggregated into its racial/ethnic components, as of 2015. The national version of each generation is also shown, which allows us to see how different the generations have become in California as compared to the rest of the US.

The baby boom generation in the US is overwhelmingly non-Hispanic white (71.6%), and Latinos make up only about one-tenth (10.7%) of baby boomers nationally. In California, non-Hispanic whites comprise a comfortable majority (52.4%) of baby boomers, and Latinos are about one-quarter (25.2%). Generation X, at the national level, is also largely non-Hispanic white (60.3%), and only one-sixth (18.6%) Latino. By contrast, in California, generation X has no majority racial/ethnic group. In fact, the non-Hispanic white (37.6%) and Latino (38.7%) groups are nearly equal in size. The millennial generation, at the national level, is still majority non-Hispanic white (56.3%), with Latinos making up barely one-fifth (20.8%); but California's millennial generation is quite different, in that non-Hispanic whites comprise only one-third (32.2%), whereas Latinos comprise almost half (44.5%).

In the post-millennial generation, however, the future has already arrived in California: in this state, the new majority is Latino (50.0%). With the addition of African Americans (5.9%) and Asians and others (15.5%), nearly three-fourths of the post-millennials (71.4%) are what used to be called "minorities." Non-Hispanic whites make up just over one-fourth of the post-millennials in California (28.7%). Even at the national level, the future is not far away; non-Hispanic whites make up about half (51.8%) of this generation, while Latinos (24.4%), African Americans (15.4%), and Asians and others (8.4%), combined, form close to the other half of post-millennials. Post-millennials in California are thus largely neither the children of the non-Hispanic white generation X nor the grandchildren of non-Hispanic white baby boomers, but instead are the children of Latino parents who are, in turn, the product of 250 years of Latino civil society in California. Researchers of America's generations will need to take this fact into consideration.

FORMATIVE EXPERIENCES OF THE GENERATIONS

One way to define a generation is to consider its exposure to shared "formative experiences" when its members were adolescents and young adults. These social-psychological formative experiences have their greatest impact on members of a generation just when their "awareness of the wider world deepens and personal identities and value systems are being strongly shaped." As the members of a generation progress through their life cycle as young adults, middle-aged parents, and retired pensioners, the influence of their formative experiences continues to color their values, attitudes, and behaviors.[5] The formative experiences of three generations—baby boomers, generation Xers, and millennials—have been well described by researchers, and are summarized below.

Atlantic American Formative Experiences

The Baby Boom Generation (1945–1964). The formative experiences of the baby boom generation included being the first generation who were largely raised in the new suburbs and who were exposed to television all their lives. They also experienced, either firsthand or vicariously, the Civil Rights movement, the divisiveness of the Vietnam War, the Summer of Love, and violent social conflict in urban America.

Generation X (1965–1980). Generation Xers lived in the shadow of the "mammoth Boomer generation" before them, and the "behemoth Millennial generation" behind them." Many of them had formative experiences of being part of "blended families" due to increased divorce and remarriage rates, and of being "latchkey" children, as in many households both parents had to work. They entered the age of sexual activity just as the AIDS epidemic broke out.[6]

The Millennial Generation (1981–1995). Children of the baby boomers, the members of the millennial generation initially were called "digital natives," as one of their formative experiences was having computers, the Internet, and smart phones as fundamental features of their daily lives. Their highly educated baby boomer parents were actively involved in their children's education and development, to the point of being satirized as "helicopter parents" constantly hovering over their children and rescuing them from their difficulties.

Latino Post-Millennial Formative Experiences

Given the predominance of Latinos in the post-millennial generation in California, we need to understand the formative experiences of Latino adolescents and young adults born from 1995 through 2015 in order to understand how the post-millennial generation in the Golden State will likely respond in the rest of the twenty-first century. Even at this early stage of Latino post-millennial emergence, some major formative experiences can be identified. No doubt they will be augmented by additional formative experiences during the period 2015 to 2030.

- They *are not the children of non-Hispanic white generation X or the grandchildren of non-Hispanic white baby boomers.* While the Pew Research Center considers millennials to be the children of baby boomers, by and large the post-millennials in California are not the grandchildren of baby boomers or the children of generation X. Therefore one cannot extrapolate from baby boomers or generation Xers to understand the formative experiences of Latino post-millennials.

- Latino *post-millennials are the descendants of eight waves of immigration.* As noted in chapter 7, the most recent of eight waves of immigration from Mexico and Central America to California occurred from 1965 to 1990. Latino post-millennials are, by and large, those immigrants' children. This means that, as children, they constructed their knowledge of American society and culture from their experience, and their parents' experience, as the heirs to 250 years of Latino civil society in California. Their secondary socialization into more general American society began only in grade school.

- They *were born in the US.* While the popular public conception of Latinos is that most are immigrants, the fact is that nearly all Latino post-millennials (94.3%) were born in the United States.[7]

- They *form a Latino majority, with a non-Hispanic white minority.* Earlier generations, at the national level, have been predominantly non-Hispanic white (from 71.8% to 51.8%), so the formative experiences of each generation were largely those of the majority, non-Hispanic white members. The post-millennial generation in California, however, is predominantly Latino (50.0%), and non-Hispanic white post-millennials are a minority (28.7%). In some parts of the state, such as Los Angeles, the Latino post-millennial majority is even larger (59.4%) and the non-Hispanic white minority even smaller (16.4%). Unlike the Chicano generation, whose formative experiences often included the situation of being the "only brown face in the room," Latino post-millennials often have the experience of brown faces being the vast majority in their classrooms.

- They *tend to be first-generation university students.* Unlike the highly educated millennials, who are the children of highly educated baby boomer parents, Latino post-millennials are, by and large, the highly educated children of far less educated parents, many of whom did not even graduate from high school. In spite of this low parental educational attainment, nearly 70% of Latino post-millennial high school graduates are going on to higher education.[8] As a result, they mostly have not had the experience of hovering parents providing support as they grew up, offering summer enrichment activities, access to private counselors and tutoring, and assistance filling out the multitudes of forms for admission to higher education.

- They *are the target of nativists' attacks.* From the day they were born, Latino post-millennials have been the target of ongoing attacks, as the embodiment of the alleged threat that the "illegal alien" poses to the US, as viewed through the lenses of Anglo-Saxonism and the new nativism. As detailed in chapter 5, the construct of the "illegal alien" or "illegal immigrant" was used to underpin the notion of an "invasion," largely of Mexican origin, which threatened to drown the state in social problems unless deterred by the provisions of Proposition 187. US-born Latinos perceived the "dog whistle" effect of this anti-illegal immigrant rhetoric, in which "illegal immigrant" and "Mexican" were used virtually interchangeably, and understood that it was really about Latino presence in California.

As Latino post-millennials in California are largely the children of the eighth wave of immigration from Mexico to the state, they, too, have heard this anti-Latino rhetoric since they were born. A 2014 Pew report estimated that 6.9% of school-age children in the US live with an undocumented parent.[9] Applying their figures to California, I estimate that about one out of every four Latino post-millennials in California—over 94% of whom are US-born—lives with an undocumented adult in the household. Birth records show that around two-thirds of Latino post-millennials born in California have an immigrant—although not necessarily an undocumented—mother. The birth record provides no information on the nativity of the father, so we cannot estimate presence of immigrant fathers.[10] So when public figures talk about the undesirability of undocumented immigrants, it hits close to home for the Latino post-millennial generation.

This twenty-first-century nativism often confuses perceived "foreign" and "criminal" characteristics with "immigrant" characteristics. The impression left by the Proposition 187 campaign in 1994 was not only that most Latinos were immigrants, but also that they were "illegal immigrants" whose presence was causing all manner of social disruption. As a result, many twenty-first-century anti-immigrant groups tend to attack undocumented immigrants, documented immigrants, and all Latinos indiscriminantly. For example, a talk radio duo known as Ken and John, hosts of a conservative radio show in Southern California, on the evening of July 30, 2008, referred to "illegal alien ... Honduran crack dealers," and then enlarged the focus of their anti-immigrant commentary to "the Mexicans," who, they alleged, suffer from obesity because "the Mexican diet is what's shot up the obesity rates in Los Angeles," particularly in "these areas ... now taken over by the Mexicans."[11] The intent of the term "illegal alien" was to call up a mental model, used by anti-immigrant discourse since 1993, which framed their following comments for their audi-ence. The way these talk show hosts used the term *Mexican* was very broad, potentially including undocumented immigrants from Mexico, legal perma-nent resident immigrants from Mexico, and ninth-generation Mexican Americans whose families have lived in Southern California for over 240 years. Such nativist attacks at times even resort to language suggesting that physical violence might be used to stop alleged "Mexican invaders." In 2006, before he was elected as a Republican state assemblyman, Tim Donnelly—then a mem-ber of the Minutemen, an anti-immigrant vigilante group—made a speech in which he claimed to be a descendant of Jim Bowie, who had died at the Alamo in Texas, but only after "he took a dozen Mexican soldiers to their deaths before they finally killed him." Donnelly then asked his audience, "How many of you will rise up and take his place on that wall?"[12]

Due to their sheer numbers, Latino post-millennials will help determine the values, attitudes, and behaviors of the post-millennial generation as a whole. They are heirs to 250 years of Latino civil society in California. Compared to their mostly immigrant parents, they will be highly educated, but they also will have experienced being the target of anti-immigrant nativ-ist attacks all their lives. This is the future of California.

LATINO POST-MILLENNIALS ON CAMPUS

"Hispanic High School Graduates Pass Whites in Rate of College Enrollment," the Pew Research Center announced in 2013. Nearly seven out of ten (69%) of Latinos in the nation who graduated from high school in 2012 enrolled in college in the fall of that same year, two percentage points higher than the 67% of non-Hispanic whites who also graduated and then enrolled in college.[13] The same report also noted that the Hispanic high school drop-out rate had hit a record low. When the Public Policy Institute of California asked a sample of adults if they thought that "a college education is necessary for a person to be successful in today's work world," Latinos were far more likely (80%) to agree than were non-Hispanic whites (50%).[14] Clearly, college education is an important topic for Latinos in California. The leading edge of the Latino post-millennial generation is already entering the state's college campuses. It would, therefore, be prudent to understand their formative experiences relating to education and campus life.

For all their optimism about higher education, Latinos, on the whole, have been poorly served by California's public education system. From 2001 on, while Latino post-millennials were in grade school, approximately half of all Latino and African American students were enrolled in low-performing schools, while only about a tenth of non-Hispanic white students and 15% of Asian American students were. Approximately a quarter of Latino and African American students were in overcrowded schools, as opposed to only 4% of non-Hispanic whites.[15]

In spite of these obstacles, Latino post-millennials have been enrolling in postsecondary education at significant rates. In the fall of 2012, nearly two-thirds (65%) of Latino post-millennials enrolling in college for the first time matriculated at one of California's 113 community colleges.[16] These institutions were developed and expanded as part of the 1960 California Master Plan in Higher Education to provide access to higher education for all who wished to continue their studies, without grade-point average or SAT score requirements.[17] Another 16% enrolled in one of the state's twenty-seven California State University (CSU) campuses, which are selective in their enrollments, generally requiring a 3.0 high school grade-point average out of a possible 4.0 for freshman admission without minimum SAT or other test scores.[18] Only 6% enrolled in one of the ten highly selective University of California campuses. Freshmen admitted to highly competitive UCLA in 2015, for example, mostly had GPAs ranging from 3.7 to 4.3.[19]

Intellectual Life

A common complaint of the Chicano generation, as noted in chapter 5, was that their high school curricula rarely offered any material on Latinos in California history or contemporary society. Even in the twenty-first century, high school curricula rarely include any Latino-centric materials. Nearly every community college, CSU, and UC campus, however, as well as many private universities, offers courses in Chicano/Latino studies; and enrollment in these courses has surged in recent years. I interact with three to four hundred Latino undergraduates every year, from a variety of campuses—community colleges and CSU campuses, in addition to UCLA—and I frequently hear what an eye-opener their first courses in Chicano/Latino studies have been to them. I teach one undergraduate course at UCLA, about the health of Latino populations and communities, with an enrollment of 120 students. Comments on the course evaluations for my class in 2015 were typical of the comments I have heard over the twenty years I have taught this class.

Knowledge. The most common comment was that the students had gained knowledge about Latinos and their role in US history, society, and policy to which they had not been exposed previously. One student noted, "I have learned so much about my ancestors, my identity, and . . . health policies affecting the nation."

Attitudes. Literature on leadership development states that a potential leader's self-awareness is the starting point for authenticity in clarifying values and for a vision that will inspire team members. The first step in such self-awareness is introspection, but an immediate second step is to include the "looking-glass self," seen in the responses of others, including both team members and the larger society. Integrating images created by self, group, and society yields a comprehensive self-awareness; once that has been acquired, a leader does not have to try to inspire team members by imitating the values and visions of someone else.[20] Between the lack of content about Latinos in elementary and high school and the high levels of nativist rhetoric in the media, many Latino students have not had much opportunity to become very self-aware until they take a Chicano studies course. One student hinted at having begun this process of self-awareness: "I learned a lot about history, health, and what it means to be Latino."

Behavior. The production of new knowledge requires that researchers be stimulated to think new thoughts. Chicano studies courses often provide a place for future researchers to link new knowledge to their growing self-awareness, and to start to think new thoughts. One student indicated that this process of linkage had begun in my class: "The info makes you think in depth and question what we have always been taught." Or as another student put it, "It was always exciting to learn something new about Latino culture and health. It made me think in ways I had never thought before."

Not Just for Latinos. While my course is on the health of Latino populations in California, it is not meant for Latino students alone. Indeed, as half the juvenile population in twenty-first-century California is Latino, one should think of it as a course in the health of mainstream California. Thus, non-Latino students taking my class learn about health in the state as a whole, not just the health of any particular population. One student said, "As a non-Latino, I learned a very large amount about Latinos in America." Another non-Latino student had integrated the knowledge into a growing self-awareness: "I'm not Latino, but I have grown such a great appreciation for the culture. . . . Great reminder why I chose to minor in Spanish."

Social Life

Since the 1960s, Latinos on state campuses have created a vibrant social life and cultural activities. Some organizations established by the Chicano generation still function, nearly fifty years later. Some provide an outlet for artistic endeavor, such as the Grupo Folklórico de UCLA (established 1966) or Mariachi UCLATLAN (1963). Others are pre-professional groups, such as Chicanos/Latinos for Community Medicine (CCM, 1969) and the Society of Hispanic Engineers and Scientists (SHPS, 1978). The Movimiento Estudiantil Chicano de Aztlan (MECHA, 1970) is a student political organization. Graduate students also have long-established organizations, such as the Latino Medical Student Association (LMSA, descendant of the National Chicano Health Organization, 1970), the Raza Graduate Student Association (1985), and the Raza Law Student Association (1985).

Since the 1990s, a new generation of Latino sororities and fraternities has taken off. These offer some of the trappings of the classic "Greek" life, such as rushes, initiations, and an active social calendar that includes attendance at campus sporting events. But a major feature of Latino sororities and fraternities is their focus on Latino policy issues, such as combatting racial micro-aggressions on campus, participating in voter registration drives, volunteering in community organizations' activities, and supporting the activities of undocumented immigrant students on campus.

Childhood Arrival: Undocumented Life on Campus

During the US Civil War, the Immigration Act of 1864 threw open America's doors to all comers, with no restrictions on origin or numbers, except for Asians, who were specifically excluded by subsequent legislation between 1875 and the middle of the twentieth century. In the US, before 1921, there was no such thing as an "undocumented immigrant"; meeting a national-origin quota or obtaining a visa was not part of America's immigration process until the emergency immigration act of that year. Suddenly, the number of immigrants from any given country was limited, with larger quotas allowed for persons from northern European countries. The expansion of the law in 1924 put in place a system of consular control that required a potential immigrant to obtain a visa from the US consul in his or her country of origin before being allowed to journey to the United States. The 1965 Hart-Celler Act eliminated specific country-of-origin restrictions, but substituted hemispheric and other restrictions. Subsequent amendments capped the number of visas from any single country at twenty thousand, created worldwide visa limits, increased restrictions of various types, and focused on keeping out immigrants from Mexico by erecting physical barriers at the border.[21]

The eighth wave of immigrants from Mexico and Central and South America, from 1965 through the 1990s, had to deal with increasingly stringent documentation requirements for entry to and residence in the US. As a result, some immigrants who originally had arrived with documentation fell into undocumented status for a wide variety of reasons, such as visa expiration. Others could not cope with the increasingly stringent entry requirements and costs, and arrived without the acceptable documentation. Wanting to keep their families intact, a number of immigrants brought their children with them. These childhood arrivals, who sometimes were brought to the US when just a few months of age, had no say in the conditions of their arrival. They went to school, played sports, and joined clubs, often blissfully unaware of their undocumented status. Nonetheless, they were subject to the same immigration strictures as their parents. At some point in their lives, they would find a seemingly routine interaction—applying for a driver's license, to community college, or for a job—suddenly interrupted, or even stopped altogether, because they could not provide a Social Security number or some other form of accepted documentation.

I have heard many stories of how this stunning news hit these childhood arrivals. They suddenly felt banned from society, their road to adulthood shut off, themselves painted with the stigma of being one of the much-scapegoated "illegal immigrants." Unable to continue on to college with their classmates, unable to work at jobs that required a Social Security number for payroll tax purposes, many drifted from informal job to informal job, unable to acquire the base of experience and assets that might carry them into adulthood. By the turn of the twenty-first century, a few childhood arrivals did manage to wriggle into higher education, sometimes by allowing themselves to be classified as international students, which required them to pay the high tuition demanded of other, generally more affluent, international students. Some of them felt a need to keep their situation a secret from their classmates, which led to feeling isolated during a normally socially active time in a young adult's life.

In 2001, California assemblyman Marco Firebaugh managed to shepherd Assembly Bill 540 through the state legislature and onto the governor's desk, to open the door to higher education for these childhood arrivals by regularizing their enrollment in colleges, allowing them to pay in-state tuition, and making them eligible for some limited financial aid. During the debate about the bill, some administrators in the University of California's Office of the President, still influenced by images of the Proposition 187 campaign a decade earlier, expressed concerns that the university would be flooded by a wave of childhood arrival applicants. CESLAC made some "back of the envelope" estimates of the possible number of UC-eligible childhood arrivals, and estimated something between a few hundred and one or two thousand. If all of them had enrolled, they would have amounted to 0.1% of the UC student body—hardly a numeric threat to the integrity of the university.[22]

A small group of about fifteen childhood arrival students at UCLA, most of them Latinos and Asians, met in 2003, initially to provide support to each other, as they were all familiar with the feelings of isolation, secrecy, and shame they had had to contend with. Within a few years, the group became a formally established student group—Improving Dreams, Education, Access, and Success (IDEAS), numbering about a hundred members. They were a small part of the 6% of post-millennials not born in the US, but their presence had important meaning for the 94% who were US citizens by birth. As most undocumented Latino post-millennials had arrived as very young children, they were, culturally, virtually indistinguishable from the other Latino post-millennials; they listened to the same music, watched the same television shows, attended the same classes, and joined the same clubs, associations, and fraternities and sororities as other Latino post-millennials. But they were different in one important way: the fact that they were, technically speaking, among the "illegal aliens" that were the targets of frequent public political debate. Not only did most Latino post-millennials have undocumented immigrant adults in their homes, but they also now had fellow students who were undocumented.

A Surprising Show of Strength

Buoyed by their presumed success at stopping "illegal immigration" in California, the proponents of Proposition 187 initially targeted Texas for their next efforts; but governor-elect George W. Bush emphatically rejected them, earning plaudits from both Latinos in the US and officials in Mexico, who viewed the proposed initiative and its advocate, California Governor Pete Wilson, as "symbols of bigotry and xenophobia."[23] Early in his presidential administration, and against vigorous opposition from his own party, Bush met with President Vicente Fox of Mexico to craft an immigration bill, "the whole enchilada," which would legalize undocumented Mexican immigrants. But just six days later, Al-Qaeda operatives hijacked several US civilian aircraft and slammed them into the Twin Towers in New York and the Pentagon in Washington, DC; abruptly, the focus of immigration shifted to keeping dangerous undesirables out of the country.

Afraid that terrorists would slip into the US by crossing its long border with Mexico, alarmists in Washington demanded that the border be "sealed" to keep the US safe. Lumping together concerns about "illegal aliens," a porous Mexican border, and terrorists, the House of Representatives produced a bill titled the "Border Protection, Antiterrorism, and Illegal Immigration Control Act of 2005-H.R. 4437," otherwise known as the Sensenbrenner bill. This bill made a felony out of the act of having an "illegal presence" on US soil, required employers to re-verify the immigration status of all previously hired employees, increased penalties for hiring individuals without proper documentation, and required state and local police to take part in these immigration enforcement efforts. To add insult to injury, the bill ordered construction of seven hundred miles of fencing at the Mexican border.[24] The president and CEO of the Leadership Conference on Civil Rights, Wade Henderson, denounced that bill, and its senate companion, S. 2454, as they "would instantly criminalize 11 million hardworking immigrants and those who help them." He also pointed out that under these bills, merely providing housing to an undocumented person would be a felony as well.[25]

It was as if Proposition 187 had been intensified and stretched out from California to cover the entire country. But the experience of Proposition 187, and of continuing nativist attacks, had also intensified Latino communication networks and political involvement. Spanish-language radio talk shows and Spanish-language television covered the progress of the bills and community reactions to them. Old-line Chicano-era organizations such as the National Council of La Raza (NCLR) and the Mexican American Legal Defense and Education Fund (MALDEF) joined more recently founded immigrant community organizations such as the Central American Resource Center (CARECEN) to apprise their members and supporters of the ominous potential of the bills. Latino post-millennials proved to be prodigious producers and consumers of online social network communications.

On the morning of March 25, 2006, Los Angeles found its downtown streets filled by the largest recorded demonstration in its history. An estimated five hundred thousand opponents of the Sensenbrenner bill turned out to voice their displeasure. US-born and immigrant, young and old, speaking in Spanish and English, half a million Latinos contested the nativist narrative of Latinos as eternal strangers in the state two-thirds of them had been born in. The streets of Denver, Phoenix, Atlanta, and dozens of other towns and cities across the country also filled with people protesting the nativist sentiments behind H.R. 4437.[26] The English-language media seemed surprised that Latino communities could make such a unified public statement. The question that intrigued many non-Latinos was, if the bill was only about "illegal aliens," why would US-born Latinos feel threatened by it? After all, they were not immigrants.

AMERICAN OR LATINO?

In 2011, CESLAC convened focus groups of US-born Latino young adults aged twenty-five to thirty who had attended college, in order to probe their notions of American identity and Latino identity, and their reactions to the discussion about immigrants. A card-sort methodology was used, in which the facilitator showed a group a sheet of paper with a one-word descriptor, such as *Chicano,* written on it. Members of the group had thirty seconds to write down their gut-level reactions to the word on a blank card. They then were shown the next paper, containing a different one-word descriptor.

The first descriptor shown was the single word "American." After the participants had silently writen reactions to all the descriptors, the facilitator returned to the first one, "American," and asked the participants to share how they felt when they saw that word. One participant said that the word *proud* popped into her head. Another participant said, "me," which she followed with other spontaneous associations: the US flag; red, white, and blue; the Fourth of July; fireworks. Yet another member of the group wrote that she was an American; she then related that when she heard the "Star Spangled Banner," she sometimes got chills.[27] Given these focus group respondents' pride in and affirmation of being American, some social analysts, such as Samuel Huntington, might have concluded that they had shed their Latino identity and were now completely assimilated (see chapter 7).

Yet, when shown the word *Latino,* one female respondent's first reaction was "Proud. I definitely identify as a Latina." She went on to describe how she liked to share her culture and background with others. Another in the group, who was also proud to be Latina, named other things she associated with the word "Latino": "culture," "happy," and "mixed."[28] This unambiguous pride in being both American and Latino would surprise Anglo-Saxonist nativists. In their view, being Latino is incompatible with being American: one is either American or Latino. But these respondents saw the two as being completely compatible. They were proud to be American, and proud to be Latino, just as Texans are proud to be American and proud to be Texan.

One of the criteria for inclusion in the focus group was that the participants had been born in the US. By definition, this meant that they were not immigrants. Reflecting the demographics of young adult Latinos in California at the time, however, the vast majority were children of the eighth wave of immigration, so they felt closely connected to immigrants. One participant explained the simple demographic reality beneath her written response to the one-word descriptor *immigrant:* "I wrote 'parents' and 'grandparents.'" Another focus group member explained that because her parents were immigrants, she could identify with the immigrant group and felt that she was very much a part of them. At the time the focus group was held, the state of Arizona had been cracking down on immigrants, and one member of the group, the same one who had earlier described herself as a "proud American," was moved to tears of anger and hurt as she explained her reaction to Arizona's anti-Latino policies. "I've really been affected by what has been happening in Arizona. It's such a travesty. [*Wipes tears from eyes.*] I think it's unfair. I think it's a type of a modern-day persecution. It just really upsets me."[29]

A proud American (who happened to be Latina) was angered and hurt by how other Americans were treating Latinos in Arizona. This is one of the most significant formative experiences of Latino post-millennials. The participants in this focus group strongly contradicted two of Huntington's nativist conclusions about Latinos. In 2004 Huntington declared, citing no data as evidence, that any show of "ethnic, race and gender" awareness meant a rejection of the idea of a "national identity." Each of the participants in our focus groups expressed deep feelings of attachment to the idea of being American; and as detailed in chapter 7, this strong sense of American identity has been evident in survey after survey that I have conducted. Furthermore, I doubt many Texans would agree with Huntington that a show of Texan regional identity is incompatible with American identity. Huntington also asserted, again citing no evidence, that "Mexicans and other Latinos . . . [reject] the Anglo Protestant values that built the American dream."[30] This updated edition of *La Nueva California* began with José Antonio Carrillo's assertion, in 1849, that he was as American as any delegate to the California Constitutional Convention that year. He and his fellow Latino delegates held firmly to the universalist principles of equality, freedom, democracy, and bilingualism. Many of the non-Hispanic white delegates, on the other hand, believed in an Anglo-Saxonist concept of America that allowed slavery, denied civil rights to nonwhites, and insisted on speaking only English. If there was any rejection of values going on in California in 1849, it was that many non-Hispanic whites—themselves very recent immigrants to the state—were rejecting the values of freedom and equality for all races and of civil rights irrespective of race; while native-born Latinos, to the contrary, rejected an Anglo-Saxonist view of America that condoned slavery, white supremacy, and elitist government.

For Latino post-millennials, Huntington's choice between being "American" and "Latino" is a meaningless dichotomy. For them, being Latino *is* being American, just as most Texans consider themselves Americans. And just as Texans distinguish Texan Americans from other regional types of Americans, so do Latinos distinguish Latino Americans from other regional types of American. In their view, Latinos are Americans, but not all Americans are Latino. Yet all are Americans. The anti-immigrant rhetoric they have heard all their lives conflates "Latino" with immigrant, and thence with "illegal immigrant," and with being "un-American." Thus, when these Latino post-millennials hear themselves and their parents, grandparents, and siblings described as undesirable foreigners who reject American values, they react quickly and angrily. Hence the five hundred thousand demonstrators in the streets of Los Angeles in March of 2006.

LATINOS INFLUENCE THE DIRECTION OF CALIFORNIA

The immediate Latino reaction to Proposition 187 was to mobilize the Latino vote for Latino-supportive candidates at the city, county, and state levels. The number of Latino representatives elected by outraged Latino voters increased dramatically, at all levels, during the 1990s. By the 2000s, these representatives had acquired knowledge of the legislative process; and at the state level, through the Latino Legislative Caucus, began to weigh in on issues important to the entire state, not just to Latinos.

Latinos Contest the Nativist Narrative

Over the course of the twentieth century, Anglo-Saxonist nativists in California erected barriers to Latino and other nonwhite participation in American society. Latinos in the California legislature have been removing these barriers one by one.

Restrictive Covenants Contested. In 1949, the builder of a suburban tract in South Gate, Los Angeles County, wanted to ensure that only non-Hispanic whites would ever occupy the houses in the tract. He legally segregated the area by attaching a restrictive covenant to the deed of each and every house offered for sale. This restriction in the deed mandated that only persons "entirely that of the Caucasian race" could live in the tract. The restriction specified that persons who were "Japanese, Chinese, Mexican, Hindu ... Ethiopian, Indian or Mongolian" were not to be considered Caucasian, and hence could not reside there.[31] Assemblyman Hector de la Torre bought a house in the tract and was offended to find the restrictive covenant still featured in the deed. In the 2009–2010 legislative session, he proposed a law, AB985, to expunge these restrictions, so as to "wipe away the stain of that time in our history."[32] Unfortunately, his bill was vetoed by Republican Governor Arnold Schwarzenegger, on the grounds of administrative costs.[33]

Proposition 187 Repealed. The infamous Proposition 187 intended not only to withhold public services from "illegal aliens" but also to require state and local agencies to "report persons who are suspected illegal aliens" to the INS and the California attorney general. The initiative made the possession of "false citizenship or residence" documents a felony.[34] As noted in chapter 5, some proponents of the proposition assumed that anyone who was Latino was likely to be "illegal." By 2014, some parts of Proposition 187 had been repealed as unconstitutional; that year, Senator Kevin de Leon introduced a bill to erase Proposition 187 entirely from California's law books so as to rid the state of a reminder of "the xenophobic sentiments that spurred" its passage. Senator Paul Fong added that "Proposition 187 was a racist and unjust law."[35] Governor Jerry Brown signed the new bill into law in the fall of 2014, with his office commenting that "this is a long overdue fix to a law that has no place on the state's books."[36]

English-Only Instruction Overturned. Passed in 1998, Proposition 227 prohibited the instruction of "limited English proficient" students in any language other than English, banning bilingual instruction for those students learning English.[37] In 2014, Senator Ricardo Lara concluded that children's multilingual abilities should be built upon, rather than banned, to help create a workforce for a globalized economy. He introduced SB1174, the "Multilingual Education for a 21st-Century Economy Act," building upon research showing that bilingual students in San Francisco performed better academically than monolingual students. Lara added that English was the "official language of California," but that the state's economy would be better served by a multilingual workforce.[38] His bill will be decided by the California electorate in the November 2016 general elections.

"[Two] Latinos Will Lead Legislature," announced the *Los Angeles Times* late in 2015. The report detailed a "generational shift in the highest ranks of the legislature."[39] The state senate elected Kevin de Leon to be its president pro tem in 2014. De Leon was raised in San Diego by a single, immigrant mother who cleaned houses to support her young son. In 1994, de Leon participated in a massive rally protesting Proposition 187. The *Los Angeles Times* story describing his background also added, offhandedly, that he was "the first Latino to hold the position since 1883."[40] The article gave no further information about that previous Latino president pro tem 132 years before; but he was none other than the Reginaldo F. del Valle who figures so prominently in chapter 1, who throughout his life contested his own era's periodic outbreaks of Anglo-Saxonist nativism in California. In the assembly, Anthony Rendon was elected to take over as Speaker in 2016. The grandson of Mexican immigrant grandparents, Rendon had a less than exemplary high school experience, at one point achieving a grade-point average of only 0.83. But he took advantage of California's embattled, underfunded higher education system, attending Cerritos Community College, then earning a master's degree at California State University, Fullerton. Finally, he completed a PhD at the University of California, Riverside. He was proud to be a product of "California's low-cost higher education." (*Los Angeles Times* reporter George Skelton added, "at least it used to be low cost.") Skelton ended his story of this

Latino assumption of power in the senate and assembly by adding, as if refuting Huntington, "It's a nice America [*sic*] Dream story in California's Capitol."[41]

Latinos Promote a Universalist Narrative

Huntington feared that "Mexicans and other Latinos" were forming separatist "political and linguistic enclaves" apart from other Americans. The behavior of Latino voters and elected officials, however, demonstrates just the opposite. California State Assembly Speaker Rendon's legislative agenda indicates that Huntington's fears were groundless. One of his top priorities has been environmental issues, from a massive $7.5 billion statewide water-use bond to reducing the impact of polluted air in small communities in his district. Another legislative focus has been the education of all California's students, not just Latinos: for example, ensuring better funding for, and lower tuition in, the state's higher education system.

The Public Policy Institute of California (PPIC) has conducted public attitude surveys for two decades and has seen two noteworthy recent trends in the state's population. The PPIC September 2015 survey of attitudes appears to demonstrate a tectonic shift in attitudes toward immigrants; nearly two-thirds (65%) of the survey's respondents agreed that immigrants are a benefit to California. As discussed in chapter 5, almost 60% of the non-Hispanic white electorate supported the anti-immigrant Proposition 187. The 2015 survey showed that 86% of Latinos agreed that immigrants were beneficial to the state, while only about half (49%) of non-Hispanic whites did. When disaggregated by political party affiliation, Democrats overwhelmingly agreed (72%) that immigrants were a benefit, while only 35% of Republicans agreed. Opinions about undocumented immigrants showed similar trends. Overall, three-fourths (75%) of respondents agreed that undocumented immigrants should be allowed to live and work legally in the state, "if they pay a fine and meet other requirements" (the "other requirements" were not specified in the questionnaire); Latinos agreed nearly unanimously (92%), and nearly two-thirds (63%) of non-Hispanic whites also agreed. Democrats gave a solid (83%) support for that idea; Republican support was much lower, though still a slim majority (53%) in favor. Respondents' perceptions of the role of government in solving social problems showed similar trends. When asked if government should "do more to reduce the gap between the rich and the poor," more than two-thirds (68%) of all respondents agreed. Latinos were more likely to agree (80%) than non-Hispanic whites (56%), and Democrats were more likely to support the idea (84%) than Republicans (32%).[42] These results show that Latinos—who have tended to register disproportionately Democratic in reaction to the nativist overtones of Proposition 187 and similar legislation—clearly favor a government more active in resolving social problems than do non-Hispanic whites, who tend to register Republican. Latinos also have more positive views of immigrants and more strongly support some form of legalization for undocumented immigrants.

The Latino post-millennial generation consists largely of the children of the eighth wave of immigration to California, which occurred between 1965 and 1990 (see chapter 7). Over 94% of Latino post-millennials were born in the US; they are citizens, and they can register to vote once they turn eighteen years of age, which hundreds of thousands of them will do every year for next two decades. Many of these Latino post-millennials have family members who are undocumented or who have been the target of anti-immigrant rhetoric. Those family members stand to benefit from programs such as President Barack Obama's currently stalled Deferred Action for Parents of Americans (DAPA) program. A recent USC Dornsife study called these Latino post-millennials with undocumented family members "DAPA-affected voters" and projected their increasing numbers to the 2032 elections. The study estimated that by the 2016 elections, over one-half million (531,000) Latino post-millennials eligible to vote in California will have at least one member of their household who is directly affected by DAPA, and indirectly by anti-immigrant rhetoric. This number will grow to nearly three-quarters of a million voters by 2020.[43] These new voters, the Latino post-millennials, feel themselves to be American. They support a universalist conception of America based on the values of equality, freedom, and democracy, and can be expected to actively reject attempts to impose nativist definitions of America upon them or their families. They will be California's future elected officials, business leaders, and parents. They will be Americans, Latino style.

NINE

Latino Post-Millennials Create America's Future

IN JUNE 2015, DONALD TRUMP announced his candidacy for the upcoming Republican presidential nomination, and he wasted little time in laying down his nativist platform, announcing in a campaign speech, "When Mexico sends its people ... they're bringing drugs. They're bringing crime. They're rapists."[1] Just before Game Three of the 2013 National Basketball Association finals in San Antonio, eleven-year-old Sebastien de la Cruz sang the US national anthem, dressed in a mariachi suit. As soon as his televised image appeared, nativists exploded in anger on social media. "Who let this illegal alien sing our national anthem?" demanded one such tweet.[2] The blog *Public Shaming*, mentioned by a CNN article on the national anthem flap as an archival source, preserved a number of the tweets, in which Sebastien was described as a "beaner," "foreigner," "wetback," "illegal," "Mexican kid," "illegal alien," "little beaner," "lil Mexican snuck in the country like 4 hours ago," and "9 out of 10 chances that kid ... is illegal."[3] Yet young Sebastien was a native-born US citizen, and his father was a US military veteran. In 2012, Angel Rodriguez, a US citizen born in Puerto Rico, playing guard for the Kansas State basketball team against Southern Mississippi, stepped up to the free throw line. In an attempt to distract him, Southern Miss band members chanted, "Where's your green card?" A *USA Today* report on the incident added parenthetically, "A quick geography lesson: Puerto Rico is a part of the United States. If you're born in Puerto Rico, you're an American citizen."[4] That same year, NBC Latino reported on a study showing that, partly as a result of nearly twenty years of nativist complaints about the growing Latino presence in the US, for many Americans "the words 'Latino' and 'illegal immigrant' were one and the same." NBC Latino also quoted the president of the National Hispanic Media Coalition complaining about the disservice the media were doing by presenting "coverage that is misleading the public about Latinos who live in the U.S."[5]

LATINO POPULATION HAS BEEN GROWING
FOR FIVE HUNDRED YEARS

The idea that "Latino" is synonymous with "illegal immigrant"—and many more such beliefs, broadcast daily—reinforces the widely promulgated nativist perception that Latinos are nearly all fairly recently arrived immigrants, most of whom did not have authorized entry. But this perception is erroneous. Twenty-first-century Latinos are heirs to nearly five hundred years of settled presence within the boundaries of what we now call the United States. Chapters 1 and 7 of this book examined the 250-year Latino presence in California. After California was acquired by the United States in 1848, Latinos, through a process of ethnogenesis during the Gold Rush and the American Civil War, created a bilingual, bicultural Latino civil society in the state that has continued into the twenty-first century. California's Latino experience is not unique. The same experience of mixed-race, Spanish-speaking settlers bringing Western society into territories now part of the US was repeated widely. The oldest city in US territory has been continuously inhabited for nearly five hundred years, since its founding in 1521: San Juan, in Puerto Rico.[6]

For three hundred years after San Juan was founded, groups of multiracial, Spanish-speaking settlers set out from Mexico, Cuba, Puerto Rico, and the island of Hispaniola, bringing Western society to the landmass to the north. By the time the United States was recognized as an independent country, in 1783, Spanish-speaking populations residing in pueblos, presidios, missions, ranches, and farms were scattered from St. Augustine in Florida to San Francisco in Alta California, their daily activities informed by the Indo-Afro-Oriento-Ibero experiences of Western society. During the nineteenth century, the young US expanded in size, acquiring further territory and people with origins in this Spanish-speaking version of Western society. Its first acquisition, in 1803, was the Louisiana Purchase, which was part of the Spanish Empire from 1762 to 1803.[7] This acquisition of Spanish-speaking peoples continued, sporadically, throughout the nineteenth century. The Adams-Onís Treaty in 1819 led to the acquisition of Florida and its people; the Texas Annexation of 1845 brought in the *tejanos;* the Treaty of Guadalupe-

Hidalgo, in 1848, acquired California, Nevada, New Mexico, Arizona, Utah, and Colorado, with their respective Spanish-speaking populations. Finally, with the 1898 Treaty of Paris, the US acquired the islands of Puerto Rico and the Philippines, and established a protectorate over Cuba. In each of the acquired territories, the Spanish-speaking population began a process of ethnogenesis, creating local variants of the bilingual, bicultural society of the Latinos of the US. Chapters 1 and 7 of this book provide an overview of the process in California, but much the same process took place wherever Spanish-speaking populations found themselves placed by political decisions in a new country without their having to take one step.

But those earlier population movements from Mexico and Latin America did not stop once the US acquired these new territories. Indeed, new waves of immigration occurred after each acquisition. At times these were spurred by events in the US, such as the Gold Rush, the US's need for labor, or changes in immigration law. At other times, they were driven by events in the immigrants' home countries, such as the French Intervention in Mexico in the 1860s, the Mexican Revolution in the early twentieth century, and the Cuban Revolution in the 1950s. Those post-acquisition immigrants generally settled into Latino communities that had taken root prior to their acquisition by the US, and largely learned about American society and identity from their already established neighbors. The newer immigrants tended to live in the same neighborhoods as the established Latino populations, to worship in the same churches, to shop in the same stores, and to attend the same local civic events, such as Puerto Rican Independence Day or the Cinco de Mayo. The children of each wave of Spanish-speaking immigrants tended to marry the children of the earlier, established groups; and as these new families were formed, the bilingual, bicultural society formed generations earlier was renewed, with each new US-born generation giving it new twists and turns.

Most educational curricula in the United States have largely ignored the experiences of these populations acquired by a century of US expansion; as a result, the erroneous general public perception of Latinos is that most of them have only recently arrived in this country. The fact is that from 1980 to the present, the majority of Latinos in the US were born in the US. In 2013, nearly two-thirds (65%) of all Latinos in the US were born in the country; only a little over one-third (35%) were immigrants.[8] Moreover, a 2014 Pew Research Center report announced that the percentage of the population who were Latino was returning, in some western states, to what it had been in the historical past. In 1870, for example, New Mexico was overwhelmingly (89.9%)

Latino. By 1910, however, Latinos made up scarcely more than one-third (35.4%) of the state's population; by 1950, the proportion of Latinos had dropped to only about a fourth. Yet by 2012, it had grown again, to almost half the total population (47.0%). In 1870, Arizona likewise was nearly two-thirds (60.9%) Latino. The proportion dropped to about a third (35.4%) by 1910, and fell nearly to 20% by 1970. Since then, however, the Latino population has grown to be nearly a third (30.2%) of the state's total. In 1870, Colorado's population was over a quarter (29.8%) Latino, but by 1910, it was only 3.2% Latino. Yet from that point on, Colorado's Latino population has grown, slowly and steadily, and in 2012 was moving toward being one-fourth (21.0%) again. This report attributes these increases to immigration, but the example of California suggests that a good deal of it is due to natural increase as well.[9]

Far from being nearly all recently arrived undocumented immigrants, Latinos have a long-established presence in what is now the US. The wave of immigration from Latin America to the US from 1965 to 2005 was only the latest during nearly five hundred years of population growth. That wave has now receded, and Latino population growth presently comes primarily from births. The US Census Bureau recently estimated that the Latino population of the US will grow over the next forty years, from the 2014 total of 55.4 million to a projected total of 119.0 million by 2060. At that point, nearly one out of every three Americans will be Latino.[10]

LATINOS STRENGTHEN AMERICAN VALUES:
A US SNAPSHOT

What kind of America will Latinos help create in the twenty-first century? National-level data on topics often mentioned by the new nativists—work ethic, independence from welfare, and health behaviors—give some clues as to how the 55 million Latinos of 2015 may influence the course of American society over the rest of this century.

Work Ethic. A common nativist claim in the immigration discussion is that Latinos are poor because they do not believe in the work ethic, and that this disdain for work is passed on to their children. Yet the data indicate just the opposite (fig. 30). In 2015, Latino males across the US had the highest labor force participation of any group, echoing the seventy-five-year trend in California shown in figure 3.

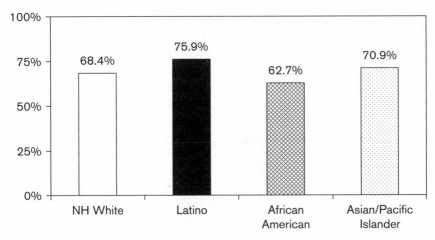

FIGURE 30. Labor force participation, male 16+ years, United States, 2015. Source: Schink custom analysis, data from Flood et al., IPUMS CPS (2015), and Ruggles et al., IPUMS (2015).

Independence from Welfare. Another commonly voiced nativist claim is that Latino immigrants are attracted by generous US welfare benefits. Mike Huckabee reinforced this image when he claimed that he wanted to "'stem the tide' of people from Mexico who have 'heard there's a bowl of food just across the border.'"[11] Again, the data demonstrate just the opposite. In 2015, across the US, Latinos in poverty were a little less likely than non-Hispanic whites or African Americans to be receiving welfare benefits (fig. 31). The notion of Mexican women crossing the border in order to give birth to future welfare users also has been disproven by data-based research.[12] In fact, statistical research has shown that today's young Latino workers will be supporting the aging baby boomer generation for most of their professional lives.[13]

Healthy Profiles. Another nativist claim is that sickly undocumented immigrants come to the US for "free health care." When the Affordable Care Act was being debated, the Obama administration explicitly excluded undocumented immigrants from participation in the health exchanges, even if they wanted to purchase insurance with their own funds. Despite this, as the president assured a session of Congress in 2009 that his proposed legislation would *not* provide free health care to the undocumented, Representative Joe Wilson of South Carolina interrupted, shouting, "You lie!"[14] Yet the data show that immigrants generally, and "especially the undocumented," in fact use far

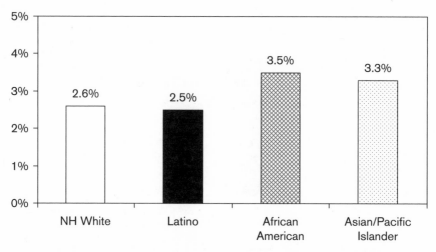

FIGURE 31. Public assistance as percent of the poverty population, United States, 2015. Source: Schink custom analysis, data from Flood et al., IPUMS CPS (2015), and Ruggles et al., IPUMS (2015).

fewer services and generate far lower costs than the rest of the population. The authors of one study said the likely reason for this lower use was "the better relative health" of Latino immigrants.[15] The 55 million Latinos in the US exhibit the same Latino Epidemiological Paradox seen for decades in California. In a 2015 *Vital Statistics Report,* the National Center for Health Statistics provided age-adjusted death rates for the entire country for 2013. For all causes of death, the age-adjusted rate of 535.4 deaths per 100,000 Latinos was 28% lower than the non-Hispanic white rate of 747.1 per 100,000 (fig. 32).[16]

Long Life Expectancy. In a nativist outburst in September 2015, presidential candidate Donald Trump railed against the alleged phenomenon of "anchor babies," in which "a woman who's nine months pregnant walks across the border, has a baby, and you have to take care of that baby for the next 85 years."[17] The only part of Trump's statement supported by data, however, was that regarding Latino life expectancy, although, typically, he exaggerated. Nationally, Latinos have a longer life expectancy than either non-Hispanic whites or African Americans. With a life expectancy at birth of 81.6 years, a Latino baby born in 2013 likely will live over two and a half years longer (2.7, to be exact) than the non-Hispanic white baby in the next crib in the same neonatal unit, who has a life expectancy of 78.9 years (fig. 33).[18]

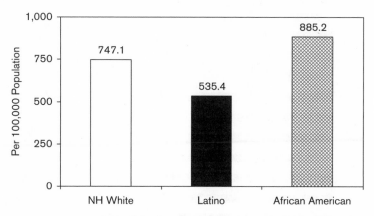

FIGURE 32. Age-adjusted death rates for all causes, United States, 2013. Source: Detailed tables, *National Vital Statistics Reports,* vol. 64, no. 2 (Hyattsville, MD: National Center for Health Statistics, 2015), p. 7, table 2.

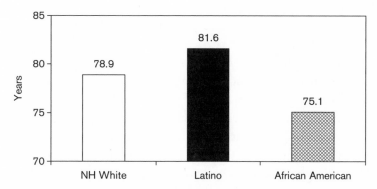

FIGURE 33. Life expectancy at birth, United States, 2013. Source: Detailed tables, *National Vital Statistics Reports,* vol. 64, no. 2 (Hyattsville, MD: National Center for Health Statistics, 2015), p. 31, table 8.

LATINO POST-MILLENNIALS—LARGEST
LATINO MARKET

The profile of the 55.4 million Latinos in the US as of 2014, with their strong work ethic, independence from welfare, and good health profiles, hardly promises the catastrophic end-of-America future that nativists decry. But because America's future is being created today in large part by the Latino post-millennial generation, it is well worth turning our attention to this

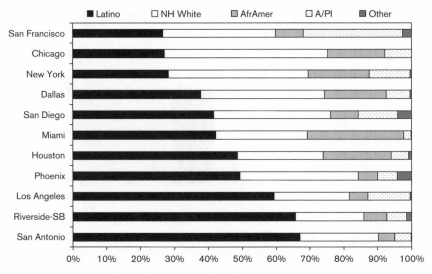

FIGURE 34. Race/ethnic composition of post-millennials in the top eleven Latino metropolitan areas, 2015. Source: Schink custom analysis, data from Flood et al., IPUMS CPS (2015).

generation, and its formative experiences from 1997 to 2015. Those experiences, unfortunately, have included large doses of nativist invective about their presence in American society.

The 19 million Latino post-millennials comprise about one-fourth of the entire post-millennial population of the US. They are not, however, evenly distributed geographically. Just as the general Latino population is concentrated in a relatively few states, so Latino post-millennials are concentrated in those same states, where they make up a much higher percentage of the total post-millennial generation. Figure 34 shows the representation of Latino post-millennials in the overall post-millennial population in the top eleven Latino metropolitan areas (MSAs, in census terminology) of the United States. The bars are in ascending order of Latino percentage in the post-millennial generation in each MSA. In almost all these areas, a Latino presence has existed for centuries, so a brief historical sketch of that presence accompanies each area.

San Antonio, Texas. In 1718, Governor Martín de Alarcón established the presidio of San Antonio de Béxar, and the city of San Antonio, which grew up around that military nucleus, has been a thriving Latino center for nearly three hundred years.[19] In 1779, the Spanish Crown decided to assist the

American rebels against the British monarchy. As part of this effort, Bernardo de Gálvez, governor of Louisiana—which belonged to Spain at that time—requested two thousand head of cattle from Texas governor Domingo Cabello in San Antonio. The resulting first long-distance cattle drive in North America wound its way from San Antonio to Opelousas, Louisiana, to feed Gálvez's troops in New Orleans. Gálvez subsequently commanded seven thousand soldiers against the British at Pensacola, along with Major-General Gerónimo Girón and his aide-de-camp, Francisco Miranda, a Venezuelan who would later be a leader in several South American independence movements.[20] With a total Latino population of 1.3 million in the MSA, San Antonio has been an important hub for commerce between Mexico and the rest of the US. Latinos are a super-majority of the post-millennial generation at 67%, and non-Hispanic whites are nearly one-fourth, at 23%.

Riverside–San Bernardino, California. Native Americans used the Riverside–San Bernardino area as a corridor for commerce between the Pacific Ocean and the Rocky Mountains for centuries before Western society was established here in 1775 and 1776, when Juan Bautista de Anza led a group of Spanish-speaking Indian, African, mestizo, and mulatto Catholics from northern Mexico to settle in Alta California.[21] The 2.2 million Latinos of this MSA alone comprise a larger population than that of West Virginia. Latinos are a super-majority (66%) of the post-millennial generation in this region, and non-Hispanic whites comprise a small minority, at 20%.

Los Angeles–Long Beach–Santa Ana, California. The pueblo of Los Angeles was founded in 1781, and the nearby mission of San Gabriel even earlier, in 1771, both in what is now Los Angeles County. During the American Revolution, the Spanish Crown requested donations from the inhabitants of all its pueblos, presidios, and missions, in the amount of one peso each, to help the rebel cause against Great Britain. San Gabriel gave 134 pesos, and the eight struggling families of *pobladores* (settlers) of recently founded Los Angeles jointly donated fifteen pesos, just months after arriving from northern Mexico.[22] Father Junipero Serra noted, "We prayed fervently last evening for the success of the colonists under one George Washington, because we believe their cause is just and that the Great Redeemer is on his side."[23] Since the founding of Los Angeles, this MSA has been joined by a growing number of Latino communities. The Latino population in this MSA of 6.4 million, in 2015, is as large as the entire state population of Indiana, Missouri, or

Massachusetts. In the post-millennial generation, there are nearly three Latinos (59%) for every non-Hispanic white (22%).

Phoenix–Mesa–Scottsdale, Arizona. In 1691, a delegation of indigenous Sobaipuris from San Xavier del Bac and San Cayetano de Tumacácori asked two Jesuit missionaries, Eusebio Kino and Juan María de Salvatierra, to travel to today's Arizona to baptize them.[24] Nearly two centuries later and about 150 miles to the north, the town of Phoenix was incorporated, in 1881. In 1889, the Latinos of Tempe, Arizona, within the Phoenix MSA, announced a program for an all-day celebration of the Cinco de Mayo and the *glorias de México* (glories of Mexico), starting with a twenty-one-gun salute to the Mexican flag at 5:00 A.M. and ending with a dinner dance lasting into the wee hours of the morning.[25] The 1.4 million Latinos in this MSA, largely of Mexican origin, are about the same size as the whole population of New Hampshire. Latinos make up nearly half (49%) of the post-millennial generation, while non-Hispanic whites are slightly over one-third (35%).

Houston–Baytown–Sugar Land, Texas. Some time between 1528 and 1536, the shipwrecked Alvar Núñez Cabeza de Vaca and his party passed through what would become the Houston–Baytown–Sugar Land MSA. In 1783, as the American Revolution was winding down, Governor Bernardo de Gálvez of Louisiana asked Spanish naval officer José Antonio Evia to prepare a map of the Gulf Coast. During the ensuing mapping project, Gálvez was named viceroy of Mexico, so Evia honored him by calling the bay he was mapping Bahía de Galvezton (Galveston Bay), for the neighboring small settlement named for Gálvez. The nearly 2.5 million Latinos in this region, largely of Mexican and Central American origin, form a population as large as that of Mississippi. In the post-millennial generation, there are nearly two Latinos (49%) for every non-Hispanic white (25%). One out of every five post-millennials in this region is African American.

Miami–Fort Lauderdale–Miami Beach, Florida. Three hundred years before Miami was incorporated (1896), Latinos established a settlement at San Agustín (St. Augustine) in 1565, as well as Pensacola and more than a hundred Catholic missions in Florida.[26] José Mariano Hernández was born in San Agustín in 1788; after Florida was acquired by the US from Spain in 1819, Hernández was elected by the Florida legislative council to serve as its first territorial delegate to Congress, in 1823. He sought improvements to

Florida's infrastructure, especially a road between St. Augustine and Pensacola, Florida's two largest settlements at that time. Hernández ran unsuccessfully for the US Senate after Florida became a state in 1845, then served as mayor of St. Augustine in 1848. He later retired to Cuba, where he died in 1857.[27]

A hundred years after his death, hundreds of thousands of Cuban refugees began to settle in Florida, mostly in Miami rather than St. Augustine. Despite this history, Tom Tancredo, once a Republican presidential candidate, returned to his native Colorado in 2006 and announced that because Spanish was spoken by so many people in Miami, he did not consider it to be an American city any longer.[28] The 2.8 million Latinos in this MSA are equivalent in size to the total population of the state of Kansas. While Cuban-origin Latinos used to be a sizable majority (59%) of the MSA's Latino population, by 2010, Cubans were simply a majority (54%), and those of Puerto Rican, Colombian, Dominican, and Mexican origin jointly made up a sizable minority.[29] In the post-millennial generation, Latinos have a plurality, at 42%; African Americans are the next largest component of this generation, at 28%, and non-Hispanic whites come third, at 27%.[30]

San Diego–Carlsbad–San Marcos, California. In the late spring of 1769, Captain Gaspar de Portolá led a company of Europeans, Indians, Africans, Asians, mestizos, and mulattos from northern Mexico to San Diego to establish the first permanent presence of Western society in Alta California. Included in his party was a university-trained medical provider, surgeon Pedro Prat, who arrived in one of the ships under Portolá's command. These ships also carried provisions, seeds, agricultural tools, and church supplies to jump-start the settlement process.[31] Father Junipero Serra came by foot in one of the same expedition's overland companies. Portolá's expedition established presidios and missions along California's coast from San Diego to Monterey, nearly six hundred miles to the north.[32] The 1 million Latinos in this MSA have continued ever since to be primarily of Mexican origin. Latinos here form a plurality of the post-millennial generation (42%), with non-Hispanic whites at a little over one-third (35%) and Asians/Pacific Islanders at just over one-tenth (12%).

Dallas–Fort Worth–Arlington, Texas. Dallas was incorporated in 1871; two years later, the town was connected to Galveston and Houston by Texas's first north-to-south railroad. Almost simultaneously, Dallas was connected to the

Pacific by an east-to-west railroad, thus becoming a major transportation crossroads. Railroad construction needed labor, and Latinos initially came to Dallas, in the early 1870s, as railroad workers. They settled in an area called "Little Mexico," often locally referred to as La Colonia (the colony), a "distinct and vibrant neighborhood of modest homes, small businesses, churches and schools" where Spanish was spoken. The Mexican Revolution (1910–1930) prompted thousands of new immigrants to relocate from Mexico to Dallas's Little Mexico. After World War II, hundreds of returning Latino veterans used the GI Bill to get an education and better jobs, and to move to new Latino neighborhoods.[33] The population of 2.1 million Latinos in this MSA in 2015 is a little larger than the entire population of the state of Nebraska. Latinos hold a slight plurality in the post-millennial generation, comprising 38%, to the 37% that is non-Hispanic white; African Americans make up nearly one in five of that generation, at 18%.

New York–Northern New Jersey–Long Island, New York. Juan Rodríguez, a mixed-race man from Santo Domingo, today's Dominican Republic, helped bring Western society to the New York–Northern New Jersey–Long Island MSA in 1613, when he established a trading post on the shores of Manhattan island.[34] In 1645, Spanish- and Portuguese-speaking Sephardic Jews founded the Congregation Shearith Israel in New York, the "oldest Jewish Congregation in the United States."[35] In 1785, the first Catholic church, St. Peter's, was built in New York, with funding from Mexico City, the city of Puebla in Mexico, and King Charles III of Spain.[36] As New York became the United States's commercial capital during the mid-nineteenth century, merchants and politicians from Mexico, Central America, South America, the Caribbean, and Spain were attracted to the city; by 1870, the US census counted over 3,600 residents from those areas. This energetic population published over a hundred newspapers in Spanish during the nineteenth century.[37] Yet, at the 2013 All Star baseball game, New York native Marc Anthony sang "God Bless America," and the Internet "dark mob" immediately attacked him for doing so because, in their view, he was not "American," and only an "American" should sing that song. The blog *Public Shaming* archived the tweets, in which native-born US citizen Marc Anthony was called a "non-American," "somebody not from America," "not even American," a "spic," a "Spanish guy," and a "damn Mexican." Of the twenty-one tweets archived, one-third called this native New Yorker of Puerto Rican origin a Mexican.[38] The 4.6 million Latinos in this MSA in 2015 made up a population as large as that of South Carolina, Alabama, Kentucky, or Louisiana. In the post-millennial generation of this MSA, there is no ethnic or racial majority. Latinos comprise 28% and non-Hispanic whites 41%. Although at one point Puerto Ricans made up the majority of its Latino population, today it consists of Puerto Ricans, Dominicans, Colombians, and Mexicans.

Chicago–Naperville–Joliet, Illinois–Indiana–Wisconsin. When the American Revolution broke out, St. Louis—at that time, officially called San Luis—was the capital of Spanish Illinois in Alta Luisiana. Bernardo de Gálvez, its governor, used St. Louis as a base from which to send supplies to George Washington's army. After Spain declared war on Britain in support of the American rebels, the British attacked St. Louis in 1780 to interrupt the flow of supplies. The Spaniards repulsed the attack; and the following winter Lieutenant-Governor Francisco Cruzat ordered a reprisal assault on the British fort at St. Joseph, on the eastern shores of Lake Michigan. A force of about 120 Spanish soldiers and indigenous allies traveled in pirogues up the Mississippi River, until ice forced them to land around Moline and march across the Illinois plains in the dead of winter. They would have passed near the site of the future city of Chicago. They took the fort by surprise, raised the Spanish flag, then burned the fort and its supplies, before returning to St. Louis.[39] The 1850 US census enumerated about thirty Mexicans in Illinois's population; but as Chicago grew into an industrial center, so many Latinos moved in that, by 1920, Chicago had at least three Latino barrios, including Hull House, the University of Chicago Settlement colony, and the South Chicago colony.[40] The 1.8 million Latinos in 2015 are largely of Mexican and Puerto Rican origin. The post-millennial generation is quite diverse in this MSA: about one-fourth (27%) Latino, one-sixth (17%) African American, and slightly less than one-half (48%) non-Hispanic white.

San Francisco–Oakland–Fremont, California. The presidio of San Francisco and the mission of San Francisco de Asís—often referred to as Mission Dolores for the creek that runs by it—were established in 1776. During the Gold Rush, this was the port of entry for Latino gold seekers from Mexico, Central America, and South America.[41] This cosmopolitan quality of San Francisco's Latino population persists in the twenty-first century, with significant numbers of Central and South Americans; while outside of San Francisco itself, the nearly 1 million Latinos of the San Francisco–Oakland–

Fremont MSA are primarily of Mexican origin. The post-millennial genera-tion in this MSA is very diverse: Latinos make up a little over one-fourth (27%) of the population, non-Hispanic whites about one-third (33%), and Asians/Pacific Islanders right in between (29%).

LATINO POST-MILLENNIALS BECOME VOTERS

Sociodemographics

Latinos in the US are generally characterized by three important demo-graphic variables: they are young, Catholic, and tend to vote Democratic. In contrast, non-Hispanic whites are older, Protestant, and tend to vote Republican. With a median age of twenty-nine years, Latinos in the US are nearly a generation younger, on average, than non-Hispanic whites, who, with a median age of forty-three years, are the statistically oldest group in the nation.[42] In religion, Latinos are about twice as likely to be Catholic (48%) as Protestant (26%), whereas non-Hispanic whites are half as likely to be Catholic (19%) as Protestant (48%).[43] In the 2014 national midterm elections, nearly two-thirds of Latinos (62%) reported voting for Democratic congres-sional candidates, while slightly over one-third (36%) voted for Republicans. Among non-Hispanic whites, the proportions were nearly reversed, although not quite as polarized: 38% voted for Democratic candidates, and 60% for Republicans.[44] In examining current Latino voting preferences, particularly where they differ from those of non-Hispanic whites, it is difficult to under-stand which of these three factors is most important to the difference. Keeping this caveat in mind, we will look at long-term political secular trends by generation and race/ethnicity, understanding that religion (Catholic or Protestant) and party affiliation (Democratic or Republican) usually track very closely with age and race/ethnicity.

Long-Term Social Trends. All societies change over time. US society is expe-riencing a number of important long-term changes in values, attitudes, and behaviors. For example, a recent Pew Center report summed up America's changing religious profile: "The Christian share of the U.S. population is declining, while the number of U.S. adults who do not identity with any organized religion is growing." This change is taking place across all racial/ethnic groups, across all generations (baby boomers to millennials), and across all religious affiliations.[45] Another significant social trend is a growing

198 • CHAPTER NINE

acceptance of homosexuality. In 2007, a minority (44%) of all Christians supported the notion that "homosexuality should be accepted"; but by 2014, the pendulum had swung far enough that a majority of all Christians (54%) supported that idea.[46] Within these long-term secular trends, millennials tend to report a greater level of change than baby boomers on a number of issues. For example, millennials are much less religious than baby boomers. They report being less likely to pray daily (39% for millennials, 61% for boomers) and less likely to feel that religion is "very important in their lives" (38% for millennials, 59% for boomers).[47]

Latino versus Non-Hispanic White Political Views. Latinos in the US often express more confidence in the future of the US than do non-Hispanic whites. This was captured in a national 2015 Pew Research Center poll, in which 54% of Latinos had "'quite a lot' of confidence in U.S future," compared to 43% of non-Hispanic whites.[48] Latinos also consistently express a favorable view of an expanded role of government in their daily lives, captured in the same poll: 71% of Latino respondents supported the notion of "bigger government, more services," while only a small minority (27%) of non-Hispanic whites did.[49] There is an important exception, however, to this generally positive Latino view of government and its services: Latinos' perception that police treat them, and other people, badly. In a national poll, only 45% of Latinos had confidence that police would not use excessive force on suspects, while a large majority (74%) of non-Hispanic whites were confident that police would not do that. More pointedly, only 46% of Latinos had confidence that police would treat them the same as they would non-Hispanic whites, while a strong majority (72%) of non-Hispanic whites believed the police would treat Latinos and non-Hispanic whites equally.[50]

On the contentious issue of what to do about undocumented immigrants, a recent Pew Research Center report indicated that a super-majority (72%) of Americans agree that undocumented immigrants should be provided some sort of legal status, although not necessarily citizenship.[51] But there are cleaer differences by generation and race/ethnicity. Millennials overwhelmingly (81%) supported legalization, while boomers supported the notion but with a much smaller majority (62%). As might be expected, Latinos largely (86%) supported legalization, while non-Hispanic whites were somewhat less supportive (69%).[52] In a different Pew-sponsored report, a vast majority (81%) of Latinos saw immigrants as a strength to the country, while only a minority (46%) of non-Hispanic whites agreed with that opinion.[53]

For all the importance given to immigration issues in elections since California's Proposition 187 in 1994, immigration still is not the most important issue for Latino voters. In December 2015, the National Institute for Latino Policy (NiLP) conducted a national survey of Latino leaders. NiLP released the findings, with the caveat that the opinions of "community leaders and advocates" could not be generalized to the Latino population as a whole. The respondents were primarily baby boomers in age (75%), but not baby boomer in political affiliation (74% were Democratic, 5% Republican). Just as it was for then-Speaker of the California Assembly Cruz Bustamante in 1996 (see chapter 5), the most important issue in the 2016 presidential election for these Latino leaders, by a wide margin (50%), was identified as "the economy and jobs." Immigration was considered a substantive issue by only 14%, although, as a "litmus test" for candidates, immigration continued to be important; 72% said that a candidate's stance on immigration reform would be "most important/very important" in deciding for whom to vote.[54] Latinos can still hear the "dog whistle" that candidates blow when they start to talk about immigration reform: they usually are really talking about the role of Latinos in American society, from a nativist perspective.

LATINO POST-MILLENNIALS: THE US-BORN OLD ENOUGH TO VOTE

As repeatedly noted, the vast majority of Latino post-millennials are native-born citizens. The National Center for Health Statistics recently released a report on births in the US, presented in figure 35. Although keeping in mind the Pew Millennial Research Project's caution that the years chosen to divide one generation from another are somewhat arbitrary, and may not be identified as such until decades after a generation's birth, we have used the Pew's general rule of thumb that the post-millennial generation consists of those born from 1997 onward. In 1997, about three-quarters of a million (709,767) Latino babies were born in the US. The number of Latino babies increased rapidly, though, and in 2006 a little over 1 million (1,039,077) were born. After staying above the 1 million mark for three years, the number of births then decreased, to a little under 1 million, reaching a low in 2013 of 901,033, then rebounding slightly to 914,065 in 2014. In essence, since 2003, about 1 million Latinos have been born every year.

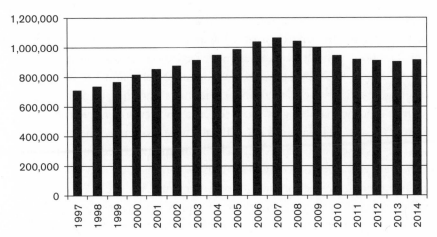

FIGURE 35. Latino births in the United States, 1997–2014. Source: *National Vital Statistics Reports,* vol. 64, no. 12 (Hyattsville, MD: National Center for Health Statistics, 2015), p. 23, table 5.

The Latino babies born in 1997 turned eighteen in 2015. This means that about three-quarters of a million Latino US citizens became eligible to vote in 2015. A slightly larger number will become old enough to vote in 2016, and the number will increase each year until 2024, by which time nearly 1 million Latinos born in the US will turn eighteen and be of voting age. Every year after that, just under 1 million US-born Latinos will turn eighteen, up to the elections of 2032. The coming-of-age of Latinos born in the US will add nearly 18 million new voters to the US electorate by that year.

In their 1985 book *Habits of the Heart,* Robert N. Bellah and his colleagues pondered the twentieth-century tug-of-war between individual and community stemming from "habits of the heart" that de Tocqueville described in the early nineteenth century as stemming from American daily family life, religious convictions, and civic participation.[55] In trying to understand the tug-of-war between self and society in America, however, de Tocqueville and Bellah pondered only the habits of the white, Protestant, English-speaking heart. Given the large presence of Latinos in the post-millennial generation, particularly in the large metropolitan areas, we would do well to understand the habits of the Latino heart as well. These young people entering adulthood are heirs to traditions forged in nearly five hundred years of the Indo-Afro-Oriento-Ibero version of Western society in what is now the United States. Thanks to their primary socialization as young children with their families, they have absorbed norms and mores that have produced, for seventy-five years, high labor force participation, low welfare use, vigorous family formation, and positive health outcomes. Since beginning their secondary socialization in schools, jobs, sports teams, organizations, and use of English-language media, these Latino post-millennials have had to contend with nativist rhetoric that denigrates and rejects their very presence in the United States. Yet since 1849, Latinos in California have proclaimed their adherence to a universalist vision of an America built on equality, freedom, and democracy, even when confronted by the nativist vision that has tried repeatedly to exclude them from the community of Americans. As of 2015, a Latino-post millennial born in the US turns eighteen approximately every thirty seconds, and officially enters adulthood. In those same thirty seconds, approximately two non-Hispanic whites die. The "habits of the Latino heart" are becoming an increasingly larger part of society, and the electorate, every day. The tug-of-war between nativist exclusiveness and universalist inclusion may well be decided by Latino post-millennials in the struggle for America's soul in the twenty-first century.

Appendix

The data presented in the second edition of *La Nueva California* is drawn primarily from four sources: Vital Statistics, the US census (1940 through 2000), the American Community Survey (2010 and 2014),[1] and the Current Population Survey.[2] Each of these sources has a different level of accuracy. Vital statistics data such as births, deaths, and life expectancy are tabulated for the entire population and are not samples. Consequently there are no "sampling errors" associated with these data. All of the census, American Community Survey, and Current Population Survey estimates are based on Public Use Microdata Samples (PUMS). The US Census Bureau has implemented a series of steps to protect the confidentiality of the data so that no individual's data can be identified. Census data for 1940 through 2000 are a 5% sample of the universe, or on average 1 in 20 persons in the total population. Since the populations for California and the United States are in the millions and multi-millions, the statistical errors associated with these data are extremely small—negligible in terms of the estimates. The US Census Bureau replaced the "long form" approach to collecting detailed data on households and individuals with the American Community Survey in 2001; and the 2010 and 2015 estimates are based on a 1% sample of the universe, or on average 1 in 100 persons. These samples are also very large. For example, the total population of California in 2010 was 36,800,011, and in 2015 it was 38,701,504. The Current Population Survey is the primary source for data on labor statistics in the United States and involves a much smaller sample than for the census or the American Community Survey. The Current Population Survey is approximately a 1 in 2,000 sample of the population and consequently has larger standard errors. The Current Population Survey provided data for two categories: labor force participation rates for males aged sixteen years and older, and race/ethnic population distributions (table 2).

Very substantially, the estimates with the greatest source of statistical error are those in figure 34, "Race/ethnic composition of post-millennials in the top eleven

TABLE 2 Percent of Latino and Non-Latino White Post-Millennials in the Top Eleven Latino Metropolitan Areas, with Estimated Standard Errors, 2015

Area	Post-Millennial Population Aged 16+	Percent Latino	Std Error Latino	Percent NL White	Std Error NL White
Los Angeles–Long Beach–Santa Ana, CA	3,310,572	59.4%	1.59%	22.3%	1.27%
New York–North New Jersey–Long Island, NY–NJ–PA	4,724,547	28.3%	1.22%	41.3%	1.25%
Houston–Baytown–Sugar Land, TX	1,789,005	48.5%	2.20%	25.4%	1.80%
Dallas–Fort Worth–Arlington, TX	2,134,566	37.7%	1.95%	36.7%	1.83%
Riverside–San Bernardino, CA	1,142,863	65.8%	2.61%	20.1%	2.08%
Miami–Fort Lauderdale–Miami Beach, FL	1,456,085	42.2%	2.41%	27.0%	2.04%
Chicago–Naperville–Joliet, IL–IN–WI	2,231,140	27.2%	1.75%	48.1%	1.85%
Phoenix–Mesa–Scottsdale, AZ	1,170,890	49.2%	2.72%	35.0%	2.44%
San Antonio, TX	611,987	67.1%	3.53%	23.2%	2.99%
San Diego–Carlsbad–San Marcos, CA	811,410	41.6%	3.22%	34.5%	2.92%
San Francisco–Oakland–Fremont, CA	1,052,724	26.7%	2.53%	33.1%	2.54%

SOURCE: Custom analysis by Werner Schink of data from Steven Ruggles, Katie Genadek, Ronald Goeken, Josiah Gorver, and Matthew Sobek, Integrated Public Use Microdata Series: Version 6.0 [machine-readable database] (Minneapolis: University of Minnesota, 2015).

Latino metropolitan areas." The standard errors in the table were computed using the formula

$$se(p, y) = \sqrt{\frac{b}{y}\, p(100 - p)}$$

where p is the estimated percentage (not decimal share), y is the estimated total population (denominator) for which the percentage is calculated, and b is a factor computed by the Bureau of Labor Statistics that is specific for each race/ethnic group.[3] As can be seen in the table, the standard errors for these estimates are relatively small compared with the estimates. With the standard errors, 90% confidence intervals for the estimates can be developed, applying a factor of plus or minus 1.65 times the standard error. Statistically, the true population will be within the confidence interval 90% of the time. Errors in estimation also may result from what is referred to as "nonsampling error." Nonsampling error can arise from many sources, including inability to obtain information about all persons in a sample, inability of respondents to recall information, and errors made in collecting or processing data.

Extensive documentation exists for census data, the American Community Survey data, and the Current Population Survey. Technical documentation for the

American Community Survey can be found on the US Census Bureau website, www.census.gov/programs-surveys/acs/technical-documentation/code-lists.html, and for the Current Population Survey at the US Bureau of Labor Statistics website, http://www.bls.gov/cps/documentation.htm.

For additional information concerning the technical documentation, contact the author at

Center for the Study of Latino Health and Culture
UCLA David Geffen School of Medicine
924 Westwood Blvd, Suite 200-Q
Los Angeles, CA 90024
(310) 794–0663
cesla@ucla.edu

NOTES

CHAPTER 1. AMERICA DEFINES LATINOS

Epigraph is from Ernesto de la Torre Villar, *La Constitución de Apatzingán y los creadores del estado mexicano* (Mexico City: Universidad Nacional Autónoma de México, Instituto de Investigaciones Históricas, 2010), p. 331. The original Spanish reads, "Bando aboliendo las castas y la esclavitud entre los Mexicanos . . . no se nombran en calidades de indios, mulatos ni castas, sino todos generalmente americanos."

   1. J. Ross Browne, *Relación de los debates de la convencion de California, sobre la formación de la constitución de estado en setiembre y octubre de 1849* (New York: S. Benedict, 1851), pp. 17, 25–26. For the English text, see J. Ross Browne, *Report of the Debates of the Convention of California on the Formation of the State Constitution, in September and October, 1849* (Washington, DC: John T. Towers, 1850), pp. 14, 22–23.
   2. John Charles Chasteen, "Introduction: Beyond Imagined Communities," in Sara Castro-Klarén and John Charles Chasteen, eds., *Beyond Imagined Communities: Reading and Writing the Nation in Nineteenth-Century Latin America* (Baltimore: Johns Hopkins University Press, 2003), pp. ix–xxv.
   3. Simón Bolívar, *Para nosotros la patria es América,* prologue by Arturo Uslar Pietri, notes by Manuel Pérez Vila, Colección Claves de América, no. 1 (Caracas: Fundación Biblioteca Ayacucho, 1991), p. 15.
   4. Hernán Venegas Delgado, "Familias de la élite e independencia (1820–1829)," in Francisco Chacón Jiménez and Ana Vera Estrada, eds., *Dimensiones del diálogo americano contemporáneo sobre la familia en la época colonial* (Murcia, Spain: Universidad de Murcia, Servicio de Publicaciones, 2010), pp. 221–222.
   5. "Documento 10: Proclama del cura Hidalgo a la nación americana," in De la Torre Villar, *La Constitución de Apatzingán,* pp. 203–204. The original Spanish reads, "¡Levantaos, almas nobles de los Americanos! . . . que ha llegado el dia de la gloria y de la felicidad pública."

6. "Documento 86: Decreto constitucional para la libertad de la América Mexicana, sancionado en Apatzingán (22 de octubre de 1814)," in De la Torre Villar, *La Constitución de Apatzingán,* p. 380.

7. Or at least for all adult males; virtually no one in either Mexico or the United States proposed political rights for women at this time.

8. Walter A. McDougall, "The Colonial Origins of American Identity," *Orbis* 49 (2006): 7–19.

9. Eric Kaufman, "American Exceptionalism Reconsidered: Anglo-Saxon Ethnogenesis in the 'Universal' Nation, 1776–1850," *Journal of American Studies* 33 (1999): 437–451. See also Paul T. McCartney, "American Nationalism and U.S. Foreign Policy from September 11 to the Iraq War," *Political Science Quarterly* 119.3 (Fall 2004): 402–407.

10. Christina González and Patricia Gándara, "Why We Like to Call Ourselves Latinas," *Journal of Hispanic Higher Education* 4.4 (October 2005): 395.

11. Reginald Horsman, *Race and Manifest Destiny: The Origins of American Racial Anglo-Saxonism* (Cambridge, MA: Harvard University Press, 1981), pp. 228–248.

12. Kaufman, "American Exceptionalism," pp. 452–454.

13. "Documento 86, "Decreto constitucional para la libertad de la América Mexicana, sancionado en Apatzingán (22 de octubre de 1814)," cap. II, art. 6, in De la Torre Villar, *La Constitución de Apatzingán,* p. 381. The requirements for citizenship are contained in cap. III.

14. Cynthia L. Chamberlin, Laura Ochoa, and David E. Hayes-Bautista, "Women's Business: *Las Juntas Patrióticas de Señoras* and Latina Women in Public Life in California, 1850–2014" (Los Angeles: UCLA Center for the Study of Latino Health and Culture, 2014), pp. 2–4.

15. Article 11, Section 21, in Browne, *Relación,* Apendice, p. XI; *Report,* appendix, p. XI.

16. Fergus M. Bordewich, *America's Great Debate: Henry Clay, Stephen A. Douglas, and the Compromise That Preserved the Union* (New York: Simon & Schuster, 2012), pp. 303–316 ; Robert E. Terrill and David Zarefsky, "Consistency and Change in the Rhetoric of Stephen A. Douglas," *Southern Communication Journal* 62.3 (1997): 179.

17. "A Trip to the Coast . . ." *Alta California,* 7 July 1857, p. 1.

18. "Comparaciones," reprinted from *El Éco del Pacífico* (San Francisco), n.d., in *El Clamor Público,* 15 March 1856, p. 2. The original Spanish reads, "Nada mas gracioso que ver a una parte de la prensa de esta ciudad hablar de la superioridad de la raza sajona, sobre todo cuando se trata de compararla con la nuestra. ¡Como se pondera su habilidad, su perfeccionamiento, su jenerosidad! y en cambio cuanto atraso, cuantos vicios, cuanta incapacidad para gobernarnos en nuestros pueblos y cuanta crueldad desplegamos para martirizar a sus *libertadores,* nosotros los pícaros, que tenemos el pecado de defender de sus garras nuestros paises, nuestros recuerdos, nuestras creencias, nuestra historia en fin!" (Nothing is more amusing than to see part of this city's press talking about the superiority of the Saxon race, above all

when it tries to compare it with our own race. How it praises their ability, their perfection, their generosity! And in contrast, what backwardness, how many vices, what incapacity for governing ourselves in our communities, and what cruelty we display when we make martyrs of their *liberators*—we rascals, who commit the sin of defending from their talons our lands, our memories, our beliefs, our history, in short!).

19. Untitled editorial, *El Clamor Público,* 24 April 1858, p. 2. The original Spanish reads, "La raza Anglo-Sajona le quitará la porcion mas rica de nuestro continente, y hara de México lo que la naturaleza la designó que fuera; mientras que sus miserable habitantes estarán obligados a refugiarse en los trópicos ó los háremos nuestros esclavos, como su color bien lo justifica."

20. Ramírez allowed that most nations of the world had had similar origins; his objection was that the Anglo-Saxons appeared not to have progressed beyond the freebooting stage. "Expedicion de Walker," *El Clamor Público,* 28 August 1855, p. 2. The original Spanish reads, "La historia del mundo dice quo los Anglo-Saxones en su orígen éran ladrones y piratas, el mismo que todas las naciones en la era de su infancia. . . . El instinto pirático de los antiguos Anglo-Saxones está activo todavia."

21. Stacey L. Smith, "Remaking Slavery in a Free State: Masters and Slaves in Gold Rush California," *Pacific Historical Review,* 80.1 (February 2011): 28–63.

22. Browne, *Relación,* pp. 67–77, 314–315; *Report,* pp. 61–73, 304–307. Due to the Atlantic American transcriber's misunderstanding of the Hispanic custom of using two surnames—the first, and primary one, being that of the individual's father and the second that of the mother—Pablo de la Guerra y Noriega is here called "Señor Noriego [*sic*]," instead of the more correct "Señor de la Guerra."

23. "One Language" (editorial), *Alta California,* 2 December 1850, p. 2. With complete lack of historical perspective, the editor here equates *Anglo-Saxon* with English; *nervous* is a nineteenth-century usage meaning "sinewy" or "flexible."

24. "Summary of the Events of the Fortnight," *Alta California,* 16 January 1854, p. 1.

25. Untitled letter to the editor, *El Éco del Pacífico,* reprinted in *El Clamor Público,* 25 September 1858, p. 2.

26. Paul Bryan Gray recently completed a biography of Ramírez: *A Clamor for Equality* (Lubbock: Texas Tech University Press, 2013). Ramírez was born in 1842 in Los Angeles and died in Ensenada, Mexico, in 1909.

27. "Convencion Nacional de los Know Nothings," *El Clamor Público,* 14 August 1855, p. 3. Ramírez's Spanish translation of Article VIII of the Know-Nothing platform reads, "Resistencia a la política agresiva . . . de la Iglesia Católica Romana en nuestro pais, elevando á todos los puestos políticos . . . a aquellos solamente que no tienen sumision directa ò indirecta a ninguna potencia extranjera . . . y que son Americanos de nacimiento . . . 'los Americanos solos gobernaràn a la América!'" The other Know-Nothing goals mentioned appear in Articles V and XII of the platform.

28. "Los Know Nothings," *El Clamor Público,* 3 July 1855, p. 2. The original Spanish reads, "Se llaman así mismo 'Nativos Americanos,' cuando sus bisabuelos

emigraron á América del mismo modo que lo hacen en nuestros dias los habitantes de Europa. . . . [H]an hecho una liga para . . . abolir el derecho del sufragio y electiva á todos los individuos . . . que tengan la *desgracia* de profesar la religion Católica Apostólica Romana."

29. Untitled article, *El Clamor Público,* 30 October 1855, p. 1. The original Spanish reads, "'Hermanos, tengamos libertad americana y religion americana.'—*Discurso del Hon. K. Rayer.* Creemos que nunca se ha sospechado que Jesucristo era nativo americano y por consiguiente su religion no es la que quiere Mr. Rayer. Ciertamente no nos oponemos a que los Know Nothings tengan una religion 'americana'—la que nos vino de Jerusalen es incompatible con su carácter."

30. Untitled editorial, *El Clamor Público,* 4 September 1855, p. 2.

31. Peyton Hunt, "The Rise and Fall of the 'Know Nothings' in California," *California Historical Society Quarterly* 9.1 (March 1930): 16–49.

32. "Exposicion," *El Clamor Público,* 6 September 1856, p. 3. The original Spanish reads, "El Know Nothing, envolviendo ideas egotistas de nativismo y contrarias al Catolicismo se opone á los intereses de los individuos que han adoptado por patria à los E.U. de America."

33. Gerald Stanley, "Slavery and the Origins of the Republican Party in California," *Southern California Quarterly* 60.1 (Spring 1978): 1–16; Hunt, "The Rise and Fall," p. 48; Bruce Levine, "Conservatism, Nativism, and Slavery: Thomas R. Whitney and the Origins of the Know-Nothing Party," *Journal of American History* 88.2 (September 2001): 455–488.

34. "To Our Spanish-American Friends," *El Clamor Público,* 18 June 1859, p. 3.

35. David E. Hayes-Bautista, *El Cinco de Mayo: An American Tradition* (Berkeley and Los Angeles: University of California Press, 2012).

36. "WHITE MEN MUST RULE AMERICA!" *Sonora (CA) Union Democrat,* 2 January 1869, p. 2, advertisement urging subscription to the *New York Day Book for 1869,* a publication self-described as "Devoted to White Supremacy, State Equality, & Federal Union," as "the paper of the people," and as "A Political Newspaper—A Family, Literary Paper, and an Agricultural Paper," in that order. The lengthy text of the advertisement makes it clear that the political affiliation of the *New York Day Book* was Democratic, which in the 1860s was the conservative party in the US.

37. "The Mongrel Republics of America," *Sonora (CA) Union Democrat,* 2 November 1867, p. 1.

38. "The Constitutional Amendment," *Sonora (CA) Union Democrat,* 6 March 1869, p. 2.

39. "The Universal Suffrage Question," *Amador Dispatch,* 31 August 1867, p. 2. This expression of virulently racist attitudes was somewhat more common and unabashed in Northern California, where the majority of the population since the Gold Rush had been Atlantic American immigrants, than it was in Southern California, where Latinos continued to be the majority of the population until ca. 1880. Such expression was, however, far from unknown in Southern California even before 1880.

40. Martha Menchaca, *Recovering History, Constructing Race: The Indian, Black, and White Roots of Mexican-Americans* (Austin: University of Texas Press, 2001), pp. 221–222. The full text of the legal decision is in "People v. De La Guerra," case no. 2,372, *Reports of Cases Determined in the Supreme Court of the State of California,* 40, transcribed by R. August Thompson (San Francisco: Bancroft-Whitney, 1906), pp. 311–344.

41. "Gacetilla," *La Crónica* (Los Angeles), October 3, 1885, p. 3. The eccentrically punctuated original Spanish reads, "Ya se vé; como solamente los Mexicanos roban . . . .ahí están los Gassen, Katz y otros como prueba." (What appears to be an ellipsis is not; it is the original punctuation of this passage.)

42. Letter to the editor, *La Crónica* (Los Angeles), 19 July 1873, p. 2; untitled editorial, *La Crónica* (Los Angeles), 16 August 1873, p. 2; untitled editorial, *La Crónica* (Los Angeles), 23 August 1873, p. 2. The latter source, basing its observations on data from Los Angeles County's voter registration records for the year, noted that Latinos would have an even greater number of votes if everyone eligible would register to vote.

43. As reported in an untitled article, *La Crónica* (Los Angeles), 15 February 1873, p. 2, citing *La Sociedad* (San Francisco), 5 February 1873.

44. "Notas editoriales," *La Crónica* (Los Angeles), 5 January 1878, p. 2. The original Spanish reads, "Si los que tienen á su cargos la defensa de nuestras leyes . . . con su indiferencia legalizan, puede decirse, el acto . . . ahora que se encuentran reunidos en Sacramento nuestros representes . . . [deben] ganarlos para que promulgen una ley autorizando el *linchamiento* de todo ladron, siempre que tan edificante acto sea cometido por ciudadanos americanos ébrios y que las víctimas sean de raza latina" (If those who have the defense of our laws in their charge . . . legalize the act, as it were, by their indifference . . . now that our representatives are met together in Sacramentos . . . [they should] win them over to promulgating a law authorizing the *lynching* of any thief, always provided that such an edifying act should be committed by drunk American citizens, and that the victims be of the Latino race); emphasis in the original.

45. Untitled editorial, *La Crónica* (Los Angeles), 26 July 1873, p. 2. The original Spanish reads, "Ahora bien; si lo que se quiere bautizar con el nombre de español está escrito en un idioma nuevo, en un lenguaje desconocido que—por derecho de invencion—pertenece al traductor del Concilio, claro es que la ordenanza no es legal."

46. Untitled article, *La Crónica* (Los Angeles), 2 January 1874, p. 2.

47. Untitled editorial, *La Crónica* (Los Angeles), 21 January 1874, p. 2.

48. Untitled article, *La Crónica* (Los Angeles), 21 February 1874, p. 2; untitled article, *La Crónica* (Los Angeles), 21 February 1874, p. 4.

49. Harry N. Scheiber, "Race, Radicalism and Reform: Historical Perspectives on the 1879 California Constitution," *Hastings Constitutional Law Quarterly* 17 (1989): 45.

50. Louis Rubidoux Sr. was born in St. Louis in 1796, when it was still French territory; his namesake son was born in Santa Fe, New Mexico, in 1837. Both married Latina women from New Mexico and settled in Southern California. "Campo

de Rubidoux, Distrito de Pinacate, Condado de San Diego," letter from the Sociedad Patriótica del Campo de Rubidoux, *La Crónica* (Los Angeles), 15 September 1883, p. 2; Scheiber, "Race, Radicalism, and Reform," p. 45.

51. "Constitution of the State of California. Adopted in Convention at Sacramento, March Third, Eighteen Hundred and Seventy-Nine," in *The Statutes of California Passed at the Twenty-Third Session of the Legislature, 1880* (Sacramento, CA: State Office, J. D. Young, 1880), p. xxvii.

52. "Illustrious and Illustrated: The Scions of the Legislature 'Done Up," *Los Angeles Times,* 7 March 1885, p. 4.

53. David E. Hayes-Bautista, Marco Antonio Firebaugh, Cynthia L. Chamberlin, and Christina Gamboa, "Reginaldo Francisco del Valle: UCLA's Forgotten Forefather," *Southern California Quarterly* 88.1 (Spring 2006): 5–7.

54. John Higham, "Origins of Immigration Restriction, 1882–1897: A Social Analysis," *Mississippi Valley Historical Review* 39.1 (June 1952): 77–88.

55. John Higham, "The Mind of a Nativist: Henry F. Bowers and the A.P.A.," *American Quarterly* 4.1 (Spring 1952): 16–24.

56. K. Gerald Marsden, "Patriotic Societies and American Labor: The American Protective Association in Wisconsin," *Wisconsin Magazine of History* 41.4 (Summer 1958): 287–294.

57. "Las Elecciones," *Las Dos Repúblicas* (Los Angeles), 13 October 1894, p. 2.

58. "Los 'A.P.A.' Conferencia Tenida por el Redactor de Este Periodico con el Honorable R. F. del Valle," *Las Dos Repúblicas* (Los Angeles), 20 October 1894, p. 2. The reference to the Catholic discoverer of the Americas was to Christopher Columbus, who had been supported by the "Catholic Monarchs" Isabella of Castile and Ferdinand of Aragon; Columbus himself viewed his voyages as playing a significant role in Catholic eschatology.

59. Higham, "The Mind of a Nativist," p. 20.

60. Newell G. Bringhurst, "The Ku Klux Klan in a Central California Community: Tulare County during the 1920s and 1930s," *Southern California Quarterly* 82.4 (Winter 2000): 365–396.

61. Joan M. Jensen, "Apartheid, Pacific Coast Style," *Pacific Historical Review* 38.3 (August 1969): 335–340.

62. "Manifiesto del Comité Mexicano de Auxilios," *El Heraldo de México* (Los Angeles), 8 May 1921, p. 6.

63. "Lo que es y lo que puede hacer la Liga Protector Mexicana de California," *El Heraldo de México* (Los Angeles), 13 March 1918, p. 2.

64. "Todo Va Favorable Para L. Guerra," *El Heraldo de México* (Los Angeles), 13 March 1918, p. 1.

65. "La Suscrición en Favor de L. Guerra," *El Heraldo de México* (Los Angeles), 16 March 1918, p. 6.

66. "El Gobernador Concede El Indulto de un Mexicano," *El Heraldo de México* (Los Angeles), 28 April 1918, p. 1.

67. "Instrucción y elevación moral de los socios," *El Heraldo de México* (Los Angeles), 13 March 1918, p. 2.

68. "Gran concierto y baile," *El Heraldo de México* (Los Angeles), 4 August 1918, p. 1.

69. "Comité mexicano de auxilios establecerá un comedor público," *El Heraldo de México* (Los Angeles), 6 May 1921, p. 8.

70. Paul Knepper, "Southern-Style Punitive Repression: Ethnic Stratification, Economic Inequality, and Imprisonment in Territorial Arizona," *Social Justice* 16.4 (Winter 1989): 136.

71. "Manifiesto del 'Comite Mexicano de Auxilios' a la Colonia Hispano-Mexicano de L.A.," *El Heraldo de México* (Los Angeles), 8 May 1921, p. 6.

72. Liga Protectora Latina, Diploma de Honor, 12 October 1925, Reginaldo F. del Valle Collection, box 3, item HM 43971, Huntington Library, San Marino, CA.

73. Brandon H. Mila, *"Hermanos de Raza:* Alonso S. Perales and the Creation of the LULAC Spirit" (master's thesis, University of North Texas, December 2013, Appendix A, Objectives and Aims of the Latin American Citizens League, circa 1927), pp. 108–109.

74. San Gabriel Spanish American League, Articles of Association, Reginaldo F. del Valle Collection, box 3, item HM 43898, 1934, Huntington Library, San Marino, CA. Originally sent by the league's secretary, Daniel Dominguez, to Del Valle, enclosed in a letter dated 23 March 1936, Reginaldo F. del Valle Collection, box 3, item HM 43897.

75. *Mexicans in California: Report of Governor C. C. Young's Mexican Fact-Finding Committee* (San Francisco: California State Printing Office, 1930; rpt. San Francisco and Saratoga, CA: R and E Research Associates, 1970), p. 12.

76. Ibid., p. 209.

77. United States Bureau of the Census, *Fifteenth Census of the United States: 1930; Abstract of the Fifteenth Census of the United States.* Washington, DC: US Government Printing Office, 1933), pp. 83, 29.

78. *Mexicans in California,* pp. 183–184.

79. Ibid., p. 12.

80. Francisco E. Balderrama, "The Emergence of Unconstitutional Deportation and Repatriation of Mexicans and Mexican Americans as a Public Issue," *Radical History Review* 93 (Fall 2005): 107–110.

81. Cited in Kay Deaux, "To Be an American: Immigration, Hyphenation, and Incorporation," *Journal of Social Issues* 64.4 (December 2008): 935.

82. Leroy G. Dorsey and Rachel M. Harlow, "'We want Americans pure and simple': Theodore Roosevelt and the Myth of Americanism," *Rhetoric and Public Affairs* 6.1 (2003): 55–78.

83. William Lloyd Warner and Leo Srole, *The Social Systems of American Ethnic Groups* (New Haven, CT: Yale University Press, 1945), p. 285.

84. Robert E. Park and Ernest W. Burgess, *Introduction to the Science of Sociology* (Chicago: University of Chicago Press, 1924), pp. 757–758.

85. CESLAC UW 1998, 3: US-born Latinos, some college, p. 90.

86. CESLAC UW 1998, 3: US- born Latinos, some college, p. 29.

87. CESLAC UW 1998, 7: Latino civic leaders, p. 37.

88. CESLAC UW 1998, 8: Latino business leaders, p. 25.

89. CESLAC UW 1998, 1: US-born Latinos, high school only, p. 20.

90. CESLAC UW 1998, 1: US-born Latinos, high school only, p. 21.

91. CESLAC UW 1998, 3: US-born Latinos, some college, p. 89.

92. CESLAC UW 1998, 3: US- born Latinos, some college, p. 33.

CHAPTER 2. LATINOS REJECT AMERICA'S DEFINITION

Epigraph is from CESLAC CHM 1999, 5: Latino health administrator, individual interview by Valerie Talavera-Bustillo, June 23, transcript stored at CESLAC, pp. 28–29.

1. CESLAC Chicano Health Movement (CHM) 1999, 8: Latina pathologist, individual interview by Valerie Talavera-Bustillo, July 1, transcript stored at CESLAC, p. 2.

2. CESLAC CHM 1999, 7: Latina program administrator, individual interview by Valerie Talavera-Bustillo, February–May, transcript stored at CESLAC, p. 18.

3. California Employment Development Department (CA EDD), *Socio-economic Trends in California, 1940–1980* (Sacramento, CA: Department of Health Services and Welfare Agency, 1986), p. 62, tables 24b, 24c.

4. CESLAC CHM 1999, 7: Latina program administrator, pp. 18–19.

5. CESLAC CHM 1999, 2: Latina health administrator, individual interview by Valerie Talavera-Bustillo, July 6, transcript stored at CESLAC, p. 14.

6. CESLAC CHM 1999, 7: Latina program administrator, p. 20.

7. CA EDD 1986, p. 30: tables 12A, 12B.

8. CESLAC CHM 1999, 8: Latina pathologist, individual interview by Valerie Talavera-Bustillo, July 1, transcript stored at CESLAC, p. 5.

9. CESLAC CHM 1999, 12: Latino health law attorney, individual interview by Valerie Talavera-Bustillo, June 29, transcript stored at CESLAC, pp. 1–2.

10. Philip D. Ortego, "Education and the Chicano: Moctezuma's Children," in *Voices: Readings from* El Grito, *a Journal of Contemporary Mexican American Thought* (Berkeley, CA: Quinto Sol, 1971), pp. 130–131.

11. CESLAC CHM 1999, 9: Latino family physician, individual interview by Valerie Talavera-Bustillo, March 4 and March 8, transcript stored at CESLAC, p. 8.

12. CESLAC CHM 1999, 12: Latino health law attorney, p. 1.

13. CESLAC CHM 1999, 9: Latino family physician, p. 3.

14. CESLAC CHM 1999, 3: Latino surgeon, individual interview by Valerie Talavera-Bustillo, March 24, transcript stored at CESLAC, p. 5. Ruben Salazar was a reporter for the *Los Angeles Times* who covered the Chicano moratorium. The moratorium itself ended in a police action, with tear gas used to disperse the crowd. Salazar was sitting inside a bar when a police agent on the sidewalk in front fired a tear gas canister inside, which struck and killed Salazar.

15. CESLAC CHM 1999, 11: Latino elected official, individual interview by Valerie Talavera-Bustillo, July 1, transcript stored at CESLAC, p. 9.

16. Mario Barrera, *Beyond Aztlan: Ethnic Autonomy in Comparative Perspective* (South Bend, IN: University of Notre Dame Press, 1988), p. 38.

17. CA EDD 1986, p. 10: table 2c.

18. CESLAC CHM 1999, 4: Latino hematologist, individual interview by Valerie Talavera-Bustillo, June 19–27, transcript stored at CESLAC, p. 8.

19. CESLAC CHM 1999, 7: Latina program administrator, p. 18.

20. Ibid., p. 5.

21. CESLAC CHM 1999, 9: Latino family physician, p. 43.

22. CESLAC CHM 1999, 10: Latino family physician, individual interview by Valerie Talavera-Bustillo, June 22, transcript stored at CESLAC, pp. 20–21.

23. CESLAC CHM 1999, 1: Latino dentist, individual interview by Valerie Talavera-Bustillo, June 25, transcript stored at CESLAC, p. 6.

24. CESLAC CHM 1999, 13: Latino ophthalmologist, individual interview by Valerie Talavera-Bustillo, March 19, transcript stored at CESLAC, p. 22.

25. Milton Myron Gordon, *Assimilation in American Life: The Role of Race, Religion, and National Origins* (New York: Oxford University Press, 1964), pp. 241–245; Eugene I. Bender and George Kagiwada, "Hansen's Law of 'Third-Generation Return' and the Study of American Religio-Ethnic Groups," *Phylon* 29:4 (1968): 360–370.

26. CESLAC CHM 1999, 5: Latino health administrator, p. 5.

27. CESLAC CHM 1999, 7: Latina program administrator, p. 6.

28. CESLAC CHM 1999, 5: Latino health administrator, p. 6.

29. CESLAC CHM 1999, 9: Latino family physician, p. 6.

30. CESLAC CHM 1999, 10: Latino family physician, p. 14.

31. CESLAC CHM 1999, 5: Latino health administrator, p. 10.

32. CESLAC CHM 1999, 6: Latino medical researcher, individual interview by Valerie Talavera-Bustillo, February 10–11, transcript stored at CESLAC, p. 32.

33. CESLAC CHM 1999, 7: Latina program administrator, p. 18.

34. Ibid., p. 20.

35. Ibid., pp. 20–21.

36. CESLAC CHM 1999, 11: Latino elected official, p. 9.

37. CESLAC CHM 1999, 4: Latino hematologist, p. 10.

38. CESLAC CHM 1999, 13: Latino ophthalmologist, p. 6.

39. Ibid., p. 7.

40. California Department of Finance (CA DOF), Demographic Research Unit, "Race/Ethnic Population Estimates: Components of Change, California Counties, July 1970–July 1990" (Sacramento: California Department of Finance, 1999).

CHAPTER 3. WASHINGTON DEFINES A NEW NATIVISM

Epigraph is from Franklin Frazier, Ellen Sehgal, Marie Cohen, Joanne Frankel, Gale Harris, Letitia Colston, Hannah Fein, and Joyce W. Smith, *The Urban Underclass:*

Disturbing Problems Demanding Attention (HRD-90–52) (Washington, DC: US General Accounting Office, 1990), p. 1.

1. Oscar Lewis, *Five Families: Mexican Case Studies in the Culture of Poverty* (New York: Basic Books, 1959).

2. Oscar Lewis, *La Vida: A Puerto Rican Family in the Culture of Poverty—San Juan and New York* (New York: Random House, 1965, 1966), p. xlv.

3. Ibid., pp. xlvii–xlviii, li.

4. Michael Harrington, *The Other America: Poverty in the United States* (New York: Macmillan, 1962), pp. 16–17.

5. Lee Rainwater and William L. Yancey, *The Moynihan Report and the Politics of Controversy: A Trans-Action Social Science and Public Policy Report* (Cambridge, MA: MIT Press, 1967), pp. 39–132.

6. William J. Wilson, *The Truly Disadvantaged: The Inner City, the Underclass and Public Policy* (Chicago: University of Chicago Press, 1987), p. 8.

7. Helen Rowan, "A Minority Nobody Knows," in John H. Burma, comp., *Mexican-Americans in the United States: A Reader* (Cambridge, MA: Schenkman Publishing and Canfield Press, 1970), p. 295.

8. Armando Rendon, "La Raza—Today, not Mañana," in Burma, *Mexican-Americans in the United States,* p. 307.

9. Rowan, "A Minority Nobody Knows," p. 295; Rendon, "La Raza," p. 318.

10. Rendon, "La Raza," p. 315.

11. Armando Navarro, *Mexican American Youth Organization: Avant-Garde of the Chicago Movement in Texas* (Austin: University of Texas, 1995), p. 243.

The term *Aztlán* was popularized during the Chicano movement. The historical term refers to the quasi-mythical home of the Aztecs before they journeyed to Tenochtitlan, on the site of present-day Mexico City. Activists used the term to refer to the modern-day, heavily Latino region of the US Southwest, seeing it as a spiritual homeland. Some Chicano activists place Aztlán near the Four Corners region of the United States, where Arizona, Utah, New Mexico, and Colorado meet; most recent scholarship places a possible historical Aztlán closer to today's Mazatlán, on the Pacific coast of Mexico.

12. David E. Hayes-Bautista and Jorge Chapa, "Latino Terminology: Conceptual Bases for Standardized Terminology," *American Journal of Public Health* 7.1 (1986): 64.

13. See note 1 of this chapter.

14. Melvin H. Rudov and Nancy Santangelo, *Health Status of Minorities and Low-Income Groups* (Washington, DC: Department of Health, Education, and Welfare, Public Health Service, Health Resources Administration, Office of Health Resources Opportunity, 1979), p. 23.

15. Ibid., p. 33.

16. Melvin H. Rudov, Jeanne A. Klingensmith, Nancy Santangelo, and Margaret W. Pratt, *Health Status of Minorities and Low Income Groups,* US Department

of Health and Human Services (Washington, DC: US Government Printing Office, 1985), p. ix. Emphasis added.

17. *Eliminating Racial and Ethnic Disparities in Health* (Washington, DC: US Department of Health and Human Services, Initiative to Eliminate Racial and Ethnic Disparities in Health, 1998), formerly available at http//www/raceandhealth.hhs.gov/sidebars/sbinitOver.htm (dead link); screen capture (2003) stored at CESLAC.

18. National Institutes of Health, Office of Research on Minority Health, "New Web Site Provides Information about the NIH Minority Health Initiative," 14 April 2000, http//www.nih.gov/news/pr/apr2000/od-14.htm [accessed 28 April 2016].

19. Charles Murray, *Losing Ground: American Social Policy, 1950–1980* (New York: Basic Books, 1984), pp. 179, 185, 219.

20. Lawrence M. Mead, "The New Politics of the New Poverty," *Public Interest* 103 (Spring 1991): 7. Emphasis added.

21. Ibid., p. 5. Emphasis added.

22. Lisbeth M. Schorr, with Daniel Schorr, *Within Our Reach: Breaking the Cycle of Disadvantage* (New York: Anchor Press/Doubleday, 1988), p. 149. Emphasis in the original.

23. Murray Weidenbaum, "It's Up to Individuals to Fight the War on Poverty," *Los Angeles Times,* 23 September 1990, p. 2.

24. Charles Murray, *Coming Apart: The State of White America, 1960–2010* (New York: Crown Forum, 2012), p. 210.

25. David E. Hayes-Bautista, "Latino Health Conditions: Policies for Future Research" (paper delivered at the annual meeting of the American Public Health Association, Los Angeles, 16 October 1978).

26. David E. Hayes-Bautista, Werner O. Schink, and Jorge Chapa, *The Burden of Support: Young Latinos in an Aging Society* (Stanford, CA: Stanford University Press, 1988), pp. 36–41.

27. Ibid., pp. 1–10, 145–150.

28. State of California, Department of Finance, *Revised Race/Ethnic Population Estimates: Components of Change for California Counties, July 1970–1990* (Sacramento, CA: Department of Finance, September 2007), http://www.dof.ca.gov/research/demographic/reports/estimates/race-ethnic_1970–90/ [accessed 29 April 2016]. The UCLA School of Medicine is now the David Geffen School of Medicine at UCLA.

29. Los Angeles County Department of Health Services, Public Health Programs and Services, Programs Coordination and Support Services, Data Collection and Analysis Division, "Vital Statistics of Los Angeles County, 1985," May 1985.

30. California Economic Development Agency (CA EDD), "Socio-Economic Trends in California, 1940 to 1980" (Sacramento: California Employment Data and Research Division, Estimates and Economic Research Group, 1986).

31. Mead, "The New Politics of the New Poverty," p. 4.

32. United States Department of Commerce (US DOC), *Census of Population and Housing, 1990: Summary Tape File 3 on CD-ROM (California)* (Washington, DC: US Bureau of the Census, 1990), p. 1.

33. Jens Manuel Krogstad and Mark Hugo Lopez, "Hispanic Population Reaches Record 55 Million, but Growth Has Cooled" (Washington, DC: Pew Research Center, 25 June 2015).

34. Rudov et al., *Health Status* (1985), p. 54.

35. United States Department of Health and Human Services (US DHHS), *Report of the Secretary's Task Force on Black and Minority Health,* vol. 1 (Washington, DC: US Department of Health and Human Services, 1985), p. 174.

36. Kathryn Riedmiller and Kamal Bindra, *Vital Statistics of California, 1998* (Sacramento: California Department of Health Services, 2001), table 2–11.

37. Melinda L. Schriver, "No Health Insurance? It's Enough to Make You Sick: Latino Community at Great Risk" (white paper of the American College of Physicians—American Society of Internal Medicine, March 2000), https://www .acponline.org/acp_policy/policies/no_health_insurance_latino_community_at_ great_risk_2000.pdf [accessed 28 April 2016].

38. Henry J. Kaiser Family Foundation, "Key Facts about the Uninsured Population," 20 October 2015," http://kff.org/uninsured/fact-sheet/key-facts-about-the-uninsured-population/ [accessed 28 April 2016].

39. Henry J. Kaiser Family Foundation, "The California Health Care Landscape," 26 August, 2015, http://kff.org/health-reform/fact-sheet/the-california-health-care-landscape/ [accessed 28 April 2016].

40. Joan W. Moore and Raquel Pinderhughes, eds., *In the Barrios: Latinos and the Underclass Debate* (New York: Russell Sage Foundation, 1993).

CHAPTER 4. LATINOS DEFINE LATINOS

Epigraph is from CESLAC Mexican American Grocers Association (MAGA) 1995, 4: Latino executive, banking, with interpolations by non-Latino white female colleague of interview subject, individual interview by Maria Hayes-Bautista, January–February, 1995, pp. 2–3, transcript stored at CESLAC.

1. Advertisement, "Abarrotes por mayor y menor," *El Clamor Público,* 5 September 1857, p. 3.

2. CESLAC MAGA 2003, Steve Soto, individual interview by David Hayes-Bautista, 9 January 2003, p. 2, transcript stored at CESLAC.

3. Jeffrey M. Humphreys, "Buying Power at the Beginning of a New Century: Projections for 2000 and 2001," *Georgia Business and Economic Conditions* 60.4 (July–August 2000): 14; James Wilkie, Eduardo Alemán, and José Guadalupe Ortega, eds., *Statistical Abstract of Latin America,* no. 37 (Los Angeles: UCLA Latin American Center Publications, University of California, 2001), table 3404.

4. Arlene Dávila, *Latinos, Inc.: The Marketing and Making of a People* (Berkeley and Los Angeles: University of California Press, 2001), p. 23.

5. CESLAC MAGA 2003: Steve Soto, p. 5.

6. State of California, Department of Finance, *Revised Race/Ethnic Population Estimates: Components of Change for California Counties, July 1970–1990* (Sacramento, CA: Department of Finance, September 2007), http://www.dof.ca.gov/research/demographic/reports/estimates/race-ethnic_1970–90/ [accessed 29 April 2016] .

7. California Economic Development Agency (CA EDD), *Socio-Economic Trends in California, 1940 to 1980* (Sacramento: California Employment Data and Research Division, Estimates and Economic Research Group, 1986), p. 10.

8. State of California Department of Finance, "July Population Estimates, E-3 Race/Ethnic Population Estimates: Components of Change for California Counties, 1970–1990," http://www.dof.ca.gov/Forecasting/Demographics/Estimates [accessed 27 July 2016].

9. Mario Barrera, *Beyond Aztlan: Ethnic Autonomy in Comparative Perspective* (South Bend, IN: University of Notre Dame Press, 1990), pp. 5, 158.

10. CA EDD, *Socio-Economic Trends,* p. 10; David E. Hayes-Bautista, *The Health Status of Latinos* (Woodland Hills: California Endowment and California Health-Care Foundation, 1997), p. 28.

11. CESLAC United Way (UW) 1998, 5: Immigrant Latinos; focus group conducted by Maria Hayes-Bautista, 28 October 1998, p. 6, transcript stored at CESLAC.

12. CESLAC MAGA 1995, 2: Latino executive, processed meats, individual interview conducted by Maria Hayes-Bautista, January–February 1995, pp. 1–2, transcript stored at CESLAC.

13. CESLAC MAGA 1995, 7: Latino executive, food and beverage, individual interview conducted by Maria Hayes-Bautista, January–February 1995, p. 5, transcript stored at CESLAC.

14. CESLAC MAGA 1995, 7: Latino executive, food and beverage, p. 18.

15. Ibid., pp. 18–19.

16. CESLAC MAGA 1995, 1: Latina executive, food and beverage, individual interview conducted by Maria Hayes-Bautista, January–February 1995, pp. 4, 7, transcript stored at CESLAC.

17. CESLAC MAGA 1995, 3: Latino executive, soaps and detergents, individual interview conducted by Maria Hayes-Bautista, January–February 1995, p. 16, transcript stored at CESLAC.

18. CESLAC MAGA 1995, 1: Latina executive, food and beverage, p. 8.

19. CESLAC MAGA 1995, 2: Latino executive, processed meats, p. 1.

20. CESLAC MAGA 1995, 7: Latino executive, food and beverage, pp. 18, 10.

21. CESLAC MAGA 1995, 4: Latino executive, banking, pp. 10, 21. Emphasis added.

22. CESLAC MAGA 1995, 7: Latino executive, food and beverage, pp. 7–8.

23. CESLAC MAGA 1995, 4: Latino executive, banking, with interpolations by NH white female colleague of interview subject, p. 12. The second quotation is an interjection by the colleague.

24. Claudia Puig, "Latino Radio Surge: A Coming of Age," *Los Angeles Times,* 7 January 1993, p. F1.

25. Kirk Whisler and Octavio Nuiry, *The 1997 National Hi$panic Media Directory* (Carlsbad, CA: WPR Publishing, in association with ADR Publishing, 1996), pp. 24–33.

26. Ibid., pp. 220–229.

27. Ibid., pp. 112–115.

28. United States Department of Commerce (US DOC), *1972 Survey of Minority-Owned Business Enterprises: Minority-Owned Business Enterprises; Spanish Origin* (Washington, DC: US Department of Commerce, 1975), 84.

29. Ruth Lopez-Williams, personal communication, 1 November 2002.

30. Ibid.

31. Strategy Research Corporation, *The Hispanic Market Handbook* (Miami, FL: SRC HQ Office, 1994), p. 59.

32. CESLAC Health Definitions 1999, 9: US-born Latino college students; focus group conducted by Maria Hayes-Bautista, 29 July 1999, p. 30, transcript stored at CESLAC.

33. Ibid., pp. 30–31.

34. Ibid., p. 31.

35. Ibid.

36. CESLAC UW 1998, 3: US-born Latinos, some college; focus group conducted by Maria Hayes-Bautista, 27 October 1998, p. 36, transcript stored at CESLAC.

37. Ibid., p. 30.

38. Ibid., p. 38.

39. CESLAC UW 1998, 1: US-born Latinos, high school only; focus group conducted by Maria Hayes-Bautista, 7 October 1998, p. 55, transcript stored at CESLAC.

40. Ibid., pp. 60–61.

41. CESLAC UW 1998, 7: Latino civic leaders; focus group conducted by Maria Hayes-Bautista, 29 October 1998, p. 39, transcript stored at CESLAC.

42. Ibid., p. 40.

43. CESLAC UW 1998, 3: US-born Latinos, some college, p. 36.

44. Ibid., p. 38.

45. CESLAC UW 1998, 7: Latino civic leaders, p. 35.

46. Ibid.

CHAPTER 5. TIMES OF CRISIS

Epigraph: personal communication to the author.

1. Tamar Jacoby, *Someone Else's House* (New York: Free Press, 2001), pp. 301, 328, 533.

2. Peter A. Morrison, "Goodby Past, Hello Future: California's Demographic Shift," *Los Angeles Times,* 13 September 1993, p. B7.

3. *National Review* 44.11 (8 June 1992).

4. David E. Hayes-Bautista, Werner O. Schink, and Maria Hayes-Bautista, "Latinos and the 1992 Los Angeles Riots: A Behavioral Sciences Perspective," *Hispanic Journal of Behavioral Sciences* 15.4 (November 1993): 429.

5. Patrick J. McDonnell, "Brash Evangelist," *Los Angeles Times Magazine,* 15 July 2001, pp. 14–17.

6. Hayes-Bautista, et al., "Latinos and the 1992 Los Angeles Riots," p. 433.

7. Latino Coalition for a New Los Angeles and the Latino Futures Research Group, *Latinos and the Future of Los Angeles: A Guide to the Twenty-First Century* (Los Angeles: Latino Coalition for a New Los Angeles, 1993), p. 65.

8. David E. Hayes-Bautista, Werner O. Schink, and Gregory Rodriguez, "Latino Immigrants in Los Angeles: A Portrait from the 1990 Census" (Los Angeles: Alta California Policy Research Center, 1994), p. 8.

9. Ronald Brownstein, "Clinton: Parties Fail to Attack Race Divisions," *Los Angeles Times,* 3 May 1992, p. A8.

10. *Los Angeles Times* poll, compiled by Rob Cioe, "Study 281: L.A. after the Riots; Charter Change, May 9–12, 1992; Results Summary," *Los Angeles Times,* 9–12 May 1992, http://www.latimes.com/extras/timespoll/stats/pdfs/281ss.pdf [originally accessed 9 June 2003; dead link; printout stored at CESLAC].

11. *Los Angeles Times* poll, "Study 300: LA Six Months after the Unrest, October 9–14, 1992; Results Summary," *Los Angeles Times,* 9–14 October 1992, http://www.latimes.com/extras/timespoll/stats/pdfs/300ss.pdf [originally accessed 9 June 2003; dead link; printout stored at CESLAC].

12. *Los Angeles Times* poll, "Survey 348: California, Late October, 1994," *Los Angeles Times,* October 1994, http://www.latimes.com/extras/timespoll/stats/pdfs/348ss.pdf [originally accessed 9 June 2003; dead link; printout stored at CESLAC].

13. Ben Sherwood, "For Pete Wilson, His Political Ambition Is Never Blind," *Los Angeles Times,* 23 July 1995, p. 6.

14. California Coalition for Immigration Reform, "Our Borders Are out of Control (Huntington Beach: California Coalition for Immigration Reform, n.d., photocopy).

15. *Los Angeles Times* poll, compiled by John Brennan, Karen Wada, Susan Pinkus, Roger Richardson, Jill Milburn, Claudia Vaughn, Cecelia Barrera, and Rob Cioe, "Survey 346: California, Early October, 1994," *Los Angeles Times,* October 1994, http://www.latimes.com/extras/timespoll/stats/pdfs/346ss.pdf [originally accessed 9 June 2003; dead link; printout stored at CESLAC].

16. Voice of Citizens Together, "Why Los Angeles County Is Broke," advertisement, *Daily News of Los Angeles,* 16 July 1995, p. 9.

17. "Feinstein's TV Attack on Immigration," *Los Angeles Times,* 10 July 1994, p. A3.

18. Leo Chavez, *Covering Immigration: Popular Images and the Politics of the Nation* (Berkeley and Los Angeles: University of California Press, 2001). This book contains a detailed analysis of the described phenomenon.

19. California Coalition for Immigration Reform, "Our Borders Are out of Control." Emphasis in the original.

20. State of California, Department of Finance, *Revised Race/Ethnic Population Estimates: Components of Change for California Counties, July 1970–1990* (Sacramento, CA: Department of Finance, September 2007), http://www.dof.ca.gov /research/demographic/reports/estimates/race-ethnic_1970–90/ [accessed 29 April 2016]; State of California, Department of Finance, *Race/Ethnic Population Estimates: Components of Change for California Counties, April 1990 to April 2000* (Sacramento, CA: Department of Finance, August 2005), http://www.dof.ca.gov /research/demographic/reports/estimates/e-3/by_county_1990–2000/ [accessed 29 April 2016].

21. Voice of Citizens Together, "Why Los Angeles County Is Broke."

22. David E. Hayes-Bautista, Cynthia L. Chamberlin, and Delmy Iñiguez, "LAUSD Enrollments, 1966–1998: Shrinkage, Then Recovery, While the City Grew" (Los Angeles: Center for the Study of Latino Health and Culture, UCLA, 2001), pp. 2, [4].

23. Los Angeles County Internal Services Division (LAC ISD), "Impact of Undocumented Persons and Other Immigrants on Costs, Revenues and Services in Los Angeles County: A Report Prepared for Los Angeles County Board of Supervisors" (6 November 1992), pp. 16–28.

24. Hayes-Bautista et al., "Latino Immigrants in Los Angeles."

25. LAC ISD, "Impact of Undocumented Persons," pp. 16–28.

26. Immigration and Naturalization Services (INS), *Statistical Yearbook of the Immigration and Naturalization Service* (Washington, DC: US Government Printing Office, 1991); INS, *Statistical Yearbook of the Immigration and Naturalization Service* (Washington, DC: US Government Printing Office, 1992).

27. Hayes-Bautista, et al., "Latino Immigrants in Los Angeles," p. 4.

28. LAC ISD, "Impact of Undocumented Persons," pp. 16–28.

29. Kim Kowsky, "Welcome to Mr. G's, the Final Frontier for Smokers' Rights," *Los Angeles Times,* 18 March 1995, p. B1.

30. Paul Hefner, "Prop. 187 Exposed Cultural Clash—Swelling Latino Numbers, Assimilation, Costs of Illegals Became Campaign Issues," *Daily News of Los Angeles,* 14 November 1994, p. N1.

31. CESLAC UW 1998, 5: Immigrant Latinos; focus group conducted by Maria Hayes-Bautista, 14 October 1998, p. 25, transcript stored at CESLAC.

32. CESLAC UW 1998, 2: US-born Latinos, some college; focus group conducted by Maria Hayes-Bautista, 21 October 1998, p. 32, transcript stored at CESLAC.

33. CESLAC UW 1998, 1: US-born Latinos, high school only; focus group conducted by Maria Hayes-Bautista, 27 October 1998, pp. 81–82, transcript stored at CESLAC.

34. CESLAC UW 1998, 7: Latino civic leaders; focus group conducted by Maria Hayes-Bautista, 29 October 1998, p. 31, transcript stored at CESLAC.

35. CESLAC UW 1998, 5: Immigrant Latinos, p. 19.

36. David E. Hayes-Bautista, "Latino Profiles Study Report: American Dream Makers" (Los Angeles: Center for the Study of Latino Health and Culture, UCLA, and the United Way of Greater Los Angeles, 2000), p. 18.

37. *Los Angeles Times* poll, "Survey #389: Exit Poll: The General Election," *Los Angeles Times,* 5 November 1996,http://images/latimes/com/media/acrobat /2003–2007/8628666.pdf [originally accessed 8 January 2004; dead link; printout stored at CESLAC].

38. Aída Hurtado, David E. Hayes-Bautista, R. Burciaga Valdez, and Anthony C. R. Hernández, "Redefining California: Latino Social Engagement in a Multicultural Society" (Los Angeles: UCLA Chicano Studies Research Center Publications, 1992), pp. 65–68.

39. Hayes-Bautista, "Latino Profiles Study Report," p. 35.

40. Mark Z. Barabak, "Anti-Bilingual Drive's Tone Is Key for Latinos," *Los Angeles Times,* 16 October 1997, pp. A3, A5.

41. Hayes-Bautista, "Latino Profiles Study Report," p. 35.

42. George Skelton, "California and the West: A Wake-Up Call for GOP about a Wide-Awake Giant," *Los Angeles Times,* 15 December 1997, p. 3.

43. CESLAC UW 1998, 2: US-born Latinos, some college, p. 32.

44. CESLAC UW 1998, 8: Latino business leaders; focus group conducted by Maria Hayes-Bautista, 30 October 1998, p. 30, transcript stored at CESLAC.

45. CESLAC UW 1998, 7: Latino civic leaders, p. 24.

46. CESLAC UW 1998, 8: Latino business leaders, p. 28.

47. CESLAC UW 1998, 7: Latino civic leaders, p. 27.

48. CESLAC UW 1998, 8: Latino business leaders, p. 33.

49. CESLAC UW 1998, 3: US-born Latinos, some college, p. 17.

50. Ibid., pp. 21–22.

51. INS, *Statistical Yearbook of the Immigration and Naturalization Service* (Washington, DC: US Immigration and Naturalization Service, 1991), p. 152; (1992), p. 130; (1993), p. 140; (1994), p. 142; (1995), p. 144; (1996), p. 148; (1997), p. 156; (1998), p. 152; and (1999), p. 184.

52. National Association of Latino Elected Officials (NALEO), *2002 Latino Election Handbook* (Los Angeles: NALEO Educational Fund, 2002).

53. William C. Velásquez Institute (WCVI), "WCVI Phone Survey of Latino Registered Voters, California, N = 560; September 27–October 4, 2000 +/-4.1%," http://wcvi.org/latino_voter_research/polls/ca/ca_total_n560.html [accessed 2 August 2016].

54. CESLAC UW 1998, 7: Latino civic leaders, p. 53.

55. Fernando Guerra, personal communication, 6 June 2003.

56. Latino Coalition for a New Los Angeles, *Latinos and the Future,* p. 107.

57. NALEO, *2002 National Directory of Latino Elected Officials* (Los Angeles: NALEO Educational Fund), pp. 26–35.

58. Cruz Bustamante, personal communication, 30 May 1999.

59. Maria Elena Fernandez, "A President Sets His Own Path: Bush Tries His Hand at Spanish in Radio Talk," *Los Angeles Times,* 6 May 2001, p. A15.

60. CESLAC UW 1998, 2: US-born Latinos, some college, p. 32.
61. Ibid., p. 26.
62. CESLAC UW 1998, 7: Latino civic leaders, p. 43.
63. Ibid., p. 12.
64. Ibid., p. 9.
65. CESLAC UW 1998, 3: US-born Latinos, some college, p. 96.
66. CESLAC UW 1998, 8: Latino business leaders, p. 44.
67. CESLAC UW 1998, 7: Latino civic leaders, p. 17.
68. CESLAC UW 1998, 2: US-born Latinos, some college, p. 30.
69. Ibid., pp. 99–100.
70. Ibid., p. 29.
71. CESLAC UW 1998, 7: Latino civic leaders, p. 36.
72. CESLAC UW 1998, 3: US-born Latinos, some college, p. 90.

CHAPTER 6. LATINOS DEFINE "AMERICAN"

Epigraph is from CESLAC MALDEF 1998, 2: Non-Hispanic whites, p. 22; focus group conducted by Maria Hayes-Bautista, 13 July 1998, transcript stored at CESLAC.

1. CESLAC MALDEF 1997, 4: Non-Hispanic whites, p. 8; focus group conducted by Maria Hayes-Bautista, April–May 1997, code sheet stored at CESLAC.
2. CESLAC MALDEF 1997, 3: Non-Hispanic white evangelical young adults, p. 38; focus group conducted by Maria Hayes-Bautista, 12 April 1997, transcript stored at CESLAC. Members of this focus group were young, non-Hispanic whites who lived in a predominantly Latino neighborhood close to the University of Southern California, adjacent to downtown Los Angeles. They were members of a racially integrated evangelical church. Although they were evangelicals, their daily lived experience with Latinos was not typical of evangelicals in more suburban areas.
3. Ibid., p. 7.
4. Ibid.
5. CESLAC MALDEF 1997, 4: Non-Hispanic whites, p. 25.
6. Ibid., p. 12.
7. Ibid., p. 23.
8. Ibid., p. 31.
9. Ibid., p. 33.
10. Ibid., p. 34.
11. Ibid., p. 32.
12. Ibid., p. 29.
13. CESLAC MALDEF 1998, 2: US-born Latino professionals, p. 10; focus group conducted by Maria Hayes-Bautista, 13 July 1998, transcript stored at CESLAC.

14. CESLAC MALDEF 1998, 1: US-born Latino blue-collar workers, p. 11; focus group conducted by Maria Hayes-Bautista, 21 July 1998, transcript stored at CESLAC.

15. CESLAC MALDEF 1998, 2: US-born Latino professionals, p. 31.

16. Gaspar Villagrá, *Historia de Nuevo México (Crónicas de América),* ed. Mercedes Junquera (Madrid: Dastin, 2001), p. 22.

17. CESLAC MALDEF 1998, 2: US-born Latino professionals, p. 34.

18. CESLAC MALDEF 1998, 1: US-born Latino blue-collar workers, p. 10.

19. CESLAC MALDEF 1998, 2: US-born Latino professionals, p. 26.

20. Ibid., p. 27.

21. CESLAC MALDEF 1998, 1: US-born Latino blue-collar workers, p. 19.

22. CESLAC MALDEF 1998, 2: US-born Latino professionals, p. 18.

23. Letters, *Los Angeles Times Magazine,* 5 August 2001, p. 4.

24. CESLAC MALDEF 1998, 2: US-born Latino professionals, p. 13.

25. Ibid., p. 38.

26. CESLAC MALDEF 1998, 1: US-born Latino blue-collar workers, pp. 18–19.

27. Ibid., p. 9.

28. CESLAC MALDEF 1998, 4: Immigrant Latinos, p. 13; focus group conducted by Maria Hayes-Bautista, 28 July 1998, transcript stored at CESLAC.

29. Ibid., p. 2.

30. Ibid., p. 10.

31. Ibid., pp. 11, 13.

32. Ibid., p. 10.

33. Ibid., p. 6.

34. CESLAC MALDEF 1998, 3: Immigrant Latinos, pp. 30–32; focus group conducted by Maria Hayes-Bautista, 7 July 1998, transcript stored at CESLAC.

35. Ibid., p. 31.

36. CESLAC MALDEF 1998, 4: Immigrant Latinos, p. 28.

37. CESLAC Social Attitudes Survey (2000), p. 4. Population-based survey conducted by telephone by the UCLA Survey Research Center, Juarez and Associates, and CESLAC, under the supervision of David E. Hayes-Bautista and Paul Hsu. SPSS files stored at CESLAC.

38. Aída Hurtado, David E. Hayes-Bautista, R. Burciaga Valdez, and Anthony C. R. Hernandez, *Redefining California: Latino Social Engagement in a Multicultural Society* (Los Angeles: UCLA Chicano Studies Research Center Publications, 1992), p. 59.

39. CESLAC MALDEF 1998, 5: Non-Hispanic whites, p. 42; focus group conducted by Maria Hayes-Bautista, 22 June 1998, transcript stored at CESLAC.

40. Ibid.

41. CESLAC MALDEF 1998, 6: Non-Hispanic whites, p. 27; focus group conducted by Maria Hayes-Bautista, 15 July 1998, transcript stored at CESLAC.

42. Ibid.

43. CESLAC MALDEF 1998, 5: Non-Hispanic whites, p. 35.

44. Ibid., p. 30.

45. CESLAC MALDEF 1998, 6: Non-Hispanic whites, p. 36.

46. Ibid., p. 27.

47. Ibid., p. 23.

48. CESLAC MALDEF 1997, 6: Non-Hispanic whites, middle-aged, p. 44; focus group conducted by Maria Hayes-Bautista, April–May 1997, transcript stored at CESLAC.

49. Ibid., p. 11.

50. CESLAC MALDEF 1998, 6: Non-Hispanic whites, p. 28.

51. CESLAC MALDEF 1997, 3: Non-Hispanic white evangelical young adults, p. 13.

52. Ibid., p. 11.

53. Ibid., p. 5.

54. CESLAC MALDEF 1998, 6: Non-Hispanic whites, p. 37.

55. CESLAC MALDEF 1998, 1: US-born Latino blue-collar workers, p. 1.

56. Ibid.

57. Ibid., p. 6.

58. CESLAC MALDEF 1998, 3: Immigrant Latinos, p. 13.

59. CESLAC MALDEF 1998, 1: US-born Latino blue-collar workers, p. 40.

60. Ibid.

61. Ibid., p. 38.

62. CESLAC MALDEF 1998, 3: Immigrant Latinos, p. 22.

63. Ibid., p. 10.

64. CESLAC MALDEF 1998, 2: US-born Latino professionals, p. 7.

65. Louis Sahagun, "LA Unified Gets Dismal Ratings from Public," *Los Angeles Times,* 11 April 2000, p. A1; Louis Sahagun and Doug Smith, "Whatever His Legacy, Cortines Jolted District," *Los Angeles Times,* 30 June 2000, p. B1.

66. Robert Lopez and Rich Connell, "Special Report: The Class of '89: Journeys into the New Los Angeles," *Los Angeles Times,* 7 June 2000, p. 1.

67. Lopez and Connell, "Special Report"; David E. Hayes-Bautista, Tenzing Donyo, Dana E. McMurtry, and Sheri Courtemache, *The Health of California's Public: A Chartbook* (Woodland Hills: California Endowment and California HealthCare Foundation, 1996), p. 38.

68. Lopez and Connell, "Special Report."

69. Hurtado et al., "Redefining California," p. 59.

70. Fernand Braudel, *The Identity of France: History and Environment,* trans. Sian Reynolds (New York: Harper and Row, 1988), pp. 106–107.

71. Hurtado et al., "Redefining California," pp. 59–61.

72. Ibid., pp. 59, 61.

73. CESLAC MALDEF 1997, 4: Non-Hispanic whites, p. 6.

74. CESLAC MALDEF 1997, 3: Non-Hispanic white evangelical young adults, p. 9.

75. CESLAC MALDEF 1997, 2: Non-Hispanic whites, p. 20; focus group conducted by Maria Hayes-Bautista, April 1997, transcript stored at CESLAC..

76. CESLAC MALDEF 1997, 3: Non-Hispanic white evangelical young adults, p. 2.

77. Ibid., p. 45.

78. CESLAC MALDEF 1997, 6: Non-Hispanic whites, middle-aged, p. 8.

79. CESLAC MALDEF 1997, 4: Non-Hispanic white evangelical young adults, p. 11.

80. CESLAC MALDEF 1998, 2: Non-Hispanic whites, p. 20.

81. Ibid.

82. Ibid.

83. Ibid., p. 21.

84. Ibid., p. 30.

85. Ibid., p. 20.

CHAPTER 7. CREATING A REGIONAL
AMERICAN IDENTITY

CESLAC MALDEF, 1997, 4: Non-Hispanic whites, p. 6; focus group conducted by Maria Hayes-Bautista, April–May 1997, transcript stored at CESLAC.

1. Terry Jordan, *North American Cattle-Ranching Frontiers: Origins, Diffusions, and Differentiation* (Albuquerque: University of New Mexico Press, 1993), pp. 43–55.

2. Richard W. Slatta, *Comparing Cowboys and Frontiers* (Norman: University of Oklahoma Press, 1997), pp. 74–98.

3. Martin W. Sandler, *Vaqueros: America's First Cowmen* (New York: Henry Holt, 2001), p. 23.

4. Jordan, *North American Cattle-Ranching Frontiers,* p. 102; Sandler, *Vaqueros,* p. 43.

5. Sandler, *Vaqueros,* p. 45; Jordan, *North American Cattle-Ranching Frontiers,* pp. 256, 262.

6. Linda Chavez, "Just Another Ethnic Group," *Wall Street Journal,* 14 March 2001, p. A22.

7. Robert Bellah, *Habits of the Heart: Individualism and Commitment in American Life* (Berkeley and Los Angeles: University of California Press, 1996), p. 37.

8. Thomas Jr. Spragens, "Communitarian Liberalism," in Amitai Etzioni, ed., *New Communitarian Thinking: Person, Virtues, Institutions, and Communities* (Charlottesville: University Press of Virginia, 1995), pp. 37–51; David Hollenbach, "Virtue, the Common Good, and Democracy," in Etzioni, *New Communitarian Thinking,* pp. 143–153.

9. Peter L. Berger and Thomas Luckmann, *The Social Construction of Reality: A Treatise in the Sociology of Knowledge* (New York: Anchor Books, 1966), p. 41.

10. Ibid.

11. State of California, Department of Finance, *Report P-2: State and County Population Projections by Race/Ethnicity and 5-Year Age Groups, 2010–2060* (Sacramento, CA, December 2014).

12. David Hackett Fischer, *Albion's Seed: Four British Folkways in America* (New York: Oxford University Press, 1989), pp. 8–9.

13. *Náhua* refers to the various indigenous peoples of Mexico who spoke the Náhuatl language, which served as the lingua franca of the Aztec Empire but was widely used by other peoples as well.

14. William Madsen, *Mexican-Americans of South Texas* (New York: Holt, Rinehart and Winston, 1964), p. 70; Margaret Clark, *Health in the Mexican-American Culture: A Community Study* (Berkeley: University of California Press, 1959), p. 122.

15. CESLAC, Edward R. Roybal Institute for Applied Gerontology, California State University, Los Angeles, 1997. Roybal Immunization Consortium for Older Adults (RICO) Survey; data set on computer diskette stored at CESLAC.

16. CESLAC Diabetes 1997, 2: Immigrant Latina, pp. 1–2, individual interview by Maria Hayes-Bautista, 1 February 1997, transcript stored at CESLAC.

17. CESLAC Diabetes 1998, 5: Immigrant Latinos, p. 8; focus group conducted by Maria Hayes-Bautista, 17 December 1998, transcript stored at CESLAC.

18. Jill Leslie McKeever Furst, *The Natural History of the Soul in Ancient Mexico* (New Haven, CT: Yale University Press, 1995), pp. 111–112.

19. Ralph Bolton, "Susto, Hostility, and Hypoglycemia," *Ethnology* 20.4 (October 1981): 261–276.

20. Margarita Arftschwager Kay, "Health and Illness in a Mexican American Barrio," in Edward H. Spicer, ed., *Ethnic Medicine in the Southwest* (Tucson: University of Arizona Press, 1977), p. 139; Clark, *Health in the Mexican-American Culture*, pp. 175–78; Madsen, *Mexican-Americans of South Texas*, p. 77.

21. CESLAC Diabetes 1997, 2: Immigrant Latina, p. 6.

22. CESLAC Arthritis 2001, 3: US-born Latino males, pp. 31–34; focus group conducted by Maria Hayes-Bautista, 26 January 2001, transcript stored at CESLAC.

23. CESLAC Arthritis 2001, 10: Immigrant Latina females, pp. 32–33; focus group conducted by Maria Hayes-Bautista, 7 September 2001, transcript stored at CESLAC.

24. Furst, *The Natural History of the Soul*, pp. 129–30.

25. Alfredo López Austin, *Cuerpo humano e ideología: Las concepciones de los antiguos náhuas, II.* Serie Antropologica, 39 (Mexico City: Universidad Nacional Autónoma de México, Instituto de Investigaciones Antropológicas, 1980), p. 218.

26. Ismael Navarro Nuño, "Que Dios guie sus manos," in David Hayes-Bautista and Roberto O. Chiprut, eds., *Healing Latinos: Realidad y Fantasia* (Los Angeles: Cedar Sinai Health System and the Center for the Study of Latino Health and Culture, UCLA, 1999), p. 166; López Austin, *Cuerpo humano e ideología*, pp. 252–257; Furst, *The Natural History of the Soul*, pp. 17–19.

27. Mariano Cuevas, ed., *Documentos inéditos del siglo XVI para la historia de México* (Mexico City: Talleres del Museo Nacional de Arqueología, Historia y Etnología, 1914), doc. 13, pp. 58–62.

28. John J. Martinez, *Not Counting the Cost: Jesuit Missionaries in Colonial Mexico—A Story of Struggle, Commitment, and Sacrifice* (Chicago: Jesuit Way, 2001), p. 30.

29. Miguel León-Portilla, *Tonantzin Guadalupe: Pensamineto náhuatl y mensaje cristiano en el "Nican Mophua"* (Mexico City: Fondo de Cultura Económica, 2000), pp. 11–16.

30. Matthew Restall, "Black Conquistadors: Armed Africans in Early Spanish America," *Americas* 57.2 (October 2000): 171–205.

31. Herman Bennett, *Colonial Blackness: A History of Afro-Mexico* (Bloomington: Indiana University Press, 2009), pp. 58–85.

32. Bobby Vinson, *Bearing Arms for His Majesty: The Free-Colored Militia in Colonial Mexico* (Stanford, CA: Stanford University Press, 2001), pp. 7–46. "Free-colored" is Vinson's direct translation from the more or less interchangeable colonial Spanish terms *pardos libres*, *morenos libres*, and *mulatos libres*; ibid., p. 6.

33. Ben Vinson and Bobby Vaughn, *Afroméxico: El pulso de la población negra en México; Una historia recordada, olvidada y vuelta a recordar* (Mexico City: Centro de Investigación y Docencia Económicas, Fondo de Cultura Económica, 2004), p. 51.

34. Katherine Bjork, "The Link That Kept the Philippines Spanish: Mexican Merchant Interests and the Manila Trade, 1571–1815," *Journal of World History* 9.1 (Spring 1998): 25–50.

35. Edward R. Slack, "The Chinos in New Spain: A Corrective Lens for a Distorted Image," *Journal of World History* 20.1 (March 2009): 35–67.

36. Sherburne F. Cook and Woodrow Borah, *Essays in Population History: Mexico and the Caribbean,* vol. 1 (Berkeley: University of California Press, 1971), p. viii.

37. Bennett, *Colonial Blackness,* p. 59.

38. Carlos Fuentes, "Imagining America," *Diogenes* 160 (Winter 1992): 10–11; Raymond L. Williams, "Literary Cultures of Latin America: A Comparative History," *University of Toronto Quarterly* 77 (2008): 77.

39. Timothy Matovina, "Liturgy, Popular Rites and Popular Spirituality," in Virgilio P. Elizondo and Timothy Matovina, eds., *Mestizo Worship: A Pastoral Approach to Liturgical Ministry* (Collegeville, MN: Liturgical Press, 1998), p. 82.

40. Elizondo and Matovina, *Mestizo Worship,* p. 3.

41. Fischer, *Albion's Seed,* pp. 887–888.

42. Mardith K. Schuetz-Miller, *Building and Builders in Hispanic California, 1769–1850* (Santa Barbara, CA: Presidio Research Publications, 1994), p. 92. The list of first settlers has been reproduced in bronze at the present-day La Plaza in downtown Los Angeles.

43. Bennett, *Colonial Blackness,* pp. 23–57.

44. Barbara L. Voss, *The Archeology of Ethnogenesis: Race and Sexuality in Colonial San Francisco* (Berkeley and Los Angeles: University of California Press, 2008), p. 33.

45. Lester Singer, "Ethnogenesis and Negro Americans Today," *Social Research* 29 (1962): 419–432; William C. Sturtevant, "Creek into Seminole," in Eleanor Burke Leacock and Nancy Oestreich Lurie, eds., *North American Indians in Historical Perspective* (New York: Random House, 1971), pp. 92–128.

46. Stuart Hall, "The Local and the Global: Globalization and Ethnicity: Old and New Identities, Old and New Ethnicities," in Anthony D. King, ed., *Culture, Globalization, and the World-System: Contemporary Conditions for the Representation of Identity* (Binghamton: State University of New York at Binghamton, 1991), pp. 41–68.

47. David E. Hayes-Bautista, *El Cinco de Mayo: An American Tradition* (Berkeley and Los Angeles: University of California Press, 2012), p. 43.

48. "Casamiento," *El Clamor Público,* 29 May 1858, p. 2.

49. "To Our Spanish-American Friends," *El Clamor Público,* 18 June 1859, p. 3.

50. "El 16 de Setiembre," *El Clamor Público,* 18 September 1855, p. 2; "Dia de muertos," *El Clamor Público,* 7 November 1857, p. 3.

51. "El 4 de Julio," *El Clamor Público,* 10 July 1855, p. 2; "Thanksgiving," *Los Angeles Star,* 26 November 1853, p. 2.

52. Advertisement, "Navidad! Navidad!" *El Clamor Público,* 25 December 1858, p. 2.

53. Hayes-Bautista, *El Cinco de Mayo,* pp. 132–176.

54. Hayes-Bautista, *El Cinco de Mayo;* David E. Hayes-Bautista and Cynthia L. Chamberlin, "Cinco de Mayo's First Seventy-Five Years in Alta California: From Spontaneous Behavior to Sedimented Memory, 1862 to 1937," *Southern California Quarterly* 89 (2007): 23–64.

CHAPTER 8. LATINO POST-MILLENNIALS

1. Douglas Coupland, *Generation X: Tales for an Accelerated Culture* (New York: St. Martin's Press, 1991).

2. Carroll Doherty, Jocelyn Kiley, Alec Tyson, and Bridget Jameson, "The Whys and Hows of Generations Research" (Washington, DC: Pew Research Center, 2015), p. 16.

3. Scott Keeter, Cliff Zukin, Molly Andolina, and Krista Jenkins, *The Civic and Political Health of the Nation: A Generational Portrait* (New Brunswick, NJ: Rutgers University, Eagleton Institute of Politics, 2002).

4. Doherty, et al., "The Whys and Hows," p. 6.

5. Ibid., p. 5.

6. Joseh Dulaney and Andrew Edwards, "Gen X—A Generation Stuck in the Middle Turns 50," *LA.Com,* http://www.la.com/ci_29319999/x-generation-stuck-middle-turns-50?source = rss# [accessed 6 January 2015].

7. Campaign for College Opportunity, "The State of Latinos in Higher Education in California," November, 2013, p. 4, http://collegecampaign.org/wp-content/uploads/2015/04/2015-State-of-Higher-Education_Latinos.pdf [accessed 3 May 2016].

8. Richard Fry and Paul Taylor, "Hispanic High School Graduates Pass Whites in Rate of College Enrollment" (Washington, DC: Pew Research Center, Pew Hispanic Center, 2013), p. 6.

9. Jeffrey S. Passel, D'Vera Cohn, and Molly Rohal, "Unauthorized Immigration Totals Rise in 7 States, Fall in 14" (Washington, DC: Pew Research Center, Hispanic Trends, 2014), p. 8.

10. California Department of Public Health, "2010 California Birth Statistical Master File," August 2011. The conclusion that 94.7% of post-millennial Latinos are US-born is supplied by a custom analysis by Werner Schink of data from Sarah Flood, Miriam King, Steven Ruggles, and J. Robert Warren, *Integrated Public Use Microdata Series, Current Population Survey: Version 4.0.* [machine-readable database] (Minneapolis: University of Minnesota, 2015), https://cps.ipums.org/cps-action/samples [accessed 2 August 2016; spreadsheet stored at CESLAC].

11. Chon Noriega and Francisco Javier Iribarren, "Quantifying Hate Speech on Commercial Talk Radio: A Pilot Study" (UCLA Chicano Studies Research Center, CSRC Working Paper, no. 1, November 2011).

12. Seema Mehta, "In 2006 Speech, Tim Donnelly Compared Illegal Immigration to War," *Los Angeles Times,* 7 April 2014, Local Section, http://www.latimes.com/local/la-me-donnelly-minutemen-20140408-story.html [accessed 1 January 2016].

13. Fry and Taylor, "Hispanic High School Graduates," p. 6.

14. Mark Baldassare, Dean Bonner, Sonja Petek, and Nicole Willcoxon, *PPIC Statewide Survey: Californians and Higher Education* (San Francisco: Public Policy Institute of California, 2010), p. 15.

15. Deborah Reed, *Educational Resources and Outcomes in California by Race and Ethnicity* (San Francisco: Public Policy Institute of California, 2005), table 4, p. 9.

16. The Campaign for College Opportunity, "The State of Higher Education in California—Latino Report" (Los Angeles, April 2015), p. 11, figure 8.

17. Hans Johnson, *Higher Education in California: New Goals for the Master Plan* (San Francisco: Public Policy Institute of California, 2010), pp. 4–6.

18. Admission for students whose GPA is between 2.0 and 2.9 requires acceptable test scores in addition; individuals with a GPA below 2.0 are not admitted. California State University, First-Time Freshman Admission Requirements, http://www.calstate.edu/apply/undergrad/first-time-freshmen.shtml [accessed 2 May 2016].

19. Advanced placement courses can raise a student's GPA above the usual maximum of 4.0. UCLA Profile of Admitted Freshmen, Fall 2015, https://www.admission.ucla.edu/Prospect/Adm_fr/Frosh_Prof15.htm [accessed 3 May 2016].

20. Raymond T. Sparrowe, "Authentic Leadership and the Narrative Self," *Leadership Quarterly* 16 (2005): 419–439.

21. Pew Research Center, "Modern Immigration Wave Brings 59 Million to U.S., Driving Population Growth and Change through 2065: Selected U.S. Immigration Legislation and Executive Actions, 1790–2014" (Washington, DC: Pew Research

Center, 2015). The information regarding restrictions on Asian immigration to the US is contained in the interactive timeline available only in the electronic version of this report, at http://www.pewhispanic.org/2015/09/28/selected-u-s-immigration-legislation-and-executive-actions-1790–2014/ [accessed 7 January 2016].

22. David E. Hayes-Bautista and Paul Hsu, personal communication to the University of California Office of the President, 2003.

23. Jesse Katz, "Prop. 187 Gives Texas a Selling Point in Mexico," *Los Angeles Times,* 6 February 1995, http://articles.latimes.com/1995–02–06/news/mn-28768_1_mexico-city [accessed 13 January 2016].

24. Border Protection, Antiterrorism, and Illegal Immigration Control Act of 2005, H.R. 4437, 109th Congress, 2nd session (2006), http://www.ncsl.org/research/immigration/summary-of-the-sensenbrenner-immigration-bill.aspx [accessed 13 January 2016].

25. Leadership Conference on Civil Rights, "The Contentious Immigration Debate of 2006: H.R. 4437, S. 2454, and S. 2611," *Civil Rights Monitor* 16.1 (Fall 2006), http://www.civilrights.org/monitor/fall2006/art2p1.html [accessed 13 January 2016].

26. Teresa Watanabe and Hector Becerra, "500,000 Pack Streets to Protest Immigration Bills," *Los Angeles Times,* 26 March 2006, http://articles.latimes.com/2006/mar/26/local/me-immig26 [accessed 13 January 2016].

27. David E. Hayes-Bautista, executive producer, "Exploring the American Identity of Young Adult Latinos," digital video recording, Center for the Study of Latino Health and Culture (CESLAC), Los Angeles, 5 April 2011. Video recording stored at CESLAC.

28. Ibid., 7 April 2011.

29. Ibid., 5 April 2011.

30. Samuel Huntington, "The Hispanic Challenge," *Foreign Policy* 141.2 (March–April 2004): 30.

31. Kitty Felde, "Legislation Would Remove Racist Language from Real Estate Deeds," 25 June 2008, http://www.scpr.org/news/2008/06/25/2553/legislation-would-remove-racist-language-real-esta/ [accessed 5 May 2016].

32. Jessica Garrison, "Living with a Reminder of Segregation," *Los Angeles Times,* 27 July 2008, http://articles.latimes.com/2008/jul/27/local/me-covenant27 [accessed 14 January 2016].

33. Assembly Committee on Judiciary, "2009–2010 Bill Summary," California Assembly, Paper 253 (2010), pp. 67–68, http://digitalcommons.law.ggu.edu/caldocs_assembly/253 [accessed 14 January 2016].

34. "California Proposition 187: Illegal Aliens Ineligible for Public Benefits (1994)," http://ballotpedia.org/California_Proposition_187,_Illegal_Aliens_Ineligible_for_Public_Benefits_(1994) [accessed 5 May 2016].

35. Patrick McGreevey, "Pushing to Erase Prop. 187," *Los Angeles Times,* 5 June 2014, p. AA3.

36. Patrick McGreevey, "Bill Repealing Parts of Prop. 187 Is Signed," *Los Angeles Times,* 16 September 2014, p. AA1.

37. "California Proposition 227, the 'English in Public Schools' Initiative (1998)," https://ballotpedia.org/California_Proposition_227,_the_%22English_in_Public_Schools%22_Initiative_(1998) [accessed 2 May 2016].

38. Lydia O'Connor, "Bilingual Education Ban May Be Overturned In California," *Huffington Post,* 24 February 2014, http://www.huffingtonpost.com /2014/02/21/bilingual-education-ban-california_n_4834573.html [accessed 2 May 2016].

39. Melanie Mason and Phil Willon, "2 Latinos Will Lead Legislature," *Los Angeles Times,* 5 September 2015, p. B1.

40. Patrick McGreevy, "From Activist to Leader," *Los Angeles Times,* 15 October 2014, p. A1.

41. George Skelton, "Rendon's Rise Defies His Poor Start in School," *Los Angeles Times,* 2 November 2015, p. B1.

42. Mark Baldassare, Dean Bonner, David Kordus, and Lunna Lopes, "PPIC Statewide Survey: Californians and Their Government," Statewide Survey (San Francisco: Public Policy Institute of California, September 2015), p. 18.

43. Manuel Pastor, Tom Jawetz, and Lizet Ocampo, "DAPA Matters: The Growing Electorate Directly Affected by Executive Action on Immigration" (Los Angeles: USC Dornsife Center for the Study of Immigrant Integration, November 2015), p. 11, table 2.

CHAPTER 9. LATINO POST-MILLENNIALS CREATE AMERICA'S FUTURE

1. Timothy Egan, "A Refuge for Racists: What Draws Extremist Hate Groups to the G.O.P.?" *New York Times,* 28 June 2015, p. SR11.

2. Cindy Y. Rodriguez, "Mexican-American Boy's National Anthem Sparks Racist Comments," CNN, 16 September 2013, http://www.cnn.com/2013/06/12 /us/mexican-american-boy-sings-anthem/ [accessed 13 January 2016].

3. Matt Binder, "Racist Basketball Fans PISSED a[t] Mexican-American Boy [Who] Dared to Sing Their [National] Anthem," *Public Shaming,* Tumblr (blog), 12 June 2013, http://publicshaming.tumblr.com/post/52763976629/racist-basketball-fans-pissed-a-mexican-american [accessed 13 January 2016]. Date appears in "View Page Source"; author identified in "About" section of the blog.

4. Nicole Auerbach, "Southern Miss Band Chants 'Where's Your Green Card?'" *USA Today,* 15 March 2012, http://content.usatoday.com/communities/campusrivalry /post/2012/03/southern-miss-band-chants-wheres-your-green-card/1#.Vpbp6xgrLZs [accessed 14 January 2016].

5. Sandra Lilley, "Poll: 1 out of 3 Americans Inaccurately Think Most Hispanics Are Undocumented," *NBC Latino,* 12 September 2012, http://nbclatino.com/2012/09/12 /poll-1-out-of-3-americans-think-most-hispanics-are-undocumented/ [accessed 14 January 2016].

6. Felipe Fernández-Armesto, *Our America: A Hispanic History of the United States* (New York: W. W. Norton, 2014), pp. 3–4.

7. In 1803, Spain ceded the territory back to France just weeks before France sold it to the US.

8. Gustavo López and Eileen Patten, "The Impact of Slowing Immigration: Foreign-Born Share Falls among 14 Largest U.S. Hispanic Groups" (Washington, DC: Pew Research Center, September 2015), p. 4, figure 1.

9. Jens Manuel Krogstad and Mark Hugo Lopez, "For Three States, Share of Hispanic Population Returns to the Past" (Pew Research Center report, 10 June 2014), http://www.pewresearch.org/fact-tank/2014/06/10/for-three-states-share-of-hispanic-population-returns-to-the-past/ [accessed 14 December 2014].

10. Sandra L. Colby and Jennifer M. Ortman, *Projections of the Size and Composition of the U.S. Population: 2014 to 2060,* US Census Bureau Current Population Reports (Washington, DC: US Census Bureau, US Department of Commerce, March 2015), p. 9.

11. Trip Gabriel and Julia Preston, "Trump Paints GOP in Corner on Immigration," *New York Times,* 19 August 2015, p. A1.

12. Sylvia Guendelman and Monica Jasis, "Giving Birth across the Border: The San-Diego-Tijuana Connection," *Social Science and Medicine* 34.4 (February 1992): 419–425.

13. Dowell Myers, *Immigrants and Boomers: Forging a New Social Contract for the Future of America* (New York: Russell Sage Foundation, 2007).

14. "Rep. Wilson Shouts, 'You lie' to Obama during Speech," CNN, 10 September 2009, http://www.cnn.com/2009/POLITICS/09/09/joe.wilson/ [accessed 23 December 2015].

15. Dana P. Goldman, James P. Smith, and Neeraj Sood, "Immigrants and the Cost of Medical Care," *Health Affairs* 25.6 (November 2006): 1700–1711.

16. Kathleen Sebelius, Thomas R. Frieden, and Charles J. Rothwell, *Health, United States, 2013, with Special Feature on Prescription Drugs,* DHHS Publication No. 2014–1232 (Washington, DC: Centers for Disease Control, National Center for Health Statistics, United States Government Printing Office, May 2014), p. 84.

17. Michael Finnegan and Kurtis Lee, "Cheers, Jeers Greet Trump," *Los Angeles Times,* 16 September 2015, p. B1.

18. Jiaquan Xu, Sherry L. Murphy, Kenneth D. Kochanek, and Brigham A. Bastian, "Deaths: Final Data for 2013,"*National Vital Statistics Reports,* 64.2 (16 February 2016), p. 31, table 8.

19. James E. Ivey, "The Presidio of San Antonio de Béxar: Historical and Archaeological Research," *Historical Archaeology* 38.3 (Fall 2004): 106–120; Daniel D. Arreola, "The Mexican Cultural Capital," *Geographical Review* 77.1 (January 1987): 17–34.

20. Robert H. Thonhoff, "Texas and the American Revolution," *Southwest Historical Quarterly* 98.4 (April 1995): 515–516.

21. Vladimir Guerrero, *The Anza Trail and the Settling of California* (Berkeley, CA: Heyday Books, 2006), pp. xi–xix.

22. Leroy Martinez, *"Cédula de donativo:* King Carlos III's Voluntary Donation Order of 1780 for the Alliance War against England" (unpublished manuscript, 2013), pp. 2, 6.

23. Thomas E. Chávez, *Spain and the Independence of the United States: An Intrinsic Gift.* (Albuquerque: University of New Mexico Press, 2002), p. 214.

24. Luis González Rodríguez, "Juan María de Salvatierra en el Noroeste (1680–1693)," *Anales de Antropología* 30 (1993): 246.

25. "El Cinco de Mayo," *El Fronterizo,* 4 May 1889, p. 2.

26. Bonnie G. McEwan, "The Spiritual Conquest of La Florida," *American Anthropologist* 103.3 (September 2001): 633–644.

27. United States House of Representatives, "HERNANDEZ, Joseph Marion," *Hispanic Americans in Congress, 1822 to Present,* http://history.house.gov/People/Detail/14946?ret = True [accessed 12 May 2016].

28. Sean Alfano, "GOP Rep. Calls Miami 'Third World County,'" *CBS News,* 30 November 2006, http://www.cbsnews.com/news/gop-rep-calls-miami-third-world-country/ [accessed 31 December 2015].

29. Miami-Dade County, Department of Planning and Zoning, Planning Research Section, "Miami-Dade County Facts–2009: A Compendium of Selected Statistics" (Miami: April 2009), table, "Persons of Hispanic Origin by Country of Origin, Miami-Dade County, Florida, 1990 to 2007" (Miami: Miami-Dade County, April 2009), p. 19, http://www.miamidade.gov/planning/library/reports/2009-miami-dade-county-facts.pdf [accessed 1 August 2016].

30. Seth Motel and Eileen Patten, "Characteristics of the 60 Largest Metropolitan Areas by Hispanic Population" (Washington, DC: Pew Research Center, 19 September 2012), p. 7.

31. María Luisa Rodríguez Sala, *Los cirujanos del mar en la Nueva España (1572–1820)* (Mexico City: Universidad Nacional Autónoma de Mexico, 2004), p. 221.

32. Herbert Eugene Bolton, *An Outpost of Empire* (New York: Russell & Russell, 1965), pp. 29–32.

33. Sol Villasana, *Dallas's Little Mexico* (Charleston, SC: Arcadia Books, 2011), pp. 7–8.

34. Anthony Stevens-Acevedo, Tom Weterings, and Leonor Alvarez-Francés, *Juan Rodriguez and the Beginnings of New York City,* Publications and Research Paper 17 (New York: City College of New York, Dominican Studies Institute, 2013), p. 3.

35. "The Early Spanish Jews of New York," *Nueva York, 1613–1945,* http://www.nuevayork-exhibition.org/programs) [accessed 30 December 2015].

36. "Spain Supports the Revolution and New York Welcomes the Spanish," *Nueva York, 1613–1945,* http://www.nuevayork-exhibition.org/node/10) [accessed 30 December 2015].

37. "Spaniards and Latin Americans in New York," *Nueva York, 1613–1945,* http://www.nuevayork-exhibition.org/galleries/3/spaniards-and-latin-americans) [accessed 30 December 2015].

38. Matt Binder, "Baseball Fans SUPER ANGRY Hispanic American Superstar Sang 'God Bless America' at All-Star Game," *Public Shaming, Tumblr* (blog), 17 July 2013, http://publicshaming.tumblr.com/post/5 5715208108/baseball-fans-super-angry-hispanic-american [1 August 2016]. Date in "View Page Source"; author identified in "About" section of the blog.

39. Abraham P. Nasatir, "The Anglo-Spanish Frontier in the Illinois Country during the American Revolution, 1779–1783," *Journal of the Illinois State Historical Society* 21.3 (October 1928): 291–358.

40. Anita Edgar Jones, "Mexican Colonies in Chicago," *Social Service Review* 2.4 (December 1928): 579–597.

41. David E. Hayes-Bautista, *El Cinco de Mayo: An American Tradition* (Berkeley and Los Angeles: University of California Press, 2012), pp. 6, 13–14.

42. Jens Manuel Krogstad and Mark Hugo Lopez, "Hispanic Population Reaches Record 55 Million, but Growth Has Cooled" (Washington, DC: Pew Research Center, 25 June 2015), p. 2.

43. Alan Cooperman, Gregory Smith, and Katherine Ritchey, "America's Changing Religious Landscape" (Washington, DC: Pew Research Center, 12 May 2015), table, "Growing Proportion of Unaffiliated across Racial and Ethnic Groups," p. 72.

44. Jens Manuel Krogstad and Mark Hugo Lopez, "Hispanic Voters in the 2014 Election" (Washington, DC: Pew Research Center Hispanic Trends Project, 7 November 2014), p. 1.

45. Cooperman et al., "America's Changing Religious Landscape," p. 4. Post-millennials were not included in this survey.

46. Ibid., p. 8.

47. Ibid., p. 7.

48. Carroll Doherty, Jocelyn Kiley, and Alec Tyson, "Beyond Distrust: How Americans View Their Government: National Survey" (Washington, DC: Pew Research Center, November 2015), p. 108.

49. Ibid., p. 38.

50. Jens Manuel Krogstad, "Latino Confidence in Local Police Lower Than among Whites" (Washington, DC: Pew Research Center, 28 August 2014), p. 2.

51. Carroll Doherty and Alec Tyson, "Broad Public Support for Legal Status for Undocumented Immigrants" (Washington, DC: Pew Research Center, 4 June 2015), p. 1.

52. Ibid., p. 5.

53. Doherty et al., "Beyond Distrust," p. 114.

54. Angelo Falcón, "Results of the December 2015 National Latino Opinion Leaders Survey," National Institute for Latino Policy, 21 December 2015, http://myemail .constantcontact.com/NiLP-Report- - -National-Latino-Opinion-Leaders-Survey-Results.html?soid=1101040629095&aid=T39hqWlBpRo [accessed 7 January 2016].

55. Robert N. Bellah, Richard Madsen, William Sullivan, Ann Swindler, and Stephen N. Tipton, *Habits of the Heart: Individualism and Commitment in American Life* (Berkeley and Los Angeles: University of California Press, 1985).

APPENDIX

1. US Census Bureau, "2014 ACS 1-year PUMS Accuracy," https://www.census.gov/programs-surveys/acs/technical-documentation/pums/documentation.html [accessed 13 May 2016.]

2. US Census Bureau, "Current Population Survey Design and Methodology Technical Paper 66," October 2006.

3. US Department of Labor, Bureau of Labor Statistics, "Employment and Earnings: Household Data," February 2006, "A" tables, monthly; "D" tables, quarterly.

INDEX

assimilation (continued)
rejection of, 31–33
retro-assimilation, 86–89
Atlantic Americans
arrival in California, xiv, 1, 210n39
definition of, xvii
on American identity, 1, 3–5, 11, 14, 21
in defining identity, 140, 144–45
definitions of Latinos by, 88–91
formative experiences of, 146, 167–68
and indigenous peoples, 153
See also non-Hispanic whites.
Aztlán, 45, 216n11

baby boom, 52
baby boom generation, 27, 52, 164–65, 189
cultural and political views of, 199–200
on acculturation, 139
formative experiences of, 167–68
and Latino population growth, 52–53
racial/ethnic composition of, 166fig29
and society, 164–66
banda youth and music, 82–83, 87, 140
Barabak, Mark, 109
Barrera, Mario, 77
behaviors
dysfunctional, 42–43, 44, 49–52, 56, 65, 73–74, 99
health, 22, 52–55, 59–66, 76, 146–52, 189–90
of immigrant Latinos, 73–78, 90
of immigrants, 37, 73–78, 74fig14, 75figs15–16, 90
individualist, 6, 22, 42–43, 50, 65, 120–21, 140–41
in new nativism, 22, 48, 49–51, 55–66
patterns of Latino, xiii–xiv, 6, 51–52, 55–66, 98, 145, 163, 164, 173, 183
social, 55–66, 71–72, 145–46, 163, 164, 198–99, 201–2
Bellah, Robert N., Habits of the Heart, 145, 201–2
Belmont High School, class of 1989, 135–37
Bigler, John, 8
bilingual education, 86
Chicano activism on, 29, 32
in economic success, 139–40
end of, 93, 108–10, 113

"Multilingual Education for a 21st-Century Economy Act," 182
in political awakening of Latinos, 113
bilingualism, 86
in the California constitution, 13, 14–15, 180
in civil society origins, 160–61
defense of, 10
value of, 109–10, 139–40
birth rates
of African Americans, 72, 73fig13
of Asians/Pacific Islanders, 72, 73fig13
of Latina women, 72, 73fig13
of non-Hispanic whites, 21, 72, 73fig13
post-millennial, 200, 201fig35
post-war, 164–65
"Black Legend" of Spain, 3–4, 6–7
Bolívar, Simón, 1–2
Border Protection, Antiterrorism, and Illegal Immigration Control Act of 2005 (HR 4437). See Sensenbrenner bill.
Bowers, Henry F., 16–17
bracero (guest worker) program, 37, 71, 90, 163
Brown, Jerry, 182
Brown, Willie, 113
Brown Berets, 31–32
The Burden of Support: Young Latinos in an Aging Society (Hayes-Bautista, Schink, and Chapa), xix, 53–54
Burgess, Ernest W., 21–22
Bush, George W., 114, 177
businesses, Latino-owned, 67–70, 84, 85fig19, 96, 98, 115
Bustamante, Cruz, 114, 200

California Assembly Bill 540, 176
California Coalition for Immigration Reform, 100–1, 104–5, 105fig24
California constitution, 1, 4, 5, 6, 7–8, 13, 14–15
California Constitutional Convention (1849), 1–5, 7–8, 9, 12, 22, 160, 180
California Constitutional Convention (1879), 14–15
California Fugitive Slave Act of 1852, 7
California Hispanic American Medical Association (CHAMA), 36–39

California Identity Project, 127–28, 137–38
California Master Plan for Education, 27, 172
California Rural Legal Assistance, 32
Californios, 1–2, 4–5, 159–62
Carlsbad, California, 195, 204 table 2
Carrillo, José Antonio, 1–2, 4, 22, 160, 180
Castilian language, 15, 153, 154
Catholics/Catholicism
    and Chicanos, 32
    in civil society, 152–53, 154, 158
    in identity, 3, 4, 6, 16–17, 22, 138, 158, 198, 212n58
    and indigenous beliefs, 153–54, 194
    and the Know-Nothing Party, 8–10
    immigrant, 15–16, 21
    in mestizo society, 155–56, 158, 193
    in nativism, xvi–xvii, 4, 6, 15–17, 21, 24, 160
Center for the Study of Latino Health and Culture (CESLAC)
    estimates of UC-eligible childhood arrivals, 176
    historical research by, xiv–xvii, xix
    identity focus groups, 86–90, 178–80
    Latino markets study, 79–82
    Latino Report Card, 23, 78, 106–7, 111
    MALDEF's Latino image focus groups, 119–28
    MALDEF's public service announcement focus groups, 129–35
    nativism's effects study, 23–24
    post-millennial focus groups, 178–80
Central American Resource Center (CARECEN), 177–78
Central Americans, 71, 197
CESLAC. See Center for the Study of Latino Health and Culture
Chapa, Jorge, *Burden of Support: Young Latinos in an Aging Society,* 53–54
charter group phase in civil society (1769–1848), 157–59
Chicano cultural identity, 29–36
Chicano generation, 26–36, 111, 174
Chicano physicians, 36
Chicano Power movement, 25–28, 29–31
Chicano studies programs, 32, 87, 172–73
childhood arrivals, 174–76

children
    immigrant, 99, 103fig23, 102–4, 106, 109–10, 175–76, 182
    in poverty, 43
    Latino, 129
    school age, in Proposition 187, 99, 102–4, 106, 170
    US-born Latino, 40, 102–4, 106
Chinese immigrants, 13–14
Cinco de Mayo, xv–xvi, 11, 114, 162, 194
citizenship
    in civil society origins, 161–62
    in nativism, 11–12, 25, 185, 196
    defining, 4–5, 11, 125–27, 128
    of Latino school-age children, 102–3, 106
    in universalism, 4–5, 10–11, 19, 159–60
    See also naturalization.
civil rights, defense of, 18–20, 32, 106
"Civil Rights Initiative," 108
civil society
    in identity, 145–52
    immigrants creating, 85–86, 160, 162–63
    Latinos creating, 144–52
    origins of, 85–86, 152–56, 158, 160–63
    phases of, 157–63, 186–87
El Clamor Público (Los Angeles), 7, 9, 69fig11, 161, 209nn19–20, 209n27, 209–10n28, 210n29, 210n32
Clínica de la Raza, La, 52
Clinton, Bill, 97
cocolixtli (smallpox?), 155–56
college enrollment of post-millennial Latinos, 171–72
Colombians, 195, 197
Colorado, 186–87, 188
Coming Apart: The State of White America (Murray), 51
Compromise of 1850, 6, 7
couple-with-children households, 57, 58figs, 97
La Crónica (Los Angeles), 12–13, 211nn41–42, 211nn44–45
Cruz, Sebastien de la, 185
Cuban refugees, 195
cultural change and dynamics
    demographics of, 37–40, 52–53, 67, 71–72, 139–41, 185–202
    immigration in, 37–41, 73–79, 84–91

Moynihan, Daniel Patrick, 44
"Multilingual Education for a 21st-Century
    Economy Act," 182
muralist movement, 33
Murray, Charles, 49–51
music, 18, 33, 39, 41, 82–83, 91, 140, 155, 162

Náhua people, 147–52, 228n13
Náhuatl language, 70, 148, 151, 154
Napoleon III, xv, 11, 161–62
narratives of identity, xiv, 1–5, 6–8, 9,
    10–14, 21
    See also nativism; universalism
National Chicano Health Organization
    (NCHO), 26, 35–36, 111, 174
National Council of La Raza (NCLR),
    177–78
National Hispanic Media Coalition,
    185–86
National Institute for Latino Policy
    (NiLP), 200
national-origin quotas, 37, 174–75
nativism
    American identity as defined by, xvi,
        3–4, 5, 6–8, 21–24, 119–20, 178–80
    of the American Protective Association,
        15–17
    in California, 3–8
    contested by Latinos, 180–84
    deportation in, 20–21
    and immigrants, 17–22
    of the Know-Nothing Party, 8–10
    Latino response to, 25–33
    in post-millennial experience, 169–71
    in Proposition 187, 100–1, 106
    racism in, 3, 5, 7–8, 11–12, 17, 23–24
    Reconstruction and, 11–12
    in research on Latinos, 21–22
    of the Workingmen's Party, 13–15
nativism, new
    American identity as defined by, 42–43,
        120–21, 140–41
    American values in, 49–51, 66
    and the culture of poverty, 43–45
    and immigrants, 77, 90–91
    individualist values in, 42–43, 50
    and the Los Angeles riots, 97
    Latinos and, 51–66, 121, 131–32

Latino social behavior paradox in, 55–66
minorities in, 42–51, 56
in post-millennial experience, 169–71
in Proposition 187, 99–101
in public policy, 1965–1975, 43–51
upward mobility in, 131–32
naturalization, 9, 112, 112fig25, 117, 125–28,
    127fig27
NBC Latino, 185–86
New Jersey, 196–97
New Mexico, xv, 187–88, 211–12n50
news media, 83, 87, 133, 135, 178, 185–86
New York City, 67, 192fig34, 196–97, 204
    table 2
No Health Insurance? It's Enough to Make
    You Sick (American College of Physi-
    cians), 63
non-Hispanic whites
    American identity as defined by, xvi,
        3–4, 5, 6–8, 21–24, 178–80, 119–21
    birth rates among, 21, 52, 72, 73fig13
    causes of death among, 59–62, 60fig7, 61
        table 1, 62fig8
    couples with children, 58fig5
    defining "white," 8
    definition of, xvii
    universalism rejected by, 3–4, 5, 6–8,
        11–12, 13–16, 17, 180
    infant mortality of, 63, 64fig9, 76
    on Latinos as Americans, 130–32,
        138–41
    life expectancy of, 63, 65fig10, 190,
        191fig33
    mortality rates of, 59–62, 61 table 1,
        62fig8, 191fig32
    nativism by, 3–4, 5, 6–8, 11–12, 13–16, 17
    in new nativism by, 45–51
    percentage of by generation, 166–67,
        166fig29
    political views of, 101, 108–9, 199–200
    post-millennials, 192–98
    in South Central Los Angeles, 93,
        94fig20
nonwhites
    citizenship status of, xvi, 4–5, 6–8, 25
    health status of, 47–49
    and Jim Crow laws in California, 17
    Latinos as, 17, 20, 25

and Proposition 187, 101, 107, 110–11,
    169–70
retro-assimilation of, 86–88
school age children, 102–3
and undocumented immigration, 111,
    170, 179, 183–84, 199
as voters, 110, 112–13, 117, 200–2

Valdez, Robert, 54, 109
Valencia, Pancho, 12–13
Valle, Reginaldo F. del, 10, 14–15, 16–17, 18,
    19–20, 182
Velasquez, Alec, 40–41
veterans, 17, 196
visas, 175
Vital Statistics Report (National Center for
    Health Statistics), 190
Voice of Citizens Together, 101, 102, 104
voter registration, 112–13, 184
voting
    in American identity, 125
    attempts to restrict, 9, 12, 16
    in the California constitution, 4–5,
        7–8
    during the Civil War, 10–11
    post-millennials and, 174, 183–84,
        198–201
    on Proposition 187, 100–1, 102fig21, 106,
        118
    and race, 7–8, 11–12

sociodemographics of, 12, 101, 102fig21,
    105, 108, 109, 110–13, 115, 117, 180–81,
    183–84, 198–201, 211n42

War on Poverty, 44, 51, 64
Weekly Democrat (Stockton), 7
Weidenbaum, Murray, 51
welfare dependence/independence
    of immigrants, 73, 76, 76fig17
    of Latinos, 57–58, 76, 76fig17, 189fig30,
        190fig31
    in Los Angeles County, 97
    in new nativism, 22, 49–50
    in views of minorities, 42–43, 57, 57fig4
    See also public assistance programs
Wilson, Joe, 189
Wilson, Pete, 98–101, 106, 108, 177
Wilson, William Julius, *The Truly Disad-
    vantaged,* 44
Winning of the West, The (Roosevelt), 21
Wisconsin, 197
women's property rights, 4, 5
work ethic, 22, 57–58, 120–21, 131–32, 188
work force participation. *See* labor force
    participation/desertion
Workingmen's Party, 13–15

Young, C.C., 20
young adults, 71–72, 78, 82–83
youth, 52–53, 59–60